SANTHANA

One Man's Road to the East

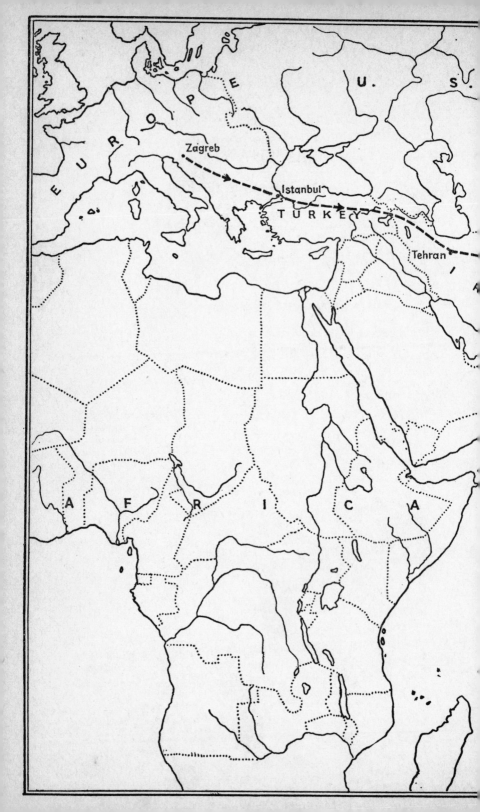

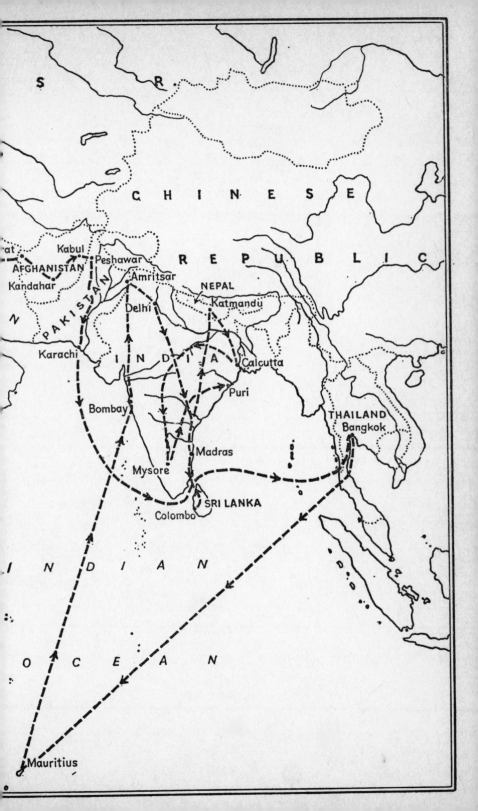

SANTHANA

One Man's Road to the East

BORNA BEBEK

THE BODLEY HEAD
LONDON   SYDNEY
TORONTO

British Library Cataloguing
in Publication Data

Bebek, Borna
Santhana.
1. South Asia—Description and travel
I. Title
915.4'04'5   DS337

ISBN 0-370-30260-5

© Borna Bebek 1980
Printed in Great Britain for
The Bodley Head
9 Bow Street, London WC2E 7AL
by Willmer Brothers Ltd, Rock Ferry
Set in Linotype Juliana
First published 1980

CONTENTS

PROLOGUE

Through the window of Puri Hospital the wind blows the sounds of the invisible Indian Ocean. I lie immobile on the white hospital bed, eyes wide open staring fixedly into emptiness. The minutes tick by endlessly. This is the final phase of the trip. There is no external movement any more.

All is still, yet inwardly awareness grows and swells, perception slowly crystallising. A year and a half has gone by. Much has happened but where is the meaning? The answer is in the quest itself, someone said, so I search through my memories.

Pictures and thoughts file past as I examine the colours, smells and moods, all carefully recorded. The rolling of the surf outside intensifies my concentration as I search for a conclusion. I relive the adventure once more.

*   *   *

The four of us were in Csarda, a gypsy restaurant ten miles outside Zagreb. We sat in a dark corner, candle-light flickering on our wine-flushed faces. The nights came cold that January in north-western Yugoslavia. Throughout the day the snow fell in heavy flakes and as night fell the sharp northerly wind turned into a gale. With the wooden shutters firmly closed and the doors bolted to protect the customers from the howling snowstorm that raged outside, the room was like an oven.

We felt good, the new graduates from Zagreb University with our girlfriends, crowded around the miniature table watching the Party functionaries also having a good time on their expense accounts. In Csarda, January is the best time for business, the month when 'grown men' worry about the 'annual plan fulfilment commission' and young men go off to the army.

With our red-sealed diplomas still in our pockets, we had gone out that night to discuss the future, take our leave and kiss our girls goodbye. Some were off to the services, and some off to graduate school. My uncle had arranged a commission for me on the troubled Albanian border.

'Become a man first,' he had said, taking the matter into his own hands. My mother thought that graduate school should come first, but my father took it for granted that I would join the Navy like him.

'We may have a military background but we are also civilised,' he would grumble every time my uncle was around. None of my friends knew that I had different plans.

In Csarda the atmosphere was rapidly growing more animated, as the usual scene evolved: a thick cloud of cigarette smoke, fires burning high, drunken gypsies playing enthusiastically. One of them, tall, thin and nimble, like an insect, leant over Anna, sawing at his violin, flashing smiles and golden teeth; in the corners sat plump officials with red faces, personalised Mercedes key-rings and platinum blonde mistresses. The tall dark band-leader crooned 'Shining Eyes'; a jilted mistress was crying into her soup, make-up running down her face. Mindless, relaxed midnight atmosphere.

The insect gypsy switched to 'The Flowers in May'. Vlado, already drunk, bought him a bottle of Dingach. The gypsy was really warming to us, playing into Anna's ear, swooping over her. Faces glowed, glasses rang. January in Csarda—time to leave for the army.

I came out tonight partly because I was expected, and partly in the hope of working up Dutch courage to carry through my decision.

I have been ready for several weeks, but have managed to change my mind on several occasions. Everything I need I have with me— passport, student card and three hundred dollars. I have told no one where I intend to go or that my train is leaving at 3.45 in the morning.

'So where are you off to?' Vlado asks, turning to me. My decision suddenly becomes definite.

'I'm off to Asia.'

The gypsy next to Anna breaks into a Hungarian *csárdás*, his loud and passionate music drowning the conversation. The *patron* comes over, fills our glasses and waves the empty two-litre flask in the air as if to ask do we want another. Vlado nods and turns to me again.

'Asia in general or some specific place?' he asks coolly.

'I guess Asia in general,' I answer, 'although I hope to turn up in India eventually.'

'Asia, India, travel—that sort of stuff is so out of date,' he grumbles.

Before he has a chance to expand his current theories, Jasna comes to my rescue.

'Passé? That's just what they said to my grandfather when he took off for India sixty years ago, which was just a few years after India and Schopenhauer stopped being all the rage at Heidelberg University. Following such logic, Asia's been passé ever since Marco Polo.'

As I looked sympathetically at Jasna, Vlado, the perpetual cynic, raised a more sensible objection.

'Yeah, I know, the eternal adventure—Ex Oriente Lux and all that—but in those days the Asia trip was a challenge, these days you just get on a bus.'

I pour myself some wine waiting for him to finish. When he does I take a sip and add: 'I'm going via Mauritius.'

Two hours after midnight they run out of food. Everybody grumbles, but that's Csarda. Anna is sent out to drive home and fetch more. Being a Commissar's daughter she carries out the mission admirably, and returns with a boot full of unbelievable things to eat. The attention of the bar is on us now; as we move up to the centre table the patron jingles: 'If you've got the food, we've got the crockery!' while assuring us that there is a cellar full of wine left. The atmosphere is really humming. The jilted mistress comes over and joins us.

'India via Mauritius,' Drazen repeats, turning to me and scratching the back of his head. 'That's an unusual route—why don't you go via Tahiti as well?'

'Tahiti's too far. I may stop off at Bangkok though.'

'Comrade Lieutenant,' says Drazen mockingly, 'pray tell us how one gets to India via Mauritius?'

I look at him and smile. 'You can start by going overland to the Bay of Sonmiani on the Indian Ocean. To get there you make your way across Turkey and Iran to Afghanistan, then down into Southern Pakistan towards the sea. When you reach the bay you raise a sunken schooner, repair her and sail her to Mauritius just in time to catch the Port Louis—Ceylon steamer. From there it's just a matter of taking the ferry across. Makes sense?'

'A bit,' he says, 'but I don't see where Bangkok comes into it.'

3

'Neither do I.' I raise my empty glass and call to the gypsy for more wine, wishing to avoid further questions. But Drazen is not sure how serious I am, and is curious.

'So when do you plan to leave?' he asks hesitantly.

'Tonight.'

'And how much money are you taking?'

'350 American dollars.'

'Where's your luggage?'

'Here,' I say, lifting a small plastic bag which contains a few books and two oranges.

Thus assured that it's all talk, he turns back to the appetising food and wine.

*   *   *

3.45 a.m. Nobody on the platform. A station attendant appears.

'Which platform for Tzarigrad?' I ask.

He remains silent and raises three fingers. I rush across the tracks. The train is already leaving. I jump on. It's O.K., the sign on the door says ISTANBUL. The whole carriage is empty. Tired and tipsy I close my eyes. The wheels sing their song. Feelings sealed in my body vibrate; kisses linger on my lips. The lights of the station disappear. It is dark. I sink into a dream.

PART ONE

Overland to Karachi

I

Istanbul

The morning breeze brought in the smell of Turkey and the Aegean Sea. I had been travelling for almost two days. The monotonous whiteness of the snow had given way to Mediterranean scenery. The sea soon became visible, a clear blue stretch that contrasted strangely with the cold grey mountains.

It was much like any riviera, the occasional lonely mosque the only suggestion of the Orient. The seaside scenery was peaceful. Quiet little villas, bays, boats and palm trees were all much less like the Orient than the eastern part of Bulgaria.

The ride was not particularly smooth, but the track was free of sharp curves and I was lulled by the pleasant monotony.

This was still Europe, the Europe so many seem to want to get away from to search for a breathing space, time to question, to review their thoughts on the kind of life that would be worth living.

There seemed to me to be several levels on which I could live. As a student I enjoyed the serene comfort of the easy flow of logic, the low-key, subtle happiness that descends late at night as slowly as a warm, engulfing mist. In formulae, in the subdued rhythm of equations there was comfort and warmth and security. My body would relax; appetites, senses, the feeling of fatigue, deprivation, thirst would dissolve, leaving nothing but soft languid forms, images, blunt edges. Yes, I could find peace in learning, yet somewhere in that abstract world of formulae and logic there was always an inbuilt flaw, something unexpected would always creep up. Perhaps it was due to carelessness brought on by fatigue: the easy rolling train of thought would start to slow down, encountering friction.

The will, and the mind would press on, but movement would cease. Through the open window of my study the wind would blow the sounds of the warm summer night. The scent of lilac, sausage and beer would creep in. At moments like that I would feel a jolt, as if a shunter had suddenly changed the points and the train were now running on a different line.

The mind brings the memory of a touch, the sensation earthy and sensual. The world of logic starts to recede, the new world to emerge.

How to live? One cannot do two or three things at the same time, or so they say. Plato wanted us to specialise, so that we should all be physicists, cobblers, violinists, poets. Yes, one might discipline one's mind and body to respond only to selected stimuli, to operate exclusively on either an ethereal or a sensuous level. Perhaps that is what civilisation, progress, nature and society demand: division of labour, specialisation, so as to allow individuals to develop their full potential.

Yet physicists, philosophers, clerks have bodies, too, that long for effort, and action, for taking strains; if left unexercised the body aches and atrophies. Ever since deciding to take University seriously I had been troubled by these thoughts. What to do, how to make decisions? To be this or that, to be here or there? Is one born to be something specific and to strive to discover what that something is? Or should one simply accept whatever is dictated by chance and circumstance?

I took out Thom's letter from Karachi well worn by now and read it again. It was this letter, or rather Thom's whimsical ideas, that provided me with an initial impetus and an excuse for this getaway. Thom had of course known for a long time of my desire to go to India but had regarded it as escapist nonsense. For a long time he was interested in South America, hence any continent or pursuit other than those in harmony with his interest of the moment was nonsense. His hostility towards Asia was further increased by the fact that Asia was at the time still in fashion. Thom always took great pains not to be considered one of the crowd. To him Asia and India until recently still meant barefoot freaks, dope and the search for self-identity, pursuits which Thom could do without. But all that was before he had discovered Bangkok. In due time he had rediscovered South-east Asia as well as the subcontinent, and now that the freaks and hippies were past history, Thom spent his time proposing ever more exotic projects that we were to undertake in Asia together.

His latest proposal had to do with raising a half-sunken yacht stranded on a sandbank in Sonmiani Bay on the Indian Ocean. I was to make my way to Pakistan where he was to meet me. At the time he wrote he was still in Bangkok, but he was going to Pakistan in a month or so to see about this boat and sort out some business with boat shackles. I wrote that I was interested, so he sent me a boatyard address in Sonmiani through which I was to contact him. He'd come to pick me up in Karachi, he wrote, and then we'd proceed to the bay, where we were to salvage the yacht, repair her and sail to Mauritius. For my efforts I was to receive enough money to make the journey to India by boat and to cover my expenses for the entire trip. The scheme was typical of Thom—unusual and challenging. He seemed to devote his life to such pursuits.

I remembered meeting him four years before in the International Youth Brigade working at the kibbutz-style collective farm. I had to go there for it was expected of me. At that time he was experimenting with Socialism. He had since tried other ideas and lifestyles, in spite of which our friendship had lasted. He came up with these proposals fairly frequently, but this time his letter caught me just at the right moment.

He wrote that if things worked out properly and we were able to refit the boat in Bangkok, we both stood to make a substantial profit. Knowing Thom, I was sceptical about things working out properly, getting to Bangkok and making money, but I did not really care— here was an excuse and the impetus to visit Asia at last.

* * *

I had been too absorbed in my thoughts to notice the approach of the big city; the increase in the number of towns, stations, cars, billboards and signposts barely registered—suddenly the city was upon me.

Istanbul, the ancient Constantinople, on the Bosphorus. The winter sun bright above; below, the azure stretch of calm sea. Then the spectacular city, one of the most beautiful sights in the world.

This was the Orient, instant and immediate. One minute I was in Europe, then I lifted my eyes and there it was—an Eastern fairy tale in white stone, marble, bricks and mortar. The sight of the city sent a shudder through my body; the picture of a thousand and one nights met and surpassed all expectations. The brilliant sun above, the white gleaming city and the blue of the bay. The tensions of a busy life, nervous energy, worries, pre-occupations block out the senses, but the night of drinking and the long ride had left me open and receptive. I breathed in the atmosphere and savoured it, open to sensation.

* * *

In Istanbul it was a crisp January afternoon. I sat in the westernised Del Mar café opposite Gunga's hotel, observing through the glass wall the colourfully-dressed young Westerners going in and out. I lingered over a beer before launching myself into a new world.

The cold winter sun was changing the soft burgundy colours of the café unholstery, making it look a cheap glaring red. There was still a drop of beer in the glass. The waiter took his time bringing me yet another one—the last one for a long time, I said to myself, looking at my small plastic bag, the only piece of luggage I had.

I paid and walked out through the revolving door.

Gunga Din runs one of the more famous overland hotels west of Kabul. Were it not for Yenesh with his dingy establishment just down the road, Gunga would have had perhaps the second place in the catering hall of fame of the overland world—second only to Baba, the superstar of Kabul.

The electric buzzer that sounded automatically as I walked into his hotel brought me Gunga's prompt attention. He eyed me quizzically. I could see the impression that I gave reflected in his eyes—nothing alarming about me, just another young man with several days beard, wearing blue levis.

'So you are from Yugoslavia,' he said as I showed him my passport. 'Dobrodosli,' he added, speaking in Croatian with a faint foreign accent. Glad to find a friendly face, I engaged him in conversation.

'Do you get many visitors from Yugoslavia?' I asked.

'Of course. I even had two Czechs here, and several Poles. Never figured out how they ever let them out—it's different with the Yugoslavs, I get them often.'

Gunga, it turned out, had been a prisoner of war in Yugoslavia. He was very friendly and invited me and a group of Swedes for a coffee.

The Swedes were there to make a TV film called 'Ten Years After'. It was a part of a nostalgia series dealing with the student revolts of the late Sixties and early Seventies—the Maharishi, the Beatles and the hippy exodus to India.

They were disappointed to find out that there was no exodus of

10

that type any more. The overland trail to Asia is still well-trodden but today's traveller is a different kind of person. No longer identifying with the hippies or freaks, he calls himself simply an overlander, thus avoiding ideological or cultural identification.

Gunga himself was something of a legend in the overland world and a much-quoted authority. He had appeared on German TV and had been featured in *Rolling Stone*. Although very nostalgic for the days gone by, he seemed well on top of the new developments in the overland world. He said that the former freak trail had become the adventurers' trail: the new travellers had no 'common politics', no 'common talk' or 'appearance', their age-range and educational background was wider; formerly most of them came in their mid-twenties, the 'post-university types', but now anything goes, one met people from late teens to mid-thirties, some well into their forties and older types coming from all walks of life. Surprisingly, Gunga's advice to all of them was that they should not go. It did not make sense, this attitude of his—his business depended on the overland traffic—but that's what he'd tell them, and that's what he told us. He went on telling us how it was: the long weeks of the journey, the sleepless nights, the people and the smells of the earth that confuse the traveller and get him down.

'Brainwash you, man—the bad mensies and womansies, bad dopes, bad sleeps, and eats'—it was all bad, bad east of Istanbul. He conceded that there were those who did not fall prey to the lure of drugs, but then, he said, they would suffer from lack of sleep, extremes of heat and cold, dysentery, hepatitis or amoebic infections. 'That would get them, so you can't win.'

His motto was, if you want to go to India—fly.

Who knows why he took that stance—was he really so concerned for the welfare of western travellers? He spoke very convincingly, yet like everybody else I ignored his advice, thanked him and paid him fifteen lire for the clean bed in the corner of a dingy room.

Before falling asleep I went quickly over my budget. I left Zagreb with $350; with soldier's reduction it cost only $3 to cross Yugoslavia. Since then I had spent a further $20. With that kind of money one can travel from Istanbul to Katmandu—at least it was so according to a guide book I found on Gunga's table.

2

About Freak Buses

The next day, as I was sitting in Lala's pudding shop—a relic of the Sixties—I realised that I still did not know how to get to Afghanistan, let alone Southern Pakistan. Before leaving I had hardly looked at a map to see which countries were en route—but then why organise a journey? A planned trip is qualitatively different from an unplanned one; I was ready for twists and surprises. Why did I want to travel? I was not particularly concerned about getting from A to B; travel was to be simply a change of consciousness induced by external stimuli. Perhaps I was just looking for adventure. But there was more to it than that. In Europe I was faced with a set of decisions which I would not make—I wanted to attain a new perspective. I found myself unwilling to live by the decisions and choices forced on me externally, yet I lacked the criteria to make my own choices; so I had to find those criteria if I were to break onto a new plane. The abstraction of the university world and my cadet training seemed to close me in; travel could be used to open me up to new sights, smells, vibrations. To be effective it had to be hard, I decided. I would have to break a mental bubble, the cultural resistance that isolated me from new thoughts. It would take effort, fatigue, sweat. My body would have to be put through shocks of cold, hunger, pain; my mind would have to be fatigued by lack of sleep, and I would have to travel slowly, step by step, overland.

At Lala's there is always a flamboyant collection of customers. Boutique owners and students sporting exotic clothes, the men wearing big ear-rings, the girls wearing anklets; well-fed, prosperous Germans; elegantly disarrayed Italians and nonchalant English, looking slightly bored.

I must have been sitting there for over an hour when my musings were interrupted by Gunga Din who had walked in unseen by me and sat down to join me.

'No use looking at these people—they're weekenders on charter flights from Munich, all *poseurs*. The real overlanders are still lying in their nests. You want travel information? You have to come in the late afternoon or the small hours of the morning. Since Yenesh is away, you will have to come here.'

I accepted Gunga's advice, and left the café.

* * *

The tall skinny youth outside was obviously French.

'*Tu es Français?*' I asked.

'*Oui.*'

'Can I ask you some questions while we eat pudding at Lala's?'

He threw a contemptuous glance towards the pudding shop.

'*Moi je mange chez Yenesh.*'

'*Bien sûr, mais il est* busted.'

The Frenchman laughed.

'Maybe this morning, but now *c'est déjà reglé.*'

Yenesh greeted us himself. He gave Gérard a pat on the shoulder, flashed a well rehearsed 'come into my parlour' smile at me and showed us to a small wooden table inside. The place was packed, yet Yenesh had all the time in the world for any newcomer.

'Welcome, my friend. What would you like?'

'How much for two plates of *pilau?*' I asked suspiciously.

'Free for you, my friend, free. I bring now. You like a drink?'

'Free too?' I enquired jokingly, expecting some kind of trick.

His long Ghengis Khan moustache shook with laughter. 'All free for you my friend.'

'Well, OK.' I shrugged my shoulders as Yenesh danced nimbly into the kitchen.

'What's all this "free for you" nonsense?' I asked, turning to Gérard.

'Once it was free for me too—Yenesh knows what he's doing.'

I was amused and no longer cared what hidden purpose lay behind this unexpected generosity. I liked Yenesh's smile and I decided that if an innkeeper could carry on like that and still make a living there must be more to him than met the eye.

Yenesh returned carrying food and drinks. We asked him to sit down, waiting to see what he wanted. Apparently he wanted nothing. His English seemed restricted to 'You like eat, you like drink, you my friend.' Suspecting some misunderstanding I again tried to pay, but no, he wanted nothing. He got up and joined

13

another group. I gave up trying to understand and shifted my attention to Gérard.

'So you want to go to Afghanistan,' he said. 'Well, to go to Afghanistan you go to Taksim Square, you look for a freak bus—Istanbul to Kabul—and that's that. You'll have to pay a hundred dollars and for that you are allowed to sit and sleep for four weeks inside a large old Mercedes bus. You'll be with American and European guys, you'll listen to bad rock and roll, you'll stop to eat at freak places where they serve freak food, sometimes at prices much higher than in New York. You'll spend another fifty to a hundred dollars on food, grass and souvenirs. After four weeks of grass and rock and hip conversation you'll get off the bus and you'll be in Kabul, minus two or three hundred dollars.

'Of course, you could have spared yourself the trouble, added another thirty dollars and flown to Karachi.'

I was surprised.

'So that's the great Asia overland adventure—a great tourist trap?'

'No, that's for the consumer freaks,' said Gérard. 'We call them flying hogs.' Gérard spat the words out and waved his hand in the general direction of Lala's.

'Who is we?'

'Us, here.' Gérard pointed around him. 'The ten per cent who travel across Asia for fifty dollars.'

'Go on, tell me how you travel to Kabul.'

A look of indignation came over Gérard's face.

'Don't ask how to get to Kabul—we go to Erzurum, you dig?' He threw in the dated English slang.

'Look for us in Erzurum—find a place to shack down and then look around for ways to get to Tabriz and Tehran.'

'How do I get to Tehran?'

'Look, don't hassle me. I told you, go to Erzurum. We don't know how to get from Istanbul to Tehran, we only know how to get from Istanbul to Erzurum, from Erzurum to Tabriz and so on.'

'OK, OK, I dig. So tell me, how do I get from Erzurum to Tabriz?'

'Don't get smart. It changes—it depends—things come up. Besides, I forget every time I do it. I don't smoke memory.'

I was beaten.

'Right,' I said, 'tell me how to get to Erzurum.'

'Now you're talking. First you gotta look like us. That means

14

getting rid of your backpack, the one I saw you buying in Lala's earlier. Packs are a pain, you can't shove them under the seat of a bus, you can't carry them through small train compartments. If you carry them on your back you can't go through doors, if you carry them in your hand they're awkward—besides, we don't speak to pack carriers. Take a waterproof cloth bag like that one in the corner.' Gérard pointed towards a cylindrical carpet-bag.

'Then you wear good warm flannel trousers and a pullover. Levis you carry to sell. Later you wear local clothes. Long hair and beards are the trade marks of the freaks and tourists—no one else has them any more. Now for your language—'

'Listen Gérard,' I interrupted. 'I appreciate all the information but can you simply tell me how to get to Erzurum?'

'Look man, I'm telling you stuff that no hog has ever heard of. I do it 'cause I like your face, but don't push it. I'll get down to basics : if you want to get to Pakistan on twenty dollars you gotta look right, or else people won't react to you right. You gotta know that there are three prices for everything—for the locals, for us and then the crazy hog prices. Now for Erzurum—wait till Tuesday and take bus 109 to Kili Kusak. Wait there for the freak bus to Delhi to come by— three of them leave every Tuesday. Flag down the first one. If the driver's white, forget it. Wait for the Turk. Speak Turkish—say you'll give him fifty lire to go to Erzurum. Either he takes you or he doesn't. You can make private deals all the way to Laos; in Asia never buy official; never change official; make deals; give bakshish; ask around. If there's no Turk driver that day or if nobody takes you, wait for the next Tuesday. Or Friday, or Wednesday. We aren't really going to Kabul or Karachi. The hippies and the freaks wanted to go somewhere and it got them nowhere. So we are not going ... We are just ... We just ... You see ...'

He mumbled inarticulately, shrugged his shoulders and slouched back in his chair, making no more effort to communicate.

3

Across Turkey

With my levis packed in my new linen bag, I stood amongst a group of a dozen or more assorted people. The young man beside me was nervous. He kept tugging at his long reddish hair and his pretty, rather effeminate face looked excited and afraid. He talked to me in a pleasant yet agitated voice.

A sweet-looking, fattish Italian girl was furiously at work trying in vain to zip up her flaming orange anorak. Her two companions laughed at her.

I could sense the cloud of fear and excitement, the tense vibrations of the group.

'This is it, folks,' a tall, balding American announced in a deep voice. No one seemed to pay any attention. Most were silent, wrapped in their own thoughts or worries as they shuffled their feet, trying to keep warm.

This is it, the journey begins. 'The ice is moving, brothers Karamazov,' I thought.

The battered Mercedes hummed idly, shaking as if it were nervous and reluctant to go. The driver, after boarding the Turks, had locked the doors and disappeared, leaving us in the cold drizzle outside.

Nobody was putting on that cool, been-through-it-all-before routine.

'Yes, it's like this every time.' The balding American turned to me. 'It's the third time for me and it still gets me, that gut feeling. What's it going to be like this time—is the driver going to make it, is the hep going to hit me hard, will my liver start up again? I got away twice, no damage, just the usual stuff—dysentery and a mild attack of hepatitis—but it's the traffic accidents I'm afraid of. I've never made a trip without being in at least one. I never got hurt though. Don't like the look of that driver—he looks crazier than most of them. And I don't like this business of letting the Turks in first to make themselves comfortable while we wait outside.'

At around 5 p.m. the driver, a small, moustached Turk, appeared.

He had brought some more passengers with him, all Asians, but they also had to wait: the ticket-man was due in fifteen minutes. The driver leant lazily on the fender, lit a cigarette and ignored the drizzle.

Waiting there and looking at the driver's cruel eyes, I lost myself in thought. Those were the eyes that for centuries had looked across the walls and fortresses that separated Croatia from the Ottoman Empire. Fierce black eyes. The eyes in which an Eastern European could still see the history of rape, pillage and murder. I recalled what I had been taught at school about Turkish history. Their empire was based on violence, looting and robbery. Turks were never farmers or builders. Their empire was the longest-lasting, best-organised protection racket in the world's history. It had collapsed overnight, and now they are modern Turks, Kemal's children. They have all changed, they have been reborn and we've forgiven them, so I thought—but as I glanced at the narrow slits again I realised that this was no new Turk. No, this one was from the stuff the old Turks were made of.

I came to myself and smiled at this exaggerated, culturally conditioned thinking. With a feeling of guilt I turned to the driver, offered him a cigarette, smiled and asked when we were leaving.

He glanced at the approaching ticket collector and said, 'Leaving now,' and with the ease of a cat leapt onto the fender of the bus and unlocked the door.

I had not followed Gérard's advice exactly. Rather than wait for the right man to come along at Kili Kusak, I had gone to the bus company to look for him. It was not a driver I found but the man who collected the tickets before people got on. He had agreed to let me ride to Erzurum and I had given him fifty lire.

Now I was sitting in one of the best front seats, right behind the driver. My legs stretched out on the empty seats nearby, I pondered over the fortunate coincidence that had left all the best front seats available.

The driver slammed the lever into gear; the bus gave a jolt and moved off. Outside the day was turning into a foggy night.

It was already morning when I awoke. I was surprised that I had managed to sleep. The dirty drizzling panorama that had accompanied us since Istanbul had changed to the brilliant white of a snow-covered plateau. Soft, relaxing music was coming from a transistor radio held by a Persian two rows behind. The bus was warm. A ray of sunshine refracted by the frozen window spread the colours of the rainbow before my eyes. I reached into the bag for an orange. I was the only passenger whose bag had been allowed inside the bus. Gérard had given me sound advice. I leaned back and felt good.

It did not take long for my calm mood to evaporate. With a painful jolt I became aware of the Turk's driving. I tensed myself in the seat and watched his movements. We had just cleared a hilltop and were now picking up speed, rolling towards a valley below. In front of us was a red Fiat, which the driver overtook—rather too recklessly for my liking.

A series of dangerous corner-cuttings followed: the Turk would simply cross the double centre-line, hug the mountainside and proceed to clear the sharp bends, ignoring the fact that he could not see round the corners. An hour or so later he met his match—an Iranian bus which would not let us overtake. After ten minutes of angry hooting our Turk came up on the left, parallel with the Persian. He lost some ground while changing gear to gather more power, but as he crept up again the Persian managed to shift down as well. The Turk stayed level. Too bad, I thought, we will have to pull in behind, but the Turk held his ground. The next moment there appeared a red car coming towards us, headlamps flashing. Quick, I thought, get behind. The Turk stayed put, the oncoming car braked desperately and skidded off the road. A few moments later we were approaching a blind bend. Suddenly we were on top of a large lorry which loomed up in front of us. Before the Turk had a chance to react the lorry swerved into a parking bay which luckily happened to be there.

'Get back!' I screamed at the driver, as a whole column of cars appeared, heading towards us. The Turk did not budge. He sat there, his eyes flashing, his hands immobile on the wheel. The Persian finally gave in. The Turk swerved to the right, his arrogant laughter drowned by the wild hooting from the oncoming traffic.

I grabbed my bag and rushed towards the back of the bus and collapsed next to the American.

'So you thought you were smart sitting up there in death row,' the pale American whispered.

'Jesus Christ!' I exclaimed. 'How long has this been going on?'

'All night. He kept cool around Istanbul—cops, you know—but an hour later—wow! You've been sleeping, so you missed it all.'

I was amazed.

'Is this sort of thing common?'

'Well, so far I've been involved in three accidents. According to statistics dealing with Turkish freak buses, only one out of four is never involved in a major accident. They buy these buses in Germany —as they are ready for scrapping they pay next to nothing for them. One good Istanbul to Delhi run will almost cover the total investment. If they manage to make a few runs without losing the bus they've done very well. To lose a bus means nothing.

'It's the drivers that are hard to get. No sane driver would drive these death traps, not even a sane Turk, so they get these desperados; most of them have other jobs so they're pressed for time. They tell their employers they're sick or something and they do an Istanbul to Delhi run. Either they make it or they don't.

'The driver gets it first, then death row behind him. If you sit in the back as everyone else does, you're usually OK. I've been in three accidents and nobody but the driver got it. I have to tell you though, I've never seen a maniac like this one.'

'Isn't there anything we can do?'

He waved his hand casually.

'What are you going to do about it? The driver hasn't got the money to return to you, and even if he did what would you do? They're all more or less like that. We could hassle him and complain about his driving but he'll just ignore you; if you hassle him long enough he'll just walk off and go home. There's nothing to hold him—he's had fifty per cent of his wages already, he couldn't care less for you or his employer. So that's it, you pay your money and take your chance.' At least I had not paid much, I thought.

I did not get off at Erzurum as I was supposed to. The driver did not care whether I paid for another ticket or not. I was lazy and decided to stay on until Tehran. This decision led me to suffer the most insane drive I have ever experienced.

The driver followed no set route or schedule. He would stop at official bus stops, luring the local Turks away from the regular buses by offering them half-price transport.

These poor tiny peasants would climb in, laden with parcels, cold and wet from the rain and snow. He drove left and right, east and west, depending on where the locals wanted to go. Generally they were heading towards Iran.

He played wild Turkish music day and night, making it impossible to sleep. Sometimes, when he was exhausted, he would stop and sleep for a few hours. Then he would demand absolute silence, shouting and cursing at the passengers and behaving like an Ottoman despot.

After the second day, he took to sleeping a lot. If any of the locals could drive, he would let them drive the bus to wherever they were going while he slept or drank. Most of the passengers put up with all of this passively, but I could see that the two Persians were getting sick of it. On the third day they had had enough.

The tough-looking one who had been sitting behind me first made the suggestion. The Turk was blind drunk when they grabbed him. He had been driving for four hours, getting more drunk all the time. After the second bottle, he got angry with the passengers for some reasons, and periodically turned to scream and gesticulate as the bus roared along at forty miles an hour.

As he slowed down to look for a new packet of cigarettes, the Persian jumped on him, locking him with his arms. His brother grabbed the wheel. The tough-looking one whipped out a knife and made to strike the Turk, but he was only bluffing. The Turk was petrified : his small, tough, sinewy body quivered against the Persian, his clammy flesh trembling with fear. The dangerous little man, a potential mass-killer a moment ago, was now scared and pathetic.

'Throw him out,' suggested a no-nonsense Palestinian. 'We can't hold him all the time.'

Somebody pointed out sensibly that we needed him to drive us across the Turkish-Iranian border.

It was the Persian's brother who drove, slowly and cautiously, but at least he always went in the right direction. The Turk fell asleep.

At three o'clock the next morning the bus broke down. Outside it was dismally cold. I left the bus and stepped out into the darkness to see what had happened. A strong wind whipped and crackled like a lash, spraying us with glittering snow.

'Anybody know anything about diesel engines?' somebody shouted.

Inside the bus everyone was awake. The passengers had not slept for eighteen hours, ever since the Persian had grabbed the Turk; they stared, petrified, at the figure that had slept through most of the day.

Somebody repeated the question but everyone was either too cold or confused to answer.

Meanwhile the Persian lit a piece of petrol-soaked cloth that he had wrapped around a stick and lifted up the bonnet. The Palestinian woke the driver, dragged him out and asked if he knew what was wrong. The driver played stupid and said he knew nothing. The Palestinian hit him across the mouth a few times but it was obvious that the Turk was useless. Somebody checked the connections and points, the fuel leads and so on, but nobody knew much about diesel engines.

It was too cold to remain in the bus and when the Persian brother noticed lights down the road some of us decided to walk. The Italians and the American joined us, the rest chose to stay. It was a long and uncomfortable walk. I had no overcoat—the American lent me his sleeping bag which I wrapped around me.

The next morning we found a local mechanic. It took him about an hour to replace a burnt-out coil and then the engine kicked away. The driver said he had no money to pay for repairs so we all chipped in a dollar and were off at last.

Eight hours later in the bright sunshine we passed Mount Ararat where, according to the American, pieces of Noah's Ark could still be found.

Then came the Turkish border. Dirty-looking, squalid shacks, untidy officials munching greasy pieces of meat as they looked through papers, everywhere mud, knee-deep. Two hours later we were through.

It was like re-entering civilisation, with clean-shaven, tall, dark and handsome officials and clean buildings; yet those smiling border guards were tough. The American was sent back to Ankara. 'No visa,' they said.

'But I had a visa given to me at the border the last time I passed through.'

'Things here change,' answered the official in good English.

'But I've paid for a ticket to Delhi.'

'Sorry. Policy.'

I asked the American if I could do anything for him.

'Yes, 'phone my friend in Tehran and tell him what's happened, OK?'

I too had no visa and was worried. But it was all right: a smile, 'Welcome to Iran,' and I was through. With good roads and clean, efficient service stations, we drove on towards Tehran. Impressed by the border and the roads, I was expecting a beautiful, thriving, exotic city.

4

Iran

We arrived in Tehran seven days after leaving Istanbul. Except for me, everyone on board the bus had a ticket paid for through to Kabul, yet none of them wanted to continue the journey.

Tehran is the least pleasant city I have ever seen. There is nothing oriental, earthy or human about it. It has the sort of vulgar architecture that one associates with instant settlements on the West Coast of the USA, yet, unlike their American counterparts, these motel-type, cheap, modern, concrete erections are dirty, many already run-down and decaying, in spite of their recent origin.

Shah Reza and Pahlavi Avenues, the famous main streets where the fashionable French and American shops were situated, were lined on both sides by ten-foot-wide open sewers. These ran about six feet deep and it was amusing to watch the fashionable Iranian ladies step from their chauffeur-driven cars and tread carefully across make-shift bridges to the ostentatious shops.

Open sewers lined almost all the avenues. The city was an enor-mously large sprawl, extending for miles across the flat, sun-drenched land. There were no parks, trees or fountains worthy of mention, simply an endless sea of stalls and squat, pre-fabricated houses, and what must surely be the world's most irksome traffic jams. The whole unfortunate settlement was enclosed in a thick violet haze that stung the eyes and made the visitor want to sneeze. But no— if Tehran did not meet my expectations, the Persians by far surpassed them. I expected a vulgar, nouveau riche, semi-modernised people.

I saw tall quiet men and graceful women, upright, proud and beautiful; the men were polite, handsome and friendly.

A few days later, tired and disappointed with Tehran, I decided to take a train to Mashhad, a town close to the Afghan border.

In Iran, as in all Eastern countries, the number of people wanting to travel permanently exceeds the number of seats available on public transport. Different countries solve the problem in different ways. In India the situation is put right by the use of luggage racks and roofs. In Iran, people without a reserved seat don't travel. There is always a next time. Time is plentiful in the East. I got a ticket through a lucky coincidence. It cost $4 so I was well within my budget. I boarded the train in the late afternoon, and was surprised to find all classes clean and upholstered. Only a few of the people wishing to travel were able to get on the train, but those lucky few had plenty of room. The train was comfortable but ramshackle, rather like a fourth-hand Cadillac held together with bits of wire and string, but kept clean by the proud owner.

Of all the trains I was to see in Asia, this was the only one where people actually sat in the seats—obviously ill-at-ease and uncomfortable. In other countries the seats just get in the way of squatting, leaning, lying and standing passengers. This Persian train was well patrolled by truncheon-swinging guards; it was hard to tell whether they were there to keep law and order or only to make sure that the passengers remained sitting, in the Western way. There was something sad about the spectacle—a token group of travellers being forced to sit like Europeans. If you want to travel, you'd better sit like a white man. This was the trouble throughout Asia, though less in Iran than elsewhere; the despots with their colonial mentality were needlessly compelling people to sit, stand, sleep and cook in positions foreign to the natural rhythm of their culture and way of life; this was done either by force or by the design of objects and vehicles.

A little after the train pulled out of the station I fell asleep. After the nightmare of the Turkish bus, this should have been a pleasant trip, but I fell ill. I had caught a bad cold the night the bus broke down. I lay down and tried to sleep; as I started shivering, my Persian companions covered me with their coats and blankets. The last I remembered before falling asleep was a giggling little girl offering me a hot drink from a thermos. There was a tall bearded fellow saying something which sounded like Barbarella and I was asleep.

*   *   *

It was noon the next day when the train rolled to a stop in Mashhad. Stepping out of the railway station, I was blinded by the bright sunshine reflected by the dazzling snow-covered streets. The whole town sparkled white; even the snow was clean. The streets were lit by multicoloured lights and crowded with exotically dressed pilgrims. To a Westerner it seemed like Christmas.

It was startling for me to see Persians in the role of devout Muslims. At first the European-looking Iranian face and Islam make an unusual mix. The movement of the ritual, the sway in the folds of the robe of the holy men, the wailing of the *Muezzin* on the minaret. 'Rahman Rahin Ibrahim Allah Russelallah, Russelallah,' droned the voice inviting the men to the mosque, so I said why not follow the crowd—took off my shoes, washed my feet and joined the crowd.

Yet I could not join. My mind was bent on analysing what was going on. It was for depersonalisation that the white bearded *Mullah* was asking in his insistent voice, to stun the mind, arrest the brain, dissolve thought in a common action. Unlike the call of Christianity, this call was not exclusively to the heart, certainly not to the intellect. No, it was to another centre of consciousness that the ritual appealed. The message was in the sound of the prayer, in the flow of the swaying bodies. Beautiful as it was at that time, this irrational ritualistic manner of perception seemed so foreign, so basic, one recoiled from it.

I slept in a cheap hotel, a taste of things to come. They call these Asian establishments hotels, but they have little to do with the European notion of a hotel; small timber-and-mud structures with a floor made of wooden planks and straw matting.

A petrol lamp and a small smoky iron stove, with an inadequate handful of twigs, was the heating provided, and there was always an army of cockroaches to keep you company. Before falling into a dreamless coma that lasted until late next morning, I had a chance to review the objectives of my trip again. Although it only took an hour, the experience of reflection seemed novel and almost out of place. Only two weeks had passed since I had last meditated to the tune of the wheels of the Orient Express, yet it seemed a long time ago. The last two weeks I had been so absorbed in the daily business of travel that my mind had been running on a different track.

I began forming an idea of how it would be possible to live out one's whole life without stopping for introspection—a habit which in Europe one takes for granted and is very proud of, assuming it to be the basis of our morality and integrity. It was in that Mashhad hotel that I had my first doubts about this intense European self-awareness, this tendency to mull over everything. These thoughts were still so unclear at that stage in my journey, I hardly knew what questions to pose, or how. So it was a relief when the foggy blanket of fatigue finally dimmed my consciousness and I sank into a deep sleep.

*   *   *

When I awoke next morning, my mind was free of reflexions and interested only in the logistics of getting to Afghanistan and finding some hot breakfast—the latter first. I met another overlander and asked him about continuing to Afghanistan. There was no organised transport to Afghanistan, he explained, but one could take a bus from Khavar garage to Tayyebat, a town about twenty kilometres from the Afghan border. From there one could hitch a ride or walk to the border. In any case, one had to be careful. It was necessary to get there before 2 p.m. It takes a long time to get through the Iranian customs, he explained, and there was a long walk to the Afghan border outpost. 'You must get there before dusk,' he said, 'as there's no electricity at the border, so it closes early. After that, look for local transport.'

It was an old but comfortable bus that took me to Tayyebat. The driver, like the passengers, was dressed in rags but had a kind and civilised face. The journey was preceded by a prayer, with the driver and the passengers all taking part.

The passengers were local peasants with rags around their heads for turbans, rugged faces, tattered clothes. I had expected them to run around the bus, to shout, argue, spit and generally to behave the way Middle Eastern people are supposed to behave. Yet these poor, rugged men sat patient and calm in their seats; they spoke in low tones and moved with grace and dignity. Generally they ignored me except for a ruddy-faced *Mullah* sitting behind me who'd periodically lean towards me, pull me by the cuff and glancing

25

around whisper loudly: 'Very good Iran, very good Islam.' Having delivered the message he'd sit back majestically for another hour of silence.

On arrival they joined in a thanksgiving prayer and left the bus in an orderly manner, each thanking the driver and bidding him farewell.

I was slow to leave the bus station. I took time drinking my coffee and contemplating the knives, forks and the china cup. How long before I would see those things again? Out there, twenty kilometres down the road, was Afghanistan. That was Asia. Iran, with its thin veneer of modernism, was the last outpost. Until now all had been only a preparation, an apparently tough excursion, but really a picnic. By now I had heard a lot about Afghanistan and knew what to expect.

I took a last delicious gulp of coffee and walked out of the door. The adventure is about to begin, I thought, and set off hurriedly down the long, straight road.

5

Afghanistan

The fat Afghan border guard was obviously bored. He was outside on the porch, sitting in a tattered plastic chair ripped out of some confiscated freak bus. A drop of sweat formed on his forehead and as it slid across his Mongolian, eunuch-like face his fat, effeminate lips twitched. He made no effort to wipe it away; it trickled across his mouth, danced for a second on his chin and fell on to the greasy hunk of *nan* (a kind of bread) he held in his hand.

It was not a hot day but he wore a thick turban. High above his head, on top of the turban, perched an official hat. It must have been very awkward carrying those two pieces of head-gear, but he was probably used to the turban and the big, impressive officer's hat lent him a dramatic air of official importance well worth the ordeal. Apart from his hat, his uniform—converted Russian surplus—was not up to much, just one of the thousands of uniforms presented by the Soviets to the tattered Afghan army. They had dyed the uniforms blue, but he ought to have dyed his over again, because the official job did not hold out well in the rain. The previous owner must have been skinny: this one could not fasten the buttons, and a piece of string across his chest held the jacket together. It was obvious that he loved the hat but would have preferred to be without his uniform, wearing his own clothes, as in the old days before the take-over. The latest Number One was a tough customer, however, and insisted that they all wore uniforms.

Above him, over the entrance to the small dock, hung a huge photograph of the Number One. It depicted a tight-lipped, sullen man. The picture was new, and there was no glass—presumably to facilitate the frequent changes of photograph.

Five hundred yards to the left of the sitting guard was a broken-down bus; behind it were hidden about half a dozen black-marketeers. The fat guard must have known very well that they were there, for the sandy ground was covered with tyre-marks from their tyre-soled footwear. Besides, it was probably through them that the guard had acquired his shiny new Russian moped—'the only one in town', he was to boast. It would have been bad form for them to be in the public eye though. Ever since the take-over they had to make do with sitting behind the bus.

It was half-past three and the guard was looking at me resentfully, not because he had anything against me, but my being there meant getting up, writing, searching, talking. A look of indignation passed over his face.

This was Afghanistan. This guard was my first real experience of the East. The West was gone.

'Passport, give me!' squeaked the fat Mongol.

I handed him my red passport and when he saw the hammer-and-sickle emblem a smile spread across his face.

'Ah, Rooshian! My friend, my friend, come in, come in, we drink tea.' Somewhat startled I said, 'No—Yugoslav.'

'Ah, Yugoslav, Rooshian, *haracho*, very good! Come in, come in.'

I liked the treatment reserved for the Yugoslav-Russians. I had heard of the normal treatment so I did not argue and went in. There were no doors, just an old carpet nailed to the frame. It was hot and dark inside. The guard invited me to sit down and went into another room.

I had already been told about the procedure. You start in the small room on the eastern side with the passport check, half an hour later comes the central room, and more passport checking, then the west-side customs, then the long wait for the big room at the front, where I eventually found myself. I sat alone on a creaky wooden chair, and looked around. It was a dark, warm room with a single small window. The walls were grey and covered with nationalist slogans, such as 'Leader + the People = Progress', 'A Great Leader leads a Great Nation to a Glorious Future', and similar gems.

A small, obsequious Afghan appeared, carrying a glass of tea and a jar of small round white balls, apparently a sweetener. The only thing I noticed about him was a huge turban. He tasted the tea, nodded approval and passed it to me. He vanished and reappeared a moment later, bowed and said 'Customs.' He disappeared again. I realised that he was the customs official and that I had just been cleared.

My fat friend materialised, carrying a load of papers.

'Papers,' he said. 'You fill here, you friend, you no walk around.'

I was pleased with this treatment; I offered the guard a cigarette and made him keep the packet. The forms were all in Arabic script. I did not bother to ask if he had brought in the wrong ones, but just scribbled my name alternately in Cyrillic and Roman script in every blank space left. I handed them back. Now there remained only the formality of walking over to the medical building to get a yellow card stamped, and then I was through.

*   *   *

The difference between Iran and Afghanistan is the difference be-tween two worlds. Crossing the border I experienced a shock like that of walking out of an air-conditioned jet into tropical heat. On enter-ing Afghanistan's cultural and emotional atmosphere the sensory system of the receptive traveller changes. To him the cats miaow differently, the dogs bark in an unfamiliar way—even the inevitable Pepsi Cola changes, not in taste but in the way it is perceived. It is hard to pinpoint where the cultural DEW line lies—right at the border, perhaps. It is possible that the air is charged with some different vibration, emitted telepathically and unconsciously by the local population.

Afghanistan is a rugged, impoverished land. In general the Afghans have no running water, electricity, cars, railways, courts, lawyers, theatre, spoons, forks, plates doctors or police that one could take seriously. I wondered how they earned a living. Later in my journey I was to see savages eating raw flesh, but I was unaffected because those savages looked like savages and behaved in a way that one might expect. One is not emotionally open to a savage: one stands near him but there is no contact, no communication. But one is open to an Afghan's dark, peaceful eyes and slow, languid movements. Charmed like a cobra by a fakir, a visitor to Afghanistan starts to sway to the natural rhythm. Crossing the border one enters a sea of silence ... The few birds around the sparse trees are singing the same song they sing in Iran, but in Afghanistan they sing in a world of silence. The background noises disappear. Afghan life is very quiet, but it is made almost inaudible by one's attitude. One hears the occasional screech of a donkey cart, the jingle of a carriage, the sounds of women carrying water from a well: but one sees these sounds rather than hears them. One looks at the donkey and senses the bray, but no noise reaches the ear.

I did not take to Afghanistan. There was no specific reason for this. Most overlanders seem to enjoy it, but to me there was something strange and unsettling in the atmosphere. It was as if death and danger lurked in every corner. The people looked peaceful but their peace concealed something cruel and menacing. No obvious aggression or malice in their speech or gestures gave that impression—just something undefined, a general feeling of violence in the air.

*   *   *

On arriving in Herat, the first town I came to, I decided to pause and get acclimatised. I took a bed in a typical *oteli-stan*—a cheap Asian hotel. They clustered on the main road, charging thirty cents a day for bed and blanket, firewood extra. Having slept the night, I decided to familiarise myself with the town. 'Herat, the wind-downsville' in the overland jargon. It was built by Alexander the Great and updated by Ghengis Khan, Tamerlane, the Turks and everybody else who came afterwards.

I took a walk. It was still early in the morning and the streets were full of soft-treading, supple Afghans. The only noise interrupting the great silence was the chatter of horse-drawn, jingle-belled carriages and the occasional braying of a donkey. The wide main road, lined on both sides by shops, was out of a Hollywood Western set, complete with horsemen, post office and sheriff's office, which is the local police station. There the fat policemen—the only fat people in Afghanistan—lounged on the terrace, their feet on the fence. I walked through the *souk*, the market place, past shelves of massed merchandise piled high, stacks of pots, piles of bulging bags, cows' legs' hanging from dirty blood-covered hooks, swarming with flies— yet all noiseless, like a silent movie.

The *souk* and the main street apart, the rest of the town was biblical. Walking along a row of mud houses I could visualise scenes from the nativity—the Virgin Mary, completely veiled, coming into the city on a donkey, with her little boy on her lap; the shepherds, the stable, the manger. The walk soon exhausted me. I stopped two policemen who were holding hands, asked them for directions and returned to the hotel. It was a two-storey structure of timber, brick and mud. I shared a room with Yorg, a German anarchist, and Philip, a French printer. Like many but not all overlanders, those two spent most of their time in the hotel, listening to hard rock, sleeping and tripping.

The majority of overlanders are not too communicative and the general impression is one of isolation—'hands off'. Although I was initially critical of those travellers who never left the ghetto, I be- haved like them for several days and met a few interesting people. I simply did not have the courage to leave the security of the hotel. The Afghan experience seemed like having the rug of my reality pulled from under my feet, so I peeped out at Afghanistan through the window. I was still amazed at how cheap everything was, and kept the bell-hop, a turbaned, Russian-overcoated urchin, running to restaurants to bring in all kinds of local delicacies—most of them too sweet or too greasy to be edible.

Several days later I had readjusted and felt ready to venture into Afghanistan again. I wanted to go into the country, meet the people, see the land, the customs, the village life. Besides, I was anxious to get off the beaten track and to make my way to South Pakistan and the ocean.

I was told that one could buy a horse at a fair for fifty dollars, ride to Pakistan and sell it at a profit. I did not care about making a profit—even if I sold it at a fifty per cent loss it would still be a bargain. I spoke of my plans to buy a horse to a young waiter at the hotel. He explained that it was not simple—a horse would be more likely to cost a hundred dollars, or even two hundred to a foreigner. Getting about on one's own was not only dangerous but forbidden. Still, the boy was eager to help. He introduced me to his cousin Fuad, a travelling salesman of sorts, who was the hotel proprietor's nephew.

Fuad was an intelligent young man who planned to study at a German university. He asked me many questions about student life in Germany, and I promised to help him on his arrival. He was quick, bright and very practical and efficient. The son of a merchant, he conducted his own business on the side and made frequent trips into the country, often on horseback, reaching inaccessible little villages and hamlets. He was about to embark on a long trip south to Kandahar, selling razor blades to the local shopkeepers en route. Fuad was, in Afghan terms, a wholesaler, and sold the blades only in hundreds or thousands. When he had sold the blades he was to ride with me across Registan to Quetta where I could take a train to Karachi and meet Thom at the bay.

Fuad promised to help me buy a horse. As I expected, he said that I should pay about a hundred to a hundred and fifty dollars, losing about ten to twenty per cent on resale. This meant fifteen to twenty dollars for the adventure of owning an Afghan horse: I was very enthusiastic.

The next Thursday we went to a horse fair together.

6

Kandahar

In Herat the Thursday horse fair is the big event of the week, and the men put on extra big turbans. Street vendors turn out in force, setting up their little spits and barbecues and fanning the flames with big straw fans, yelling, 'Yala, yala!'

Groups of young Afghans with shaven bullet-heads walk about keeping close together, as though under magnetic attraction, caught in a common mental trance to which they all swayed, their individual brains dulled to inertia. I believed it was the complete and unnatural absence of women in these Muslim lands that created this atmosphere, a sort of misdirected sexuality, with men holding hands and a physical proximity between men and beasts, and always the threat of violence—perhaps as a result of repressed sexuality. Nevertheless I could see how others might find this atmosphere exciting and romantic.

Fire-breathers shot great tongues of flame. Dwarfs, acrobats and fortune-tellers entertained, and tough, sinewy horses ridden by skilful men exhibited their prowess.

The horse fair lasted all day and the whole day was spent in looking at horses, feeling them and examining their legs, flanks and teeth. Those Afghan horses were a dismal-looking lot. Sad-faced, abject and pathetic, they stared at you passively, fatalistically, all life and spirit beaten out of them. To the Afghan, a horse is a dire necessity, a tool, a machine that must function.

We tried many horses. I was surprised to find that rather small ones could carry me without much difficulty. A few of them even went quite fast. Having ridden them, I would have been quite happy to buy one, their looks aside, but I had seen Kandahar. In spite of his name, Kandahar did not look like an Afghan horse; instead he resembled what foreigners imagine Afghan horses to look like.

Kandahar was not offered at the fair. He belonged to Asis, Fuad's father. I had seen him the day before when we called on Fuad to make arrangements for the fair. He ran free and wild around the courtyard and one of Asis's boys was trying to catch him to take him to the blacksmith. He had the wide, scared eyes of a tense animal capable of much speed. By European standards he was not a big horse but he was by far the biggest of all the Afghan horses we had seen.

Many horses were brought to us. We appraised them and rode them and always came out with the standard line, 'Fine horse for an Afghan, but I'm too heavy for him.' This was not quite true, but plausible, for the horses were really quite small. We chose a capable-looking one for Fuad, but as the day came to a close I put on a worried look.

'So what about that Kandahar of yours?' I asked finally.

Fuad was eager that I should go with him—to be seen with a foreigner in all those villages meant prestige. Besides, he was anxious to finish our talk about student life in Germany and to find out what his possibilities were. Also a white face would guarantee that the blades were really American, and that Fuad was becoming a big man.

I got Kandahar for a camera that I had acquired by accident and which I had come to regard in a negative light. I also gave sixty dollars to Asis and a pair of levis to Fuad. I carried out the transaction quickly, fearing that the man might change his mind. Until then I had not even come close to that horse, but I knew I would not be disappointed. I sent Fuad's boy to take Kandahar to the hotel stables, then I returned to the town alone.

In the restaurant I was so excited that I could hardly sit still. Of course I now had only about two hundred and something dollars left, some of which would go towards ammunition and provisions; Fuad would get the rifles. But this is Asia: in Afghanistan the net annual per capita income is eighty dollars, and so it is all the way to South-east Asia. So I had the equivalent of almost three times a man's yearly earnings. I ordered a huge meal and gave the boy twenty Afghanis so that he would celebrate—and to make sure nothing was eaten on the way from the kitchen.

Now I had a horse, a good horse of my own. Things were looking up, I thought, as my dinner was brought in.

*   *   *

Two days later we were off. It was still dark when we rode through Herat, and the beautiful winter morning greeted us in all its glory. Herat dissolved in a brownish haze and I could see the top of the thousand-year-old mausoleum displaying its glittering blue enamelled dome.

The earth was dry and we made good progress. Kandahar and I were good friends. I was soft and gently insistent, Kandahar easy, yielding and ready to oblige. It felt wonderful to be so free. There was a long stretch of soft ground ahead.

'I'll try out Kandahar,' I said to Fuad, and gave the horse a squeeze with my thighs, bringing him to a canter. The horse was game; I stroked his neck. He was raring to go. I eased the reins and we were off. I rode in a way I had never ridden before, feeling the excitement of the horse, the strain in his muscles and the thud of hooves against icy ground.

This was the first time I felt clearly a transition that was to come at increasing intervals during the rest of my trip. This ride was one of those triggers into a higher consciousness. My mind would suddenly lose the capacity to remain isolated; it would open up and start functioning in a new way, immersed in the environment. I opened up to the horse, the ground and the frost, and they in turn opened up to me. The horse positively sensed this. There was a perceptible change in the animal as he responded to the excitement of our communion. I sensed his resistance melting, my control over him slipping, and I felt a clear tremor in his muscles as he mellowed and stretched out into a yet faster gallop. What startled, though, was not the speed but the change in rhythm of the gallop. The horse was contracting, hitting the ground, lunging forward at the rhythm of my own heart-beat. I felt as if it was I who was galloping, the horse an extension of my body. A sense of joy surged through us as I felt no me—I felt only a blend of energies and forces. The individual I melted. There was just the strain, the urge to spring, the warm horse/man blood surging over brown earth, absorbed in it, part of it. Later I was reminded of the centaurs of classical legend, and I felt the great truths behind the myths, the complex multiplicity that is a human being. I felt the horse's desire to give expression to the feeling so I cried out for both of us as we galloped in wide circles. The heat between my thighs that was the horse grew alarmingly intense, yet I let him gallop at his own speed, slowly easing off and coming to trot parallel with Fuad. I slowed to a walking pace.

I rode on next to Fuad in silence, still absorbed in the pleasure of the communion. Only gradually did I come to myself again, a single individual once more, as we continued the long trip south-east. We wore thick Afghan sheepskin coats, boots and camel-hair socks. Two second-hand Enfield rifles in leather sheaths were slung from each horse.

We carried little luggage—the bag of blades, a small tent, and the food. Fuad carried no maps: he knew the country, and his only accessory was a heavy British-army compass stashed inside the medium-sized saddle-bag. The lack of luggage made us look like Sunday trippers rather than merchants.

'Tribesmen will not take us for merchants,' Fuad had said. 'It is better this way.'

Before us was a huge expanse of brown earth and an occasional lonely mountain in the distance. There was no road, and soon the last human dwelling disappeared from sight. It was like riding across the moon's flat nothingness.

We stopped for lunch by a stream near a small hill and did not bother to make a fire. We ate *nan*, boiled eggs and chocolate, then continued the silent journey.

Four hours later the horses signalled the approach of the village, their ears pricking up and their steps growing more lively. In the distance smoke was rising into the grey sky.

The whole village came out. Fuad explained that this would happen every time, for the villagers were friendly. The headman, tall and bearded, greeted us and asked some boys to take care of the horses. We kept the saddle-bags but handed the rifles to the headman. This was the custom, Fuad said.

We were guests of the old man. It was obvious that he was giving the best of everything he had. It still took will-power to eat an acceptable quantity of foul-tasting, greasy *pilau* while wearing an expression of satisfaction. All ate from the same dish. The head man frequently dipped his fingers into the sauce to fish out the best-looking pieces of meat for Fuad and me. I could see the contrast between the dirty parts of his fingers and the tips washed clean by the sauce. Putting hepatitis and dysentery out of my mind, I did my utmost not to disappoint him.

The children showed some interest in me at first but soon seemed to forget me and clustered around Fuad instead.

'Interesting as your face may be to them, they can't forgive you your stupidity,' said Fuad. He explained that they could not understand why I did not speak Farsi. They had run into nomadic tribes who did not speak their language, but then they were assumed to be creatures of a lower caste, whereas I had the advantages of a good horse, clothes and a rifle, so it was unforgiveable that I could not speak like a man.

We slept on the concrete floor in the old man's house. There was fire underneath the floor, so it was cosy and wonderfully warm inside. I had not been so warm since Istanbul. The man brought us straw mats and a glass of hot goat's milk, and we were soon asleep.

We left at daybreak; in order to reach the next village by nightfall we had to move at a brisk pace all day.

The morning came fresh, and the violet sky had become slightly overcast. Here and there patches of morning mist still hung close above the ground as we rode along the edge of a long flat plateau to some mountains. I wondered about Afghanistan, this strange, empty, sterile land. Surely it was not meant for human habitation—yet people lived there, over twelve million of them. I had never found out what they lived on: scraping a living from those moon valleys seemed impossible. I was told that it was mostly goats and sheep, a little farming, selling skins for export, getting some aid here and there, mostly from the Russians, getting by from day to day. It seemed an inadequate explanation, however. They must eat rocks and sand, I concluded.

Chara, the next village, was considerably bigger than I had expected and in some ways more beautiful than Herat. The houses had a graceful architectural style; the mud walls were whitewashed even and elegantly curved, the flat surfaces smooth and polished. All genuine architecture is made beautiful by virtue of its intimate connection with the spirit and culture of the people, the climate, and the use of local materials. It is when one transports Greek columns to Massachusetts, I thought, and crosses them with mountain logs and Swiss cottages—when the inner sense of balance is lost—that ugliness results. Something in the slopes of those curves, the angles of the walls, was organically linked to the thoughts, behaviour, fears and aspirations of the users and makers of those dwellings. There seemed a logic in the way streets led into the square as if there were a hidden underlying pattern to local life of which these shapes were a visible manifestation.

The sale itself was unexpectedly simple. It was all over before I even had time to register what Fuad was doing. Welcomed by children and old men, we proceeded straightaway to Omar's shop. Fuad knew Omar and told him what our business was. There was tea and *jellaba*. Fuad stated the quantity and the price of the blades. Twenty minutes later the man had bought a thousand dollars' worth and handed the money to Fuad. I was amazed.

'Is it that simple?' I asked Fuad.

He said there was no problem : the man had been waiting for the blades, and other people were waiting for him. Omar's cut would be about a hundred dollars, a big profit for those parts.

We spent the night at Omar's house. This time we slept on small, uncomfortable beds, but they were the best he had.

The next trading post was only two hours away. The merchant did not know Fuad and fussed a lot, burning and rubbing the blades and opening many of the packages. Once satisfied, he counted seventy-five thousand Afghanis, fifteen hundred dollars' worth.

'Wow !' I exclaimed, as we rode away an hour later. 'You could make a fortune selling razor-blades here.'

'Hardly likely,' said Fuad. 'The market is very limited—we've just about covered a year's supply of razor-blades for the whole area. Of course, I could make a lot of money importing many different things, but operations bigger than this are difficult at the moment; one needs powerful friends, and that takes a lot of investment—but one day I'll have them.'

It was much the same in Azra and Gazni—first we glimpsed trees and then the village—a welcoming crowd, a fat jovial merchant, a large meal and ready cash. Next day we had sold almost all the merchandise so we took our time, enjoying the ride.

*   *   *

A day later we saw a caravan : it was a startling sight. My eyes, already fatigued by the lifeless, unending expanse of earth and sky, focused on this oasis of life. A sharp contrast : the clear blue sky, the whiteness of the land and the brown sprawl topped by the rising smoke from the fires.

'Let's go and visit them,' I said excitedly.

Fuad was reluctant. 'It would not be wise. Word gets round, people know we are trading and carrying money. We have taken few risks so far. We're safe in the villages and nobody can catch us in the open—besides, we carry guns, but to drop in on them like that ... Those people are wanderers; they are outside the law and recognise no borders or governments. They may be friendly or they may not be—you never know how they'll react.'

I hardly listened. I was so excited that I had to go on ahead.

'Listen Fuad,' I said, 'take Kandahar and the money and wait for me. Make sure they can see you so that they realise there are two of us. If something happens to me they know they can't catch you; you'd be sure to bring help later—they know they can't hide or escape.'

This seemed to make sense to me at the time and Fuad finally agreed. We exchanged horses. Kandahar had already made friends with Fuad. We rode together to about five hundred yards from the camp. It emerged in a rainbow of colour—red and ochre, black tents, the red dresses of the women and the black coats of the men. The fires burned invitingly.

I rode ahead alone and was greeted by the barking of the dogs but ignored by the men. They sat outside their tents, smoking, talking and minding the animals. The women were cooking. The camp was strangely silent. Nobody showed aggression—I was merely ignored. I rode about in the hope that somebody would pay me some attention and invite me to dismount.

I noticed I was being followed by two rather unpleasant-looking youths. Not knowing what to do, I dismounted, tethered the horse, took a torch and walked towards them, making an effort at smiling. I got to within twenty feet from them when one of them started shouting. I saw that he was not a youth but a slight, middle-aged man; the other, taller and younger, bent down to pick up a stone. I realised I was getting nowhere and turned around, still smiling, and walked back towards the horse. A stone whistled past me : I ignored it and walked on. I heard footsteps running up from behind and flexed my body as the man flung himself on my back. I was ready : I whipped round, bringing the butt of my rifle down on to his shoulder. He screamed with pain. The other one jumped and danced around me, brandishing an ineffective-looking stick and waiting for a chance to spring. More of them came out of their tents.

The impending fight was averted by a commanding voice. The smaller man dropped his stick and walked away. I turned in the direction of the voice and met with the cool but not unfriendly gaze of a tall, well-built man. Unlike the rest, he wore no turban but a large impressive fur hat. He gestured, inviting me to a large red tent that obviously belonged to the chief. The women around the fire immediately withdrew inside the tent as we approached but I caught a glimpse of them and realised that they wore no *chador* : their faces were uncovered. In the tent they giggled nervously behind the curtains. They were the only creatures in the camp who smiled.

38

The man motioned me to sit down and then sat next to me in silence. I examined his face: it was hard and cruel, but not sly or mean; it was like all the other faces, a sad face. I gave him the torch. He examined it, saw that it worked and called for somebody. A woman appeared; he gave it to her and she disappeared.

A few moments later she came back carrying a pot of tea and some stale *nan*. The tea was cold and flat, and the *nan* wet and soggy—rather a poor bargain for my torch, I thought. I was only half-way through drinking the tea when the man rose and brought my horse over—rather an abrupt goodbye, but the man looked resolute.

I swung up into the saddle and disappeared in a flurry of ice and snow.

7

The Attack

It was a cold February night, fierce and pitch black. We did not reach Saresh, the small hamlet where we were supposed to spend the night. The river was flooded and we spent four hours trying to find somewhere to cross. Still, we found a good camping place—a dry cave by the high, rugged edge of a plateau about two hundred yards up from the foot of the cliff.

I took the first watch. I gathered some wet twigs and built a feeble fire that kept threatening to go out. I kept it alive by adding shots of kerosene at critical moments. With three hours of the watch to go, there was less than a pint of kerosene left. I was sitting about two hundred yards below the dry cave, protected from the wind, in which we had made our camp: the horses could not get up any higher. The fire dwindled and became almost ineffectual. Lazy and listless as I was, I forced myself to get up and look for wood. I was lucky enough to find a half-rotted tree trunk. I placed it on the fire, sat down, looked at the flames and relaxed.

My boots were wet and had shrunk and were giving me some pain.

I took one of them off and started to pick out the little pebbles. It was while taking off the other that I felt again that sudden mental switch, as if somewhere in my mind a signalman had changed the points, transferring my mind back on to the reflective track. Mechanically I went on picking out the pebbles, but my mind slipped away from where I was, from my fingers picking at the boot-soles. I looked blankly through the fire as the unanswered questions flooded back into the consciousness.

I had left on this trip in order to collect my thoughts, to reflect on the kind of life that was worth living—or so I kept telling myself. On this trip, however, I felt increasingly a certain inner resistance, a jolt of mental discontent that came whenever my mind became aware of itself. I wanted to reflect, yet my body rebelled against reflection. The senses protested as if rudely awakened every time my mind switched to an introspective channel.

Something in me was already asking, was it not better to live like 'the natives': a silent, extrovert life absorbed in the environment, functioning and feeling with the weather and the immediate circumstances? I wanted to think, but perhaps the reflection I really wanted was of a different kind. I was interrupted in these thoughts by a blast of freezing wind, and I was thankful when the flying snow hit my face and chased my mind back to occupy itself again with my freezing feet and the cold night.

Since I had left on this trip the process of reflection became so unpleasant, I almost wished that somebody would bang me on the head or stun my mind with an electric shock. It was like a premonition and little did I know how quickly my wish for non-reflective adventure was to be fulfilled.

The wood on the fire did not catch: it was too wet and the fire had practically gone out.

I looked around for something that would burn and my eye fell on the horse blanket. Oh to hell with it, I thought, tomorrow we'll be in town. I took the blanket, soaked it with kerosene, threw it on to the fire and piled the logs on top of it.

The fire surged quickly and the logs dried out. As the wave of heat thawed my body, a pleasant feeling ran through my limbs. I took a Russian can of pork, opened it and grilled the meat over the fire. It sizzled and smelled good.

I wished I had a bottle of wine with me, and as I thought of it I found myself remembering Thom and all the bottles of wine we had emptied together. I wondered what sort of stage I'd find him in this time, for Thom's life was essentially a matter of going through stages. Would he be on a Che Guevara kick, dressed in 'fatigues' and talking of revolution, or would I find him in the Sheraton bar telling the waiters off for bringing ice-cubes when he asked for crushed ice. I decided that it did not matter, and left myself open to surprises. The meat on the skewer was cooked and I put it in a piece of *nan*, letting it absorb the fat and toasting it briefly over a glowing chunk of wood. I ate slowly and with gusto. Having finished, I washed the can and brewed some delicious coffee.

I felt good. The fire crackled and sparkled. The night became a soft sensuous blanket. Alone and relaxed, I took out Fuad's mouth organ and abandoned myself to music and memories of Adriatic coasts, cool Slovenian lakes, blood-red *Dingach* and tall Dalmatian girls. After an orgy of reminiscences, my mind drifted back to the present. The sky had cleared a little and there was no sound to be heard. A strange violent land, I said to myself, and started to play again.

*　　*　　*

Perhaps it was a false note that saved me. As I played it I must have jerked my head back angrily, and consequently the powerful blow only glanced off my skull; my shoulder took the full brunt of it. I fell forward, arms outstretched, hitting my nose against a stone. I landed with my face buried in the dirt, and blood started to ooze out of my nose and collect in a small puddle. For a few moments I lay there, conscious but shocked and immobile. It took a while for me to realise that I had been attacked. My immediate reaction was not to move—play dead, I thought.

There were voices around me, about a dozen men. The one who had hit me still carried a heavy wooden club. I could not see if the rest of them were armed. The one with the club poked the fire and picked up a piece of burning horse blanket on the end of the club. Guessing his intention, I rubbed my face into the pool of mud and blood under my nose. He walked up to me, grabbed my hair and jerked me up and around. I could not help groaning, but I kept my eyes shut and my body limp. He held up the torch, lighting up my twisted blood- and mud-covered face. They must have assumed that I was badly hurt, for two of them picked me up and carried me up the cliff towards the tent. I recognised the two men who threw stones at me when I visited the caravan. On reaching the tent they threw me down like a sack. Fuad was still asleep. For a second it occurred to me to shout a warning, but I realised it was a ridiculous idea. The attackers took no precautions against being heard. The big man (I recognised my host) grabbed the top ridge of the tent and with one quick powerful jerk swept it clean into the air. Fuad lay there exposed like a snail without a shell. He did not even wake up when the first kick landed. As he sprang up in terror he was grabbed by the two men who carried me. The big one stepped towards him and gave him a loud slap. Fuad groaned and shouted something. The man continued to slap him, then paused and fired some questions. Fuad was too confused to answer. Realising this, the big man gave him a few minutes to come to himself. Meanwhile the rest of them were going through our bags and blankets. They found what remained of the razor-blades but were not interested; they were obviously looking for the money which was hidden in the linings of the saddles.

As Fuad become more composed the big man pointed at my bare feet and questioned Fuad. Thoughts flew through my head; my brain worked like a machine. I realised that he might be asking Fuad where the money was. My mind searched frantically for a way to shift the hopeless odds and give us a chance. I let out a groan, attracting attention to myself. Then in English, muffled to sound like another groan, I groaned twice, 'Money in my boots, in my boots.' Fuad obviously understood. He pointed at my bare feet, telling the man that the money was hidden in my boots, then gestured towards the horses. It worked. Only the two men holding Fuad stayed; the rest ran off down the steep slope towards the horses below.

My pulse quickened and I analysed the situation. How long would it be before they found both boots, cut them open and examined them? Five or ten minutes at the most—but at least I had bought some time. We had to act quickly.

The two men were about ten feet away. One still held Fuad, whose arms had been bound, the other set about examining the contents of the tent again. The men were talking now, both with their backs to me. This was ideal—there was no more time for thought. I looked around for something to strike with and my eye fell on a long tent pole and then a large stone. Which was it to be? The tent pole might be too light, but the stone . . . It had to be the tent pole; the stone was too awkward. Fuad's eyes widened as he saw me crawl towards the tent pole. As I grabbed it I realised that it was not light at all. Now there was distance to worry about, and I could not afford to make a mistake. What should I do—crawl up to them? No. But springing up on them would be too awkward. I would have to get up and hope that they would not look round.

The man turned around suddenly, but it made no difference. I was already on my feet, holding the tent pole up high in both hands. Covering the distance in a flash, I put the whole weight of my body into the blow. He lifted his hands to protect himself but they collapsed like straw under the blow which landed against his skull. He crumpled up like a broken doll. The second's delay gave the other man a chance. Before I could raise the stick again he was on top of me, lunging wildly with a Khyber knife. We both fell down.

His uncontrolled frenzy made him miss and gave me a chance to grab his skinny arm. He was on top of me, his face twisted, dripping sweat and cursing. I had him: the skinny arm that had aimed to kill me was weak and fragile and I felt it breaking under the pressure. With my other hand I pulled his long hair. Suddenly his elbow jerked free and he hit me on the ear. For a second I was confused: his head slipped free as he buried his teeth deep into my arm. I screamed with pain but was not going to let go. By then Fuad had realised what was happening. He threw himself with all his weight at the man on top of me. The blow knocked his head away and freed my left hand, with which I overpowered the little man and held him on his back, pinning his arms down with my knees and holding his throat while my right hand found the knife.

The little man stiffened like a monkey that at the end of the chase prostrates himself before his attackers. He froze, while his eyes burned with fear. A stone caught my eye. Lifting that stone was hard but at least I was not consciously killing a man. All my senses in revolt, my hand came down. The man lay motionless but was still groaning. I got up and cut Fuad's bonds. As soon as he was free Fuad grabbed the knife. The man on the ground moaned and made an attempt to get up, but Fuad was already there.

About two minutes must have passed since the other men had left; how much time did we have before their return? We did not stop to think but grabbed the saddle, ripped it open, took the money and the small package of blades, and ran into the night. Our hearts beating wildly, we ran, stumbled and fell. My feet were bleeding but I did not feel the frost or cold. Twenty minutes later we felt exhausted. I listened out for sounds of pursuers but there were none. We ran on, stopping every ten minutes or so to get our breath. Fuad took off his thick shirt and gave it to me to wrap around my feet.

Two hours later the dawn was breaking and as the first rays of the sun parted the morning mist we suddenly saw in the distance the curve of the Kandahar road glistening in the sun like a snake. 'Thank God,' I said, and collapsed into the snow. Cold was creeping into my bones. I shivered. Fuad unwrapped my feet and began to rub them with snow

8

The Hammam

The big hall was gloriously hot. A cloud of steam was rising from my wet clothes. I peeled them off with difficulty and threw them into a basin of hot water.

It was very dark in the Kandahar Central *Hammam*, the Afghan version of a Turkish bath. A small man, naked save for a loin cloth, handed us a thin, dirty-looking towel. I smelt it: it was clean—it only looked dirty, as did everything else in the hall.

The hot stone gave me a wonderful tingling sensation and brought my feet to life. My whole body was a block of ice slowly being thawed.

I wanted it to be as hot as could be and said to the little man, '*Bura garam, bura bura*, big hot, big, big,' handing him a ten Afghani note. He took it and motioned me to follow. We walked through the big hall filled with sprawling men wearing small towels around their waists. Nobody paid any attention to us and we reached a narrow dark passage that led off into the darkness. We had to duck as we walked through various wooden doorways. The heat grew more intense. The man stopped before number 73 and we entered. There were two adjoining cubicles. The first one, a sort of rest chamber, was considerably less hot than the second where the heat would normally be unbearable. But now I was overjoyed to step in, collapse on the rack on the floor and stretch full length, letting the heat enter every joint and bone. Only two hours previously we had been standing in deep snow, almost frozen, when we heard the rattle of the morning Kandahar bus.

I turned to Fuad. 'We've had a lucky escape! We've lost the horses and provisions though.'

Fuad waved his hand airily. 'Allah's will,' he said. 'All we've lost is three hundred dollars. We've made close on four thousand. If only every week were like that!'

He put on such a self-satisfied philosophical expression as he said it that I had to smile. Fuad looked at me and started to laugh. Still laughing, he grabbed the bucket of cold water and threw it over me, but I had already turned on the cold shower tap and a huge spray of icy water came down on him. We went on like that, rocking with laughter and splashing each other until some time later, finally exhausted, we sat down again.

'Too bad about Kandahar,' I said. 'I don't suppose there's anything we can do about it.'

Fuad became serious. 'You're joking: if we try, we stand to lose as much as the tribesmen. That self-defence talk carries little weight when used by adventure-seeking foreigners. Besides, I want nothing to do with that tribe again. They've had some losses, and in return they've got the horses. Will of Allah! Besides, in a week or so they'll be who knows where.'

This meant that I would not be able to continue south to the Indian Ocean but had to get back on to the Asia trail for a while, then break off at Peshawar and make for the coast as planned. I reconciled myself to this idea and looked for the soap.

The masseur tapped on the door and entered. He was tiny but well-proportioned, his taut, oiled body glistening like that of a snake.

'He's very good,' said Fuad. 'Always ask for Kabir when in Kandahar. Now just relax.'

The masseur crouched over me and turned me over on to my stomach. He started by lifting and stretching my legs, raising them backwards towards my head. He trod up and down my spine which crackled; he continued the motion while raising my hands. This part of the massage seemed somewhat violent and unpleasant but when he had finished I felt loose and relaxed. He knelt and dug his palms into my shoulders; he worked quickly and efficiently, finishing each set of movements with a slap. For a while I wondered if the man knew what he was doing, for I felt he was about to break every bone in my body. Unlike a Western massage, there was very little rubbing; this was actually neck-cracking, joint-pulling and limb-twisting. All this, I was to find out, is a part of life throughout Asia, and follows in one form or another a visit to the barber, a bath, etc. This first time I found it painful, but it achieved what I wanted. My body, stiff and rigid from fear, cold and exhaustion, felt wonderfully relaxed and supple. When we reached our dirty little hotel I fell asleep immediately.

Unlike my exciting horse, the town of Kandahar was sleepy, dreamy and mellow. I took to it straight away. It was softer, gentler and earthier than Herat, which in retrospect seemed somewhat cold and sterile. There was a touch of romance to Kandahar, a scent of the South, a certain erotic charge in the air. The men moved with exuberance, the palms swayed sensually, a lively rhythm pulsed in the streets.

* * *

The *Hammam* and the massage may have saved me from chronic arthritis or pneumonia—yet in spite of that invigorating experience, I fell ill.

The day after the arrival in Kandahar I woke up sick and shaking with fever. For three days Fuad stayed with me, yet there was little he could do but sit there. Most of the time I was sleeping and only half conscious, suffering the fever, waiting for it to lift.

When the worst of it was over and I found myself being able to read and converse, I saw no need for him to stay. Our plan to ride across to Quetta had fallen through, and to get across to Pakistan I had to get back to the bus route anyway. Fuad's father needed him back so I urged him to go. Before he left, he made arrangements with the *hotelier* to take care of me and my room was kept warm. The hot, invigorating food came regularly and there was *tsai* and *jellaba* whenever I asked for it.

So we said our goodbyes and Fuad left and I was alone, still bedridden, still weak, wondering how long before I would be strong enough to leave.

During the next few days, lying there hour after hour watching the sun's shadow slowly travel across the room, I'd suddenly experience intense happiness. These moments came particularly at the sunsets, when I sensed the shadows were about to disappear; the room would light up with a pale glow and then the magic was suddenly extinguished and the darkness swept across the ceiling. There was at first a sharp feeling of sorrow, but one of happiness immediately followed, as if springing from the same well; the sensations were of the same texture and colour, like two faces of the same coin.

At times I'd experience a sudden longing for a proper bed with sheets, for clean food and people who looked you in the eyes and spoke words you could understand. But there was also a cleansing aspect to my circumstances and I felt Europe drifting away further into the recesses of my mind.

My room was on the ground floor of the Hotel Serai and looked onto the street—where I could see only the necks of camels passing by and donkeys' heads. In the evening there would be children. Silent wordless Afghani children, with runny noses, close-cropped and shaven heads, pressed against the window bars, staring expressionlessly at the sick white foreigner. I was indifferent and ignored them, most of the time I would not even see them, so absorbed was I in reflection while lying in that dingy hotel. I became increasingly capable of switching the mental track from the reflective to the immediate from that of observer to that of participant. It seemed as if from the beginning of the trip I had travelled on two different planes. The further I penetrated into Asia, the less I was inclined to see the reflective aspects of the journey as superior to the merely physical experience and the adventure of travel itself. At times I found one could still experience the world in a way one did as a child. What is it, I asked myself, that happens to the mind as one grows older, that conditions it to experience the world only through the mediation of one's *intellectual* perception of it? I'd had the dubious privilege of stemming only partially from a very 'cultured' background, and the misfortune of having an aunt who was all too aware of the less 'cultured' elements of our family pedigree. The fact was ignored that if the country was free of foreign domination and my aunts were still women of note, this was thanks to the uncultivated elements who hacked and shot their way through the long years of revolution and war, civil and otherwise. So I'd had my share of being told that I was a peasant and crude and of being whipped for going barefoot and for playing with the gypsies. I was punished and screamed at till I learned to accept that reading about gypsies was O.K., but touching them was not; that being good meant having a certificate from a teacher saying so, that intelligence meant passing tests, that health required a certificate from the doctor. Everything that was indirect, roundabout, meditated, removed from the actual, was good. Yet my transition from physical into intellectual being did not seem complete, and a hidden signalman kept changing the tracks in accordance with some rhythm which I wanted to grasp. And so it was on this trip: reflection—action—intellectual experience—adventure. It was that something which held them together that I wanted to get to know. I might experience an event as an adventure free of mental connotations, or as an exercise in philosophy, but this seemed independent of the event itself. Yet this duality pleased me; the more I thought about it, the more I realised that it was not something new—it was there all along but merely ignored.

Perhaps it was for that reason that I was attracted to people like Thom: in their extrovert pursuit of different and often contradictory goals, they seemed to emerge guiltless.

Although I lay in my hotel room with no books, no friends or visitors, I was not bored. I engaged in my favourite pastime of writing letters to my friends. Like the late Pope John Paul I, I even wrote to imaginary or dead people. Whom was I to write to, though, when I had written to all my friends? It was then, in that Afghan hotel room that I decided to write a diary—but not an ordinary diary. I decided to record moods, colours, the tiniest details—the colour of a mountain at sunset; the shape of Afghan cups, the texture of the local cloth and the taste of the bread. It was to be a diary of smells, colours and sentiments; loose, unstructured sentences, using a page to describe a single sound or the feel of the wet grass on bare feet.

*   *   *

Seven days after first falling ill I finally felt strong enough to walk to Kandahar's hospital. The resident French doctor received me— in bed. Like everyone else, I had to wait an hour for this *Roi Soleil*

48

to take notice of me and of a bunch of sick wailing women. He did not bother to examine me and listened to my complaint without turning over in bed to face me. He took childish pride in 'diagnosing' my accent without looking, and convinced himself that he recognised my complaint. After mumbling a prescription to a nurse, and after correcting my mistaken use of the French conditional, he dismissed me with a regal yawn, and added 'zdrastvuyte' as I was leaving, just to show how he knew everything about me. I returned to the hotel where I spent the next three days in bed.

Perhaps the doctor's prescription was good after all because four days later the fever was gone and I got up. It was late afternoon when I went out and decided to take my first stroll in the soft twilight. Although Kandahar is quite big there is no electricity: the power lines are there but the plant is not operating. The streets were lined with shops lit by candles and kerosene lamps. Goods were piled high in front of the stores; it was a dry twilight and candles shone their soft light on tomatoes, cucumbers, oranges, eggs as well as other beautiful things rarely seen in the north. It felt good to be on one's feet again.

The next day I confidently boarded the bus for Kabul carrying my luggage: a plastic bag and some books. The drive was dull in comparison with my ride through the Afghan countryside on horseback. The bus, like all Afghan buses, was decorated like gypsy caravans, with mirrors, flags and holy pictures; it was slow, noisy and badly sprung. The driver, like all Afghan drivers, was incompetent beyond imagination. In Afghanistan a traffic accident carries a drastic penalty so drivers are cautious to a ridiculous degree, yet to no avail, because they go down like flies. The crash that we experienced seemed the height of absurdity to me, but in later conversations with other travellers I found out about even more unlikely ones: in one example a driver was heading towards a tree and began to panic; he stiffened, accelerated, went flat out for the last hundred yards and, eyes wide with fear, drove smack into the tree, too mesmerised to turn or brake.

The driver went along straight, empty roads at thirty m.p.h., his face tense and absorbed like that of a jet pilot in the middle of a low bombing dive. He would stop, wait and look round at every crossroad, an unnecessary precaution as we were driving through desert and could see for miles along the empty roads. The ritual was repeated at every crossing until we encountered the first blind junction at the foot of the Hindu Kush mountains. A huge 'Stop' sign was clearly visible. The driver, his powers of concentration exhausted, continued past the sign without a moment's hesitation. We hit an army lorry. Nobody was hurt but we lost hours waiting for another bus to come by. Nothing turned up so we all had to walk the last fifteen miles to Kabul.

9

Kabul

From a distance Kabul, the capital of Afghanistan, reminded me of a mediaeval European town. There was little about it that looked oriental or exotic. Perhaps that is why Europeans used to choose it as their base in this part of the world. Take any of the older European towns and remove the department stores, neon lights, glass and concrete structures, the traffic and the noise, and you get something like Kabul.

There was still a freak ghetto situated in Chicken Street, world famous among overlanders. I stayed in a hotel. The sign outside said, 'Hotel 99: Sauna, Hot Showers, TV, Beautiful Gardens, Discotheque, Spotless Rooms, 15 Afs/person.' It was all sham of course, but you couldn't beat the fifteen Afs. If anyone asked for a sauna the manager would direct them to the local *hamum*. The TV station was not operating, he said, but he did possess a set; the beautiful garden was a stretch of wasteland. I shared a room with an American film-maker called Bert who was to become a friend. The rooms were filthy but there really was a discotheque and, intrigued, I decided to visit it that same night.

It was after 10 pm when I entered the smoke-filled room. The place was already in full swing. The low room was dimly lit with ultra-violet light and candles, and had stained-glass windows that must have come from some Vatican supply truck. On the narrow stage two young men with shoulder-length hair played electric guitars. A third, rather older and sober-looking, played a harmonium. Many of the discotheque's fittings seemed to have been pilfered from churches. There was a fourth man who played the drums.

The music was something extraordinary called Afghan pop. The harmonium carried the melody and all the songs sounded the same—a typical Arabic wailing lamentation. The players improvised on the last three notes of the harmonic minor and produced something resembling a cats' chorus miaowing an oriental funeral march. What made the music startling was the rock accompaniment provided by the electric bass guitar. The drummer played a constant beat to every tone, punctuated at regular intervals by two heavy thuds on the bass drum. About eight young men sat on the stage behind them, smoking and talking. They were all in the band but there were only four instruments so all took turns to play, changing not by fours but individually, after each song. Only the harmonium player remained at his post. He was older than the rest and took it all very seriously. I felt sorry for him, with his fine, sensitive face, playing in this absurd band. Regardless of the change of crew, the identical beat was kept throughout: rat-a-tat-tat, then the two heavy thumps.

Although shabbily dressed, I was shown to a good table where I found Bert wearing a tie over his turtleneck '—keeping up appearances,' he said. The discotheque was full. Young men were in the majority but there were a few distinguished-looking older men. There were also some women tucked into a dark corner; from a distance they looked rather attractive.

When the waiter brought me my beer I was startled by a bill for 90 Afs, for in Afghanistan this was the price of a hotel for a week. I sent the beer back and had a double Courvoisier for the same price.

As the band began a popular song most of the men started to clap in time. A flamboyantly dressed young woman leapt into the middle of the room and started to dance. My pulse quickened at the sight of her, but she moved awkwardly, out of time with the music, and gesticulated rather than danced. She was joined by other women who moved in a similar fashion but were better dancers. I assumed that they were some kind of Afghan go-go girls. A few men got up to dance and the women retired immediately.

A short, skinny, hawk-nosed Afghan stood up. He had profoundly sad eyes set in an aggressive face typical of his people. He stretched out his arms, rather like a Greek folk dancer, snapped his fingers and proceeded to dance. He was a very good dancer. It must have been some kind of local dance, for all the men joined in afterwards, dancing in the same fashion although not so well. The hawk-like Afghan was an artist. His head shook as if an electric charge passed through it. Periodically he broke into a whirling spin, back erect, hands outstretched, working madly as if trying to gather impetus to fly away. The men danced alone, totally preoccupied with themselves. Someone insisted that Bert and I join the dance, but I refused on the excuse of ill health. Bert took them up on their invitation and, as a result of his exertions, we were swamped with free drinks.

Most people were quite drunk by this time. No one was smoking reefers, although people in Afghanistan generally do. Still, they more than made up for it with alcohol. The men who had distinguished themselves by their dancing were plied with drinks and invited to share other people's tables. As soon as the men left the floor the women would dance by themselves; men and women did not dance together.

I assumed that the women were quite good-looking by Afghan standards, but a Westerner would find fault with their thick legs and heavy thighs. They sometimes had sex appeal, if no grace.

A distinguished-looking man turned out to be the Pakistani Ambassador. He seemed to be inflamed by the hawk's dancing and kept embracing and kissing him after every dance. He concluded the evening by offering to stand everyone a drink, but less than half the people took him up on it.

As the night went on, the men got more and more drunk. It is strange to see how alcohol affects different races in different ways. One can learn much about people by looking at their animals, particularly pets, or by observing them when drunk. It is also interesting to see how and why certain cultures turn to different means of getting high. For the poor Afghan it's hashish, for the rich it's beer. Minds that have for centuries been trained to hashish adjust to alcohol in curious ways.

The men were swept periodically by waves of sorrow—it was strange to see so many of them affected simultaneously. They sank their heads down to the tables; even the dancers let out occasional sobs. The band would follow the mood of the patrons, rather than the other way round. Every half hour or so would come an aggressive period which lasted for five minutes on average. Somebody would become jealous or annoyed and strike out, then they would all jump on each other, forming instant groups and alliances. There was much gesticulating and hair-pulling. It was all done in silence and in a few minutes the fighting groups would disperse.

The fighting was so ineffectual that I thought at first that it was some kind of mime or dance, some strange local custom. I turned to the Pakistani Ambassador and asked what it was all about.

'Fighting,' he said.

'Does anyone get hurt?'

'Seldom hurt, but people have been killed. The fighting is harmless in itself, but if someone pushes his luck too far and humiliates his beaten opponent by twisting his nose or spitting on him, then the knives come out.'

I saw that after every bout many of the combatants would retire together, kissing and embracing and getting more drunk.

* * *

The next day I moved to B's hotel, a famous institution. It was a large building and rather luxurious for an overlander place. It even had a reception desk and a comfortable lounge, which had been the scene of many hash séances. It was the safest place to take your trips, not because you were safe from the law, but because the drugs were to some extent controlled for quality. When things went wrong there were plenty of people who knew what to do, and even a doctor was on hand, a Dutch medical-school drop-out who lived there free. Inexperienced as anyone with only two years of university training would be, he had at least become something of an expert in the area of drug abuse, administering both traditional Afghan and modern treatment. Things were looking bad, however: the doctor had taken one trip too many. Besides, since the Soviet advisers had moved into Kabul, no place was completely safe. B's hotel was the information centre for the overland trip and offered the best value for money.

I stayed there for three days. Again I found myself unable to cope with Afghanistan—I vegetated in the hotel. But three days of being only an observer tired me and I was eager to leave the country. On the last day I went to see the money market.

Kabul's money market is one of the world's financial curiosities. Tribesmen in turbans, swathed in blankets and rags, walk about carrying huge amounts of money in their hands. Yen, guilder, krone and rupees seems as common a sight in their hands as *nan* and *kebabs*.

I was surprised that the new government would allow them to trade like that. I asked a group how it was that they were permitted to change money in the street.

'But no, Baba ! It is forbidden, Baba !' they explained enthusiastically as they smiled politely and got on with their business.

*   *   *

Some hundred dollars and 32 days ago I was still in Zagreb; it already seemed like an eternity. But this time I was again longing for a clean bed, a shower and a good night's sleep. I was tired of the barren landscape and the frozen ground, and wanted to make my way to Thom as quickly as possible. Without Fuad and the horse I was forced to make towards Pakistan before I could get to a railway once more and travel south, down to the ocean. This meant more bus journeys, a prospect which I dreaded, but at that time my energy was ebbing and I did not have the courage to walk, ride, go down river or undertake similar heroic pursuits. I had had my fill of Afghanistan and wanted to get out, and quickly.

The next morning I found out that both the local and the Pakistan bus to Peshawar were full for weeks ahead. I knew that there was a freak bus leaving the hotel for Delhi and I thought of catching a ride to Pakistan. When I returned to the hotel I found that the Soviet 'narcs' had busted the owner as well as the freak mechanic who serviced the bus. Another mechanic was quickly found; the bus was serviced and ready to go.

'How much to Peshawar?' I asked the young English driver.

The driver, yellow-trousered, snakeskin-jacketed, ignored me for a while, took a long puff at his *chillum* and, exhaling a cloud of hash smoke, hissed, 'Fifty dollars.'

'But the normal fare is one dollar.'

'One dollar for the coons. You want to risk your life or travel like a white *bwana*?'

'Look, I just want to get there.'

'So walk. Otherwise the fare is fifty dollars.'

There were three of them who ran the freak bus—two owners, cocky Cockney types, in process of graduating from grease to the punk look, and the idiot mechanic. They had little patience with all that euphoria of love, peace and brotherhood that characterised the hippy movement of a decade or so ago. This was the new generation, raised in the post-industrial age of leisure and electronics and material excess. They had a new rhythm, danced to a new tune. Theirs was the message of the post-rock sound. To them the romantic India overland experience was the stuff that went out with the whole-earth movement, the Maharishi, the Beatles, Bob Dylan—songs now forgotten.

I wanted to get out of Afghanistan but there was no way I was going to pay fifty dollars for a one dollar trip. The problem was solved by the hotel manager, a well-dressed, intelligent young Afghan.

'Take him,' he commanded. It turned out that his hotel was decorated by surrealist paintings done by an eccentric Yugoslav artist, so he was friendly on that account.

'Give my regards to V. when you are back in Zagreb. Where are you going now?'

'The Pakistani border—I want to get down to the coast,' I said.

'Wouldn't you like to see the Khyber Pass?' he asked. 'If you want, they'll take you across and back down to Lahore. From there you can catch a train south to Karachi.'

'Sure,' I said. 'I'd love to take that route.'

'You've heard him,' said the manager as he turned to the driver. 'The man wants to go to Lahore.'

'O.K. man, Lahore it is,' said the driver, by now indifferent and lost in a cloud of smoke. The manager shook hands with me and left.

There were only twelve other passengers, all of the consumer-freak variety. They had the smell of Europe about them although they had been travelling for weeks.

As we entered the bus I distinctly sensed that feeling of entering a different reality—like stepping out of a hot bath or leaving an air-conditioned room. Was it caused by the European smells that the bus carried with it, was it the European-looking disorder and rubbish on the floor, or could it be that people emit a certain radiation that charges physical objects with their own cultural values?

The bus was huge and comfortable. I sat in the first upholstered seat I had encountered since leaving Europe. The driver started the engine and we were off.

It rolled softly and smoothly, that piece of Europe, raping its way through Asia. The expensive stereo blared music that must have been set to the same rhythm as the songs of first-century Rome. I was too much a product of my time not to feel a certain thrill induced by that music, yet I was becoming increasingly aware of the automatic feeling of emptiness and anxiety that inevitably followed indulgence in the high-pitched tingling tastes, sounds and smells of our techno-culture. Having stung the mouth with synthetic pizza and stunned the mind with TV, one felt as if one had set light to a piece of furniture in order to experience an intense momentary thrill. It was characteristic for drug addicts—intense thrill, then emptiness. So I watched the live performance. They lay sprawled over the seats, some smoking, others sniffing. Occasionally the bus would pull up for someone to give himself a fix. I looked through the window: there was Afghanistan, the outside world, but it was as far away from the inside of that bus as it was from Europe. From inside it was like watching television. We would stop to eat at tourist restaurants, my fellow-travellers paying three to five times more than I did, but they didn't seem to mind.

With only two hundred dollars in my pocket it was tempting to travel free all the way to Lahore. I felt weak and exhausted, and nothing seemed more appealing than collapsing on one of the mattresses on the floor and sleeping my way to Karachi and the ocean. I lay down on the most comfortable mattress and was still half-asleep when we crossed the Afghan border. Some time later we pulled up on the Pakistani side of the border, the engine was switched off and I decided to stretch my legs.

10

Over the Khyber

When I got off the bus I felt refreshed and strong. I walked to a nearby restaurant and ordered tea.

The crimson sun was disappearing behind the Hindu Kush mountains. In the distance the silvery Khyber Pass glistened like a snake. The Pathan men around me were big, open and warm. I looked at the bus and the small group of punks round it who were busy ordering the friendly locals about. The bus seemed a cold, mechanical, vulgar and soul-less animal. I had no idea how I would continue my journey, but I knew that I was not getting on that bus again.

A few minutes later, as it drove away in a haze of dust and rock and roll, I felt a great weight lift from me.

The street had turned a bluish red and a gentle breeze was playing in the groves above. I was still in Asia. Had I stayed a day longer on that bus I might never again have been able to free myself of the European mental environment.

In spite of the high mountains above, it was pleasantly warm in this border village. I decided not to bother to look for transport across to Peshawar but to stay the night. The village was called Landi Kotal.

Opposite the customs building was a general store built of wood, like something from the American frontier days. The sign said 'Asis Supplies'. A powerfully-built man inside greeted me with a winning smile and spoke English.

'It must be that you like our village very much to leave your friends like that.'

'Yes, I do like it. But I didn't like my friends on the bus very much. Do you do much business with them?'

'No, they have set places where they shop. The storekeepers charge treble and pay the driver a kick-back. I'd do it too, but I can't stand those young drivers, they treat you like dirt. Not that I have anything against foreigners. I served the Crown for twenty years.' He straightened up proudly. 'Even under the British we were not treated like dirt. They were gentlemen. Well ... Some of them were.' He spoke as if to himself.

'Are you English?' he asked.

'No, Yugoslav.'

'Ah, Marshal Tito!' came the usual reply. 'Great man!' he concluded, his knowledge of Yugoslavia exhausted.

'Who is a great man?' A man walked in from the back of the shop, obviously the storekeeper's brother.

'Are you praising those damn English again?'

'No, the Yugoslavs.'

An uncomprehending look came over the newcomer's face.

They were twins. Both huge and fat they behaved with easy charm. The storekeeper was a reactionary royalist and his brother was a rebel who had fought against the British as keenly as his brother

57

had served them. Still, it was plain to see that they got on splendidly.

The shop sold food, general supplies and weapons. I refused to buy a machine-gun but asked permission to look through the long racks of weapons that lined the walls. When I found out that the upper floor was a hotel I took a room.

The next day I was awoken by the singing of the loyalist brother. The morning sun streamed through the open windows and his deep voice added warmth and friendliness to the place. The rebel brother served a huge breakfast on a sunlit terrace with a view of the vast mountain range. There was orange juice, heavy, sweet home-made jam with pancakes, and a basket of fruit. The view, the sound of singing and the fruit made me feel light-hearted and positive. It was as if the heaviness of Afghanistan had evaporated from my system.

An hour later I was strolling around the little bazaar in a village a few miles up the road. There were men on horseback carrying bandoliers and rifles; shopkeepers offered hand-grenades and machine-guns for sale, exclaiming, 'Special, special good price, made in Czechoslovakia.'

The people were Pathans, a race that lives on both sides of the border, yet these Khyber Pass highlanders seemed different from their brothers on the other side of the border. It was as if different forces and sentiments resided together among those rocks. These hidden forces would combine to materialise as noiseless, somewhat creepy Afghans, frail-looking yet spirited horses, slow, deceptive rivers; a slight variation in the mix, and a new spirit emerged—fierce pride, tenacity symbolised in the rocks and waterfalls, or in the goat-skin-clad Pathan coming down from the mountains to buy a new part for his 303 rifle. The Pathan faces were hard but there was something friendly, almost childlike, about them. Like everyone else in Asia, they would run after whites shouting the familiar 'Come into my shop' line, but they would do it with no obsequious note in their voice.

I had a good time trying out the guns; I was charged heavily for the ammunition but paid gladly.

I stopped to eat in the open air. The food was the same as in Kabul, grilled garlicky meat, but there was already a touch of Pakistan about it. The spices and smells had a little more piquancy than in Afghanistan. Afterwards I found a peaceful vantage point at the edge of the village from where I could watch a soft patch of green grass and a flock of white sheep grazing peacefully. It was pleasant to find repose in the softness of the flock and the grass. Sitting there absorbed in this patch of softness and peace wedged between the heaps of rock and the noise of vigorous Pathan activity, I pondered how difficult it was to ascribe qualities to places, objects or people. Every observation was necessarily a generalisation, and every generalisation necessarily wrong. I perceived hardness in the resolute way the ram tore out the tender grass; hardness was concentrated in the ram's horns and hoofs; there was whiteness in the ravens on the porch, blackness in the snow-covered mountains above: all freely merged and interchanged.

* * *

The buses were full for the next week. A fat shopkeeper talked a bus driver into letting me climb on the roof, where I joined a group of young Pathans going to Peshawar for their night on the town. There was fun and excitement as the bus started out on its long ascent, and everyone joined in a song.

It was not long before we were rolling through the Khyber Pass, that thirty-mile-wide crack in the wall between the Indian sub-continent and the rest of the world. The tattered bus panted and gasped on its way along the steep slope, a red speck in the sea of brown. When the white roofs of Peshawar appeared, they reflected the last red rays before night filled its narrow streets.

I I

The End of the Lap

Peshawar has the exciting aura of a frontier town, but its inhabitants have lost some of that arrogant, independent swagger that characterises those from the rest of the Khyber region. In this country ruled by tribal laws, it was only in Peshawar that I felt there was a nominal acceptance of Pakistan's central government. Tribal skirmishes still fill the land with blood, and the laws are those which tribes and families make with their guns. But the system seems to work: there is no feeling of the anarchy and lawlessness that characterise parts of Thailand and Malaysia I was to visit.

Peshawar itself was a sprawl of low, grey, brick and mud buildings, dominated by the red fort of Bala Hisar and the white railway station. It felt like a town, not just a settlement. The crowded streets were brightly lit by the thousand and one kerosene lamps shining ouside little teashops, restaurants, cinemas and gun shops. The Pathans must be very narcissistic—almost every film showing there had a poster depicting the inevitable Pathan on horseback, brandishing his 303 rifle. As in most places in Muslim Asia, there were no women in the streets, so it was quite a shock to see a woman's face, if only on one of these posters.

The food was considerably better than in Kabul, and there were no idiotic policemen holding hands and gaping like cows. The people seemed much too interested in themselves to worry about following foreigners around. When they were curious they were not ashamed to show it. The Afghans pretended that they were not really interested but studied you secretly through narrowed eyelids, watching and waiting. There was none of that in Peshawar. It was all out in the open there. Chickens and oxen were being roasted on spits, and men were singing in the streets, cracking jokes and laughing.

I took a hotel room, grossly expensive at one dollar for a floor-level bed in a large room, but I liked the building, a domed Islamic creation with tall narrow windows. In the lounge, turbaned guests played backgammon.

* * *

I had an excellent view from my window so I blew out the candle and opened the window to let in the sounds of the busy night. Outside the oriental town illuminated by moonlight was living well on into the late hours.

I had difficulty in falling asleep. Part of the journey was coming to an end and soon I would be travelling by train, making my way swiftly to the ocean. And then what—a sea saga? Sailing to Mauritius, sandy beaches, Creole girls.

So this is the end of this overland trip, I kept repeating to myself; it seemed somehow incomplete. Although an eternity had passed since I had left Europe the idea that in a day's time I should be back in the city, using electricity, radios, knives and forks again, seemed too unreal. I was afraid of meeting up with those things again. How much easier and psychologically more comfortable just to pursue my overland track on into India. India, after all, was the object of my journey, but at that stage it seemed as if my goal were being reached too quickly. I felt that I had not mellowed enough to experience India in the proper way, to feel whatever it was that India was about. Somewhere in the back of my mind it was becoming clear to me that to arrive anywhere too quickly or too easily was not possible. We all want the higher things but shun the means to the higher things. Slaves, serfs, colonies, aeroplanes, drugs, computer-dating, labour-saving gadgets: all different historical expressions of mankind's basic corruption—desiring the end but not willing the necessary means. Always looking for a painless short-cut—in love, in sex, in human relationships—the factor that will avoid disappointment, conception, responsibility, pain and sorrow—as if happiness and sorrow, pleasure and pain were not intimately bound together. At that time I was far from understanding any of this, yet somehow subconsciously I must have realised some of it. The India that I could reach at that moment would only disappoint; it was that realisation that made me stick to my original plan and turn south to the ocean, to use the sea, the sails and the roll of the waves to soften up and to open and relax me yet further.

When the wailing voice of the *Muezzin* calling the faithful to prayer announced the imminent dawn, there were no more doubts in my mind. I was to meet Thom and take him up on his plan, no matter how inconvenient, difficult or awkward it turned out in reality.

* * *

I woke up late but cheerful. I paid for the room and went over to the post office to send a cable to Thom telling him I was arriving. I sent it to the agreed address c/o Ahmad Duali-Duali Shipyard, Sonmiani. It read, 'Leave an address at Karachi Poste Restante, see you soon.' With that matter arranged, I went to have my last 'overland' break-fast. I ate it, then hailed a horse-drawn carriage to take me to the railway station. As I got out of the carriage I was already thinking of the ocean and swaying palm trees.

The long line of railway tracks signified freedom, opportunity and mobility. It seemed like a father's reassuring hand resting on the shoulder of a scared little boy. I bought a ticket, put down the plastic bag containing my only possessions, two books, a torch, a knife, some underclothes and a piece of cheese, and sat down to enjoy the scenery. The modern station would not have been incongruous anywhere in Europe but the crowds of people jammed against the closed gates to the platform made it clear that this was Asia.

An impressive diesel engine drew in, hauling a long train of blue streamlined carriages, and came to a screeching halt. This was the Peshawar—Lahore express. As the gates opened it seemed as though a riot were breaking out. The unconcerned expressions of the uniformed guards and policemen assured me that this was merely a daily routine. By the time I got to the train any possibility of boarding it conventionally seemed to have gone. I read my third-class ticket to confirm my suspicion that it was only good for the day, shrugged my shoulders and took a flying leap at the train. My hands connected with the rim above window-level. Holding the plastic bag in my teeth, I swung my legs in through the window and lowered myself on to the mass of tangled bodies inside—slowly, so as not to provoke aggression.

Instead of showing annoyance, the men on whose heads and shoulders I had landed guided me to a few inches of free space left in one of the corners. I landed on top of some soft and comfortable sacks. Feeling utterly exhausted I blessed my good luck and fell asleep, dreaming of boats and the sea. Outside, the tough policemen scraped the doors free of any men who had not made it, and the plush train, which would have been so much more useful had it been less up-to-date and bigger, left on its long journey to the ocean.

As the train rolled on I filed away my Asian experiences in various compartments of my brain. Two days later, when the magnificent expanse of the Arabian Sea met my eyes, I felt like a slate wiped clean.

I was overwhelmed by the busy station, trucks, lorries, shops, streets, city life—it was all too much. I stood in front of the railway station facing Ranchi Square, feeling lost and confused. It was like watching a speeded-up film of Buster Keaton or the Keystone Cops.

I walked over to the Poste Restante to pick up Thom's message. It was there alright. I ripped open the envelope to find his Karachi whereabouts. As I read the address I could not help but smile—I wonder what he's doing there, I thought, as I hailed a cab.

PART TWO

Andromeda
and the Thais

12

Andromeda

I found Thom sitting in a luxurious chrome-and-leather armchair on the eighteenth floor of the Karachi Hilton. As I was to find out, there was no particular reason for him to be there but he'd had my telegram so he had left the boatyard and decided to receive me in style; such was Thom. He was looking very self-satisfied as usual, resting his feet on the balcony-railing. The warm sun passed the rim of the orange and black striped parasol above him, suddenly lighting up his blue eyes. As he saw me approaching, he remained seated, a big smile spreading across his face.

In spite of the sun it was not too hot. The air conditioning was full on and provided a stream of cool air. A radio in the background softly played a South American tune. Thom arranged his feet in a more comfortable position, tightened the belt of his dragon-emblazoned silk kimono and turned towards me.

'Don't just sit there looking dumbstruck—what's the matter with you? You're not sick, are you? What's the story?'

'I don't know,' I mumbled. 'Culture-shock or something, I guess. Give me a few days, I'll pick up.'

'Few days, hell . . . What you need is a few drinks.'

He gave the rail a kick and the chair rolled towards the marble-topped table. He picked up a push-button telephone and gave some instructions. I could not help but smile as he barked: 'And don't forget to bring the crushed ice as well as the cubes.' Then he turned to me. 'We'll soon straighten you out. Don't sit on that silly stool like you were a holy cooly or something. Go and take a long shower and then we'll have a drink.'

'OK,' I said.

I peeled off my clothes, closed the heavy glass-and-chrome doors and turned the taps, letting the powerful high-pressure head spray water all over me. By twiddling the elaborate controls I made the water sharp, prickly, pointed and flared. I felt exhilarated playing with this technological toy. Having finally flooded the bath, I flung a huge bathrobe around me and dashed back into the room. The next minute we were having one of our traditional pillow-fights. Leather cushions and pillows went flying and there was broken glass and ashtrays on the floor. Finally the knocking of the room-service man interrupted us. He brought in the drinks.

'I was going to order champagne,' said Thom apologetically, 'but I decided that we wouldn't drink champagne until the boat's sold—then we'll be able to take a bath in it. We won't go thirsty, anyway.'

It did not look like it. There were two exotic punch bowls topped with chunks of fruit, flower petals and other bits and pieces. I looked incredulously at everything. Thom tipped the man and told him to push the trolley into the terrace.

'We'll drink first, then we'll talk,' he said.

I passively accepted the luxuries around me, even though I had learned to live without them. I was up against the Western reality again, but not hostile to it, as I had been when I left it behind. Then the luxury would have burdened and annoyed me.

It was late afternoon. The drinks were delicious and the soft silk of the kimono I was wearing felt cool and pleasant against my skin. We were young, life was ahead of us. We felt good.

Thom began to explain about the boat. It was quite a story. The fifty-five foot schooner was built in 1976 in Thailand for a young Westernised Arab called Abdullah, a Kuwaiti. Abdullah spent most of his time in Marbella, Ibiza, Gstaad and such places. Jack, the fellow who had built the boat, was the key to the story. I had heard Thom mention him in accounts of their previous escapades. Jack was older and more experienced but Thom made up for it with enthusiasm and natural charm. Their ways had since parted—Jack came into some money and wanted to make more. Like Thom he did not think much of conventional work; he tried several things and eventually became a boat-builder.

Thom spent some time talking about Abdullah and Jack, explaining that it was the best way for me to learn about the yacht.

'She's a mirror image of those two characters—you see, Abdullah is a mess and Jack is a phoney.'

Jack, Thom explained, had bought a boatyard off Phuket Island in Thailand and specialised in building boats for the likes of Abdullah. He would find a likely customer and sweet-talk him into paying a deposit. He found his customers all over the place, from

Martha's Vineyard to Sardinia. He would explain that the labour costs in Thailand were a fraction of those in the USA; his American friends had useful connections and he could import all the spares from his army buddies. The customer would later check this and find it all true. A man in Jack's position might build excellent yachts for ridiculously low prices.

'Other men could,' added Thom, 'but not Jack. When he's hooked his fish and secured a large enough deposit, he considers his job finished, and goes fishing again. He leaves the actual construction of the yacht to his German wife and his alcoholic Vietnamese lieutenants. They turn out these sorry-looking boats put together from Vietnamese surplus junk. In the course of a year Jack has squeezed over a hundred thousand dollars out of Abdullah for the boat-building costs, but today she isn't worth a third of that.

'Anyway, the proud owner took possession and started to sail back home to Kuwait. Not that he knew anything about sailing, but Jack had assured him that there was nothing to it. It was Jack who sailed the boat down the river and out to sea. Otherwise Abdullah and his crew of eager Arabs would have quickly discovered that sailing is not all that simple. Once out on the open sea, Jack left them to their own devices. There was nothing much wrong in that—it's the quietest stretch on the Indian Ocean. Abdullah managed to get by somehow.'

In the three weeks that it took him to get to the coast of Pakistan, he had time to discover everything wrong with the boat. Sensitive child of comfort that he was, those three weeks of sailing were three too many, and he decided to give up this newly-discovered sport, get off at Karachi and let his crew continue to Kuwait. Not surprisingly, sailing round the coast proved too much for them. Entering Sonmiani Bay they hit a sandbank near the shore and took in water through the open portholes. The hull was of ferro-cement construction so the boat began to sink. Instead of manning the pumps, Abdullah and his men panicked, grabbed their possessions and left the boat, Abdullah vowing never to set foot on it again.

The boat listed and sank, or rather half sank, resting comfortably on her side on the sandbank. Luckily the crew had had enough sense to drop anchor, otherwise the tide would have carried her out. As it was, she only rolled around, but she lost both masts. It was almost a week before Jack found out. He flew to Karachi and had the boat secured to the shore with chains. All he really wanted to do was remove the engine, which was still intact in a watertight compartment, but he realised that the boat could be salvaged if there were someone to do it. That was why he contacted Thom.

'What about Abdullah?' I asked. 'Isn't he the owner any more?'

Thom explained that Abdullah had collected some money from his insurance company and had virtually abandoned the boat. Given the situation in Pakistan, the boat was of no use to anybody. There were no yacht clubs or tourists interested in chartering her or capable of salvaging her. Thom, however, had arranged a deal with the Club Méditerranée in Mauritius. They were interested in chartering a large boat for their club in Troux aux Biches, and having a boat brought over from Europe would be too complicated and expensive for them. If we equipped Andromeda properly, they might even be willing to buy her.

'This is where we come in,' said Thom. 'We raise Andromeda, pump her clean and make her seaworthy—Jack gets the engine and we get the boat. We tart her up and sail her to Mauritius. Then we'll be in business—yacht clubs, tourists . . . If we manage to sell her we'll give some money to Jack and if not we'll just make it pay by chartering her. As for me, if I didn't want to hang about, I could take my share of the money as soon as we got there and go on to India as I wanted.

Thom looked triumphant. 'Well, what do you say? Brilliant, isn't it?'

I had to disappoint him. Although it sounded straightforward I could not see how it would work. I was surprised that Thom, who was a much better sailor than I was, could not see the problems. It was the bit about Jack keeping the engine that ruined the scheme as I saw it; another problem was that she had lost her masts. I could not work out how we were to go about re-rigging the boat in Pakistan where there are no master tuners to fix the rigging, no yards, equipment or skilled men. The nearest place where masts were made was Israel. We could get local carpenters to fashion wooden ones, of course, but the design would have to be taken into consideration— how could we work out the correct height, tension and balance? There was no end to my objections and I fired them at Thom who just smiled patiently and encouragingly, as if I were repeating his own thoughts.

If we could keep the engine everything would be different. We could refloat the yacht, do all the necessary repairs in Karachi and simply motor across to Iran—a short journey, and we would probably not have any problems. I thought I knew what I was talking about, because I had worked it all out the previous night on the train. In spite of their problems after so many years of the Shah and his cousins, I had little doubt that the Persians would be well equipped for yacht repairs.

It did not take long for an experienced sailor like Thom to convince me that he had thought it all out. He said that keeping the engine was out of the question—it was a practically new 200-HP Perkins, worth almost sixteen thousand dollars. It was because of the engine that Jack went to all the trouble of securing the boat by chains and contacting Thom, but in Karachi the engine would be as useless to him as the boat would be to us.

'So what do we do?' I asked. 'Motor to Abadan and mail the engine to him?'

Thom smiled triumphantly and delivered the punch line. He said that the idea was to motor all the way to Thailand right into Jack's boatyard on Victoria Bay; in return, Jack would give us use of the boatyard. If we caught him in the right mood he might even let us use his men when they weren't busy.

'Motor all the way to Thailand!' I exclaimed. I did not know how far it was; Thom said it was about two thousand miles. It seemed a hell of a long way to go for repairs but Thom pointed out that five hundred miles across the sea to Abadan or two thousand to Thailand made no difference. I had just covered close on three thousand miles, so why not two thousand more?

'Besides, all you do is sit on your behind and wait,' he said.

I did not take to the new route quickly. Sailing three thousand or more miles to Mauritius seemed very different from motoring to Thailand. The trip to Mauritius meant adventure, excitement—and sailing.

Thom had an answer for everything.

'You want to sail—we'll have a sail.' He explained that he had salvaged one of the original masts, and had it cut down to twenty-five feet—hardly a schooner mast, but it would be sufficient to hoist a sail, gaff-rigged, which would take us at four or five knots, given a good wind.

I was still worried about the danger of putting to sea in such a wreck, but Thom pointed out that apart from the stretch between Jaffna and the Andaman Islands it would be a matter of island-hopping. It was the quiet season anyway, and there would hardly be a wave all the way across. Our biggest problem would be boredom as we sat and waited.

By the time I had more or less resigned myself to his scheme, Thom voiced his own doubts. Jack was not the type to let go of a bargain, and the rest of the deal was that we would take to Thailand some surplus boat shackles that he had had delivered from Israel. I asked how many shackles there were. Thom paused and answered reluctantly.

'Three tons.'

'We're nothing but a blasted tug boat for this guy,' I exclaimed. I asked if there were any more surprises and Thom assured me that that was all there was to it. Seeing that I looked worried, Thom got up, poured two more drinks and came back to join me.

'Well,' he said, passing me a full glass, 'What do you say? Are you in or not?'

I looked at him and smiled. 'I'm here, aren't I? I just hope we don't sink.'

Thom raised his glass.

'Here's to Mauritius, calypso and the good life.'

'Right,' I said, and clinked my glass against his. 'To Mauritius—via Bangkok,' I added with a sigh.

13

The Garden of the Heavenly Maids

By the time we had finished talking it was dark. In Karachi night falls quickly, stunning the city into silence and driving the men off the streets, like some giant stamping his foot on a mouse city. But not for long—after the initial shock the cars start to hoot again and the night life begins.

Thom and I stood on the balcony watching the transformation take place.

'How about some action tonight?' said Thom. 'First we'll go to a seafood restaurant—one with a cabaret and all—then to Madame Sin Sang's place in Chinatown.'

'It's only my first night back in civilisation,' I answered. 'I can handle a restaurant, but let's leave Chinatown for some other occasion.'

'We'll see how you feel,' said Thom, and picked up the telephone to order a taxi.

Thom assured me that the only place to eat seafood in Karachi was Mohammed's Palace on the Esplanade. It really was a palace—it had belonged to a British general, but now it seemed mostly unoccupied and very sad. The restaurant was situated on the flat rooftop. I could imagine very pukka English colonels waltzing around the big terrace, the young bloods cornering flushed maidens behind the balustrades and convincing them of their honourable intentions.

The roof had a splendid view of the sea; little boats, specks of light, were gliding in the distance. A band played Western music out of tune, the atmosphere was bogus European and I would have preferred a *tandoori* place with belly dancing and all.

We both ordered local wine and lobster, which was the cheapest dish on the menu, although at two dollars a head it was still very expensive by Eastern standards. The lobsters were greasy, overcooked and so spiced as to be inedible. What a terrible waste, I thought, and left them practically untouched. The wine tasted like curried lemonade and had a smell of incense about it. I was sure that Thom had taken me there only to tantalise me.

The show looked like turning into a long one. First the guests were treated to what the compere called Pathan folk dancing. It featured a bunch of overweight Gujaratis dressed in Grecian miniskirts who kept stumbling over the amplifier leads and hurt themselves on sharp parts of the microphone stands.

I had seen enough. I turned to Thom and asked, 'So what about this Chinese place of yours—can we eat there?'

Thom replied that we could, and for less money than in this tourist trap. We had a few more drinks and left.

In Chinatown girls were available for conversation and entertainment; they were rather like Greek *hetaeras*. In Muslim societies, wives

71

are creatures of a lower order. This should not be so according to the Koran: the inferior role of women has simply evolved according to custom. As wives were uneducated and locked up, some educated and emancipated women became hostesses; a form of business which was highly respectable and sophisticated, but officially illegal. According to the new military regime, Islamic law made these non-Muslim customs unacceptable.

Suriya Garden was indeed a better place to eat. Everyone ate in a communal room, a large domed hall with cut-glass windows and a heavy brass chandelier. We sat on cushions and girls wearing loose silken trousers and embroidered bras served the food. It was simple but delicious. I was surprised to see that all the waitresses looked foreign, and Thom explained that they were Parsee. Throughout the Islamic world Zoroastrian Parsee girls are praised for their beauty. and their refusal to mask their faces with the *chador* is much tolerated and secretly appreciated. It is a status symbol to have a Parsee, or at least Parsee-trained, hostess at one's disposal. I engaged one of them in conversation. I had rather hoped that she would indeed, be Zoroastrian so that I could discuss the fascinating religion with such an unusual specimen of the philosophic community. She stretched herself out elegantly on the silken cushions, arching her body as she did so, and made me think of Ingres' Odalisque.

For a while I listened to the sweet chirping sound of her voice without bothering to register what she was saying—my mood was too sensual—yet after a while I realised that she was talking sense. She spoke broken English but made up for it with the picturesqueness of her descriptions. She was explaining the sacred flame of life, the holy Zoroastrian symbol. Life was a struggle between Ahura Mazda and Ahriman, she said, a battle between the gods of light and darkness. It was a daily struggle to create order, a constant restructuring, a harmonious pattern recreated out of the discordant situations, events and forces which life arrayed against one.

It was a novel experience for somebody trained in the European tradition, where learning and philosophy go hand in hand with hard chairs, dimly lit libraries and bespectacled professors, to listen to this half-naked odalisque expounding theories about life and death. But why not, I thought, as I picked at delicious grapes and sipped the milky, sweet-tasting wine.

We were joined by two more girls; all three came from Iran. Ever since the days of the Mogul shahs, dancers and entertainers had been recruited from non-Islamic Parsees. Although well-versed in Zoroastrianism and Ahura Mazda's philosophy, the girls were not Zoroastrian but members of a special sect of Hasas, an offshoot tribe from which 'Huriah' ('heavenly maids') were selected for the sultans in Istanbul.

They played instruments rather like lutes and sang melancholy Farsi songs for us. We were on the verge of becoming sad when my philosophical companion laughed gaily, stood up and performed a dance.

It was very different from the belly-dancing one sees in nightclubs. There was little that was teasing or provocative in the way these girls danced. It was startling, for it was erotic yet lust-free. It was a novel sensation, lust-free Eros. It did not tickle and tingle. No, it throbbed, it hit low and provoked not desire but yearning. They called it not belly-dancing but *yakasha*. Belly-dancing is Islamic, they explained, and is performed by Omani girls; *yakasha* is a slow, sinuous dance and most of the movement was in their arms, which were stretched out above their heads. The girls rotated their hips, but in contrast with belly-dancing, where the hips appear to move independently, theirs was all one movement in which the whole body was unified. It was very fluid, like a snake swaying to a flute.

Out of curiosity I asked Thom in French whether the girls were ever available. My philosophical companion stopped the dancing, rearranged her hair and replied with a sad smile: '*On peut faire mieux dans les autres endroits si Monsieur n'est pas content avec la danse ici.*'

I replied that I was perfectly content to watch her dance and talk philosophy, but the girls took their instruments and left us to finish the meal by ourselves. Yet there was no feeling of frustration or unfulfilled appetite. Quite the contrary to a night-club show, it left one erotically fulfilled, peaceful, as if there had been a consummation of some sort. We did not go to '*autres endroits*' but, having thoroughly gorged ourselves, returned to the hotel.

The next day I moved out of the Hilton and made camp in an empty gatekeeper's hut at the boatyard. Thom sulked for a day, insisting that we stay at the Hilton since he was picking up the bill, etc., but a few days later he gave up and joined me in the hut.

*   *   *

73

A month had gone by since we had pumped out *Andromeda* and raised her out of water. The boat looked dismal without any masts. She was full of mud, slime and sand. Only the engine was still perfect: isolated in its compartment, it looked practically new. The boat was so full of slime that we decided no work would be worthwhile until we had cleaned her thoroughly. We were not sure how to do it, and for a while we contemplated sinking her again, but the water in the bay was so muddy that the exercise would have been futile. Eventually we settled for high-pressure hosing. Ahmed had no compressor but for a fee of two hundred rupees his cousin Farouk somehow managed to obtain a super-powerful mobile model that materialised one day on top of a massive truck driven by a wily-looking Korean. The truck was marked 'City of Karachi Department of Water and Canalisation'. We did not dare ask who was going without water for the two days that it took us to hose the boat clean.

After that we embarked on extensive repairs. For a day or so even the boatyard workers were inspired by Thom's enthusiasm and put in a little serious work.

The most complicated part was the mast. It was shortened to about twenty-five feet and inserted by Pakistani carpenters. We used the rusty old shrouds, that could hardly weather the slightest storm, but then we rather irresponsibly decided that the shrouds were unimportant for we assumed that there would be no great pressure exerted on the mast, as there was not much wind or bad weather at that time of the year.

We examined the hull carefully, reinforced all the weak points and made sure she was really watertight. As the hull was made of ferro-cement that was no great problem. We spent a lot of time making the boat habitable by installing wooden fittings and refurbishing the galley. By the time Thom declared her ready to sail she still did not look very pretty—more like an ugly duckling. A sailing yacht without a mast does not look right; our makeshift effort only made her look more clumsy.

Finally there was the matter of supplying the boat. In Asia I had got used to eating garbage so I was indifferent. We bought masses of Dana pork luncheon meat in tins. They were too old, so they were on special offer at the Karachi supermarket. We bought $20 worth—it was enough to last forever. We also bought local honey, dates, nuts, raisins, flour, sugar—$35 in all.

14

Slow Boat to Siam

We set off for Thailand in late March. The day dawned perfectly clear, as did all the days to follow. We finished an enormous breakfast of sausages and eggs and hung around the boatyard, doing everything in slow motion.

It was getting close to noon when we finally realised that if we delayed any longer we would lose the tide as we had the day before. Ahmed came to say goodbye and the rest of his men joined him, hoping for fat tips, but we just smiled and shook their hands. Sorry fellas, I thought, you weren't much help anyway. But it was nice of Ahmed to come and see us off. Before we left he gave us a basket of green fruit, telling us to let it ripen at sea.

We cast off and drifted away from the pier. We slid out slowly, Thom at the helm while I waved goodbye to the naked little children running along the beach. I felt a sense of loss as we severed our bonds with the shore.

I sat down at the stern, feet dangling over the water, waiting for the land to sink below the horizon. Neither of us wanted to keep close to the shore.

'To hell with sticking to the land,' said Thom. 'The sea is going to be perfectly calm.' The sight of land would just be a constant temptation—a disrupting influence.

With the shackles loaded the boat was very low in the water and looked like a barge. The excess ballast made her very stable and the small waves that we encountered could hardly roll us.

As the shore of Pakistan began to disappear I felt excitement and a sensation of fear creeping up my spine. The smells of land rapidly faded. The seagulls that had followed us started to turn back; only one or two remained.

I went below to the galley to fetch a piece of cake that I had saved from breakfast. Soon we would be eating soda bread and Dana luncheon meat. Neither of us was particularly hungry so there was quite a lot of cake left. I looked at it with distaste—somehow it represented a bond with the land: it had no place on board. As I threw it over the side I felt that I had finally cut myself loose from the land. The last seagull emitted a few cries as it wheeled and glided into the wind and back to her nest.

In the distance the shore of Pakistan was just a tiny speck catching the last rays of the blood-red sun. Then it was gone.

And so the long journey south-east had begun. There was no need to pretend that this was a pleasure trip or an adventure—it was a straightforward delivery job and the two of us felt no better than a couple of lorry drivers going down an empty highway. Day followed night followed day with a blue sameness. The unchanging round line of the horizon was our constant companion. The only movement was the sun's daily progress from one side of the horizon to the other. Days were long, but the weeks flew by.

*　　*　　*

As one goes from one country to another, the sounds and smells of the first slowly fade and new cultures, new colours and rhythms are perceived. There is a brief overlap, then the new vibrations overwhelm the old. The body chemistry of the traveller changes accordingly. At sea there were really only two highs: when the land mass sank below the horizon, and when it reappeared. The severance from land manifested itself in temporary loss of appetite, a sense of confusion, and sleeplessness. As I entered the barren emptiness of the sea, the constant roar of the engine made communication with the elements difficult.

Yachtsmen tell of the joy of entering into communion with the sea and the wind. The sea swells and the boat dances to the rhythm of the waves. Plato suggested that being gently rocked by the waves should be a necessary part of education for babies. The sea breathes in an eternal cosmic rhythm—he said, but these subtleties were lost on a barge like ours. With the ocean almost perfectly calm, the heavy boat forced the unnatural rhythm of the engine on to the waves. The smooth-running mechanical organism was essentially hostile to the natural movement of the body and soul. The $16,000 Perkins wonder was in tune with the literature that I was reading at the time, books that Abdullah and Jack had left behind. They were American books, heavy stuff, very deep and philosophical. Like new Hollywood movies they were technically perfect, with no rough edges—safe books expressing reliable ideas but spiritually dead. I longed for a rough-cut novel with some genuine warmth and feeling, something to break the monotony. I wished that the engine were an old bad-tempered one that would change pitch or break down, but no—like the books I was reading, it flowed like honey.

There were enjoyable moments, though. The sunsets were spectacular: the sky turned the ocean into a boiling purple cauldron; blue-tinged flying fish performed their evening extravaganzas, their pink wings catching the intense rays of the sun.

As the sun sank into the ocean the water became indigo but the sky glowed bright yellow, then slowly turned crimson. A calm descended on the sea. The flying-fish suddenly disappeared and the water's surface was broken only by schools of porpoises. At times like that we would sit in silence, absorbed in an inward joy.

Occasionally we saw families of whales but we could never distinguish the good kind from the bad kind. Thom had read somewhere that a mother whale with her brood should be given a wide berth; all the whales we saw seemed to be mothers and babies which gave us cause for concern. After collisions with other craft, whales are the second most common cause of deep-sea yachting disasters, I was told.

Dolphins were a great source of delight, but they never stayed with us for long. I've heard stories of dolphins keeping ships company for weeks on end. They turned up often enough, but in spite of our frantic attempts to be friendly they never stayed with us for more than an hour or so. After several forlorn attempts at socialising we felt snubbed; we began to sulk and made no further efforts to cultivate or feed them.

Our tasks during the trip to Thailand were very simple. We did not have an auto-pilot so one of us had to hold the helm; most of the time we just tied it down or held it between our legs, but someone always had to be on hand to make corrections. Navigation was the only challenge: we took up to ten fixes a day, not because there was any need, but mainly for practice. Our greatest pleasure was to draw that tiny line of the ship's progress on the chart and to watch the line lengthen towards the coast of Thailand.

* * *

It took a storm to shake me out of our land bound neutrality and put both of us finally in touch with the sea.

We were already two weeks out when it came—these were the two uneventful weeks of perfect weather, and when the first drops of rain started coming down, we felt almost relieved. Both of us were on deck—wearing only shorts, welcoming the big warm drops that freshened our bodies. The drops grew in number and we cleared the deck of loose articles and clothes. A slight wind picked up as I took the helm and let Thom adjust the gaff-rigged main sail that we picked up for $10 from Ahmed's brother. He tightened the sheet, reflecting for a moment whether to haul in the sail, but we decided against it and, having pulled in the mainsheet, we left mainsail hoisted in the south-westerly breeze which was increasing steadily.

Soon the sky grew dark as a magical feeling of calm, mystery and warmth spread across the ocean. There were sounds of thunder and flashes in the distance as the horizon lit up—blue, white, dark red.

The sail swelled and our speed increased till we were gliding across the rolling steel-grey sea raising much spray which flew about lashing cool and pleasant against our warm bodies. The thunder grew louder and the flashes were more frequent, reflecting on our faces and giving Thom a macabre look.

It was raining quite intensely now and the sea was foaming as the boat heaved and bounced through the water. In spite of leeway we lost no ground. With the strong wind from the port quarter, the sail pulled smoothly and the engine ticked over, steady and reassuring. As the crests were breaking almost opposite to our course, we appeared to be gliding at twice our actual speed. In spite of the loud noise of the surrounding sea, subjectively we could scarcely hear it. Although the noise and the wind were increasing I felt a great calm, a sense of slowing down, like a flywheel coming to a slow stop. Thom's earnest face, illuminated by the flashes and wet from the spray, glowed in absorption, radiating a certain inward peace that enshrouded both of us. We shared in silence this feeling of sinking down into the deep, into some invisible fluid, exhaling the air and settling slowly to rest. Our attention was occasionally drawn to the taut mainsail which reflected the lightning-flashes which outlined the ship against the dark ocean as by magical strobe lights.

After the weeks of abstract non-feeling, sailing in a mood of insensitive stupor, it was good to feel the streams of water running through one's toes, the thud of the rain and the angry cries of the sea and the storm mingling in the crucible of that Indian Ocean afternoon. I wished the moment would petrify, drag out into eternity. Like Wagner's sea-captain, I would continue to spite the elements, sailing through the angry ferment of clouds, unmoved and resolute. I heard the thunder of Wagner's closing chords as Senta throws herself into the ocean and *The Flying Dutchman* disappears into the fuming horizon.

And then it came unexpectedly, the sudden scream of bright, blue-white flame lighting up the dark afternoon, turning it into a dazzling white surrealist painting; it shot across our heads and plunged into the waves, disappearing suddenly as if by the flick of a switch. There was a moment of darkness and silence and then we were shaken by a shattering explosion which brought down the mast with a crunch. It all happened too quickly for me to react. As the stern lifted clear out of the water, I felt the wheel go dead in my hands and the boat turned side ways, absorbing the impact of the first massive wave that smashed into us full on. The boat reeled, shipping water over the starboard side, and in the process washing the mast and sail clear of the deck. I looked to see whether Thom was still on deck and saw his grinning face watching the mast being swept overboard; he screamed, 'Thank God for that, now bring the ship round.' I turned the dead wheel which spun freely as the stern stayed clear of the water, and the whirling propeller whined in the darkness. Suddenly there was a tremendous thud against the hull. It threw me off balance and over the helm. As I fell I just managed to grab hold of the railing. I thought that we had hit the bottom but the thud came again and again. I realised the absurdity of my idea. I looked around and saw Thom running across the deck with an axe in his hands shouting that we were being rammed by the mast. 'Quick,' he said, 'we've got to cut it loose.'

I scrambled towards him—but the ship went into a spin. It was impossible to hold one's balance and swing the axe. 'For God's sake, bring her round,' shouted Thom and I struggled back to the loose wheel. Suddenly the propeller dug in and the helm spun back, hitting me hard on the chin—but I grabbed her and held on. Quickly I collected myself, turned up the throttle well past the red mark. The engine was screaming as I fought to turn the boat into the wind. For a moment she steadied, giving Thom a chance at a few clean strokes with the axe. Suddenly he cut through; the rigging snapped and the boat reeled back, shipping yet more gallons of water. I had her back on course now. Thom was holding on to the anchor; his axe was lost overboard with the mast. He was grinning. I tried to ease the throttle but as soon as I did so the boat would start to yaw. I put her on full throttle again and she held and we sliced on course 210, the only possible direction. Thom disappeared into the cabin, and came out some ten minutes later fully dressed in our red, foul-weather gear. Only then did I feel how cold it was and realised that I was shivering. 'Go down and get dressed, it's going to be a long and a cold night,' Thom said. He took over the helm and I made for the cabin, still feeling elated and thinking how good it was that I was not sea-sick—but as soon as I entered the hatch, the cabin spun around me and my stomach turned as I groped my way to the towels and dry clothes. It took a lot of work to get dressed and even more to heat up some soup, fill the thermos and bring it out.

As Thom had predicted, it was a long night yet our spirits were high and we felt good; we were finally doing something. The wind changed direction four times that night. For about an hour or so at a time we had to keep the engine at a full throttle. It was an excellent engine and it held, but not the wooden casing around it—towards the morning it began to smoulder. We took turns at steering and splashing buckets of water over the boiling engine. It was only some hours after the sunrise that the wind let up a bit and we set the throttle at some 1,000 revs. The whine subsided and the wood stopped smouldering. We cooked some breakfast and, as the first rays of sun filtered through, we set course again for the western coast of Thailand. It was the only bad weather we encountered on that trip and it took us two days to survey the damage, secure the shackles and cut loose all the rigging. As for the mast, we accepted the loss as rather a good riddance. We were only a week or so away from the mainland and after that we'd have no use for it anyway.

Three days after the storm the sun came out again and the ocean looked as it always did. Yet I did not feel as before; the Asia 'overland' feeling had lifted—it went overboard with that stump of the mast. It was only later in Thailand that we found out about the course of our storm—it was an out-of-season cyclone formed somewhere over the Malayan Archipelago, and it raced across the Indian Ocean bringing much rain and happiness to Indian farmers and a taste of the sea to us.

15

Thailand

Three weeks had gone by since the coast of Pakistan had disappeared behind the stern. As the Thai shore started to materialise it was almost impossible to convince ourselves that this land-mass looming ahead was really the coast of South-east Asia. Only a little while ago, or so it seemed, Pakistan had vanished into the horizon; after the interlude of the sea's nothingness, land was rising up again. It did not feel right—there was no emotional arousal. It came unexpectedly: for all we cared it might as well have been the USA or China.

Yet as the boat drew closer, the wind carried a new smell and the feel of a new land. There was an aromatic softness; the air became moist and heavy and spiced with *satay*. In the distance the grey shore started to acquire new colours—dazzling green with patches of indigo and violet. It was afternoon, and a hot breeze was blowing from the land.

The shoreline started taking shape and we could make out beaches, houses and swaying palm trees. A two-second light signalled that this was indeed Pak Phrat Strait. I rushed below to get the charts. This was Thailand: the charts said so, but my body did not believe it.

We made our way past the Phuket Island, sighted the black beacon-markers and slipped into the channel. After two more hours of careful motoring. Thom pointed towards a cluster of yellow buildings.

'That's it,' he said. 'That's Jack's boatyard.'

As the sun sank into the green jungle we finally docked at Dunna Bay.

*　　*　　*

The first week flew by, and nothing happened. Jack was not there and his Vietnamese lieutenants could do nothing but smile and say: 'He come back soon, he know.'

It was not until the arrival of his wife that there was some action. She was quick and energetic, a short-legged German woman, and she knew how to put them to work. We pulled the boat up on to the slip and let the workmen get on with unloading, taking out the engine, scraping and resealing. As for Jack, he was two hundred miles up the coast and Thom left to meet him.

I was exhausted with the strains of the trip and was perfectly happy to stay on at Dunna Bay forever. It was just the right place to fall in love with. A marvellous horseshoe-shaped sandy beach stretched for fifteen miles. Along the beach lay little villages with palm-thatched houses, where tiny fishermen made their daily rounds. There was a local *sampai khana*—an inn of sorts—where these marzipan-coloured men met at night to drink a coconut-based liquor called *bada*; it tasted not unlike white rum. Sukim, the *khana* boss, fried delicious crayfish, and his stretch of the bay was my favourite place. I would spend the day fishing and diving for coral in the crystal-clear water; like everybody else I wore only a loincloth. In the afternoon I would join the fishermen and help them in their work. Being a keen diver I offered to help the women dive for coral but they declined. At first I thought that the men did not want me around their women but then I realised that that had nothing to do with it. Men simply did not dive—it was women's work. Far from being jealous, they seemed completely unpossessive about their women. I became rather fond of two sisters, daughters of Sukim's brother. They followed me about, giggling and jumping into the water after me. They wore thin sarongs which, when wet, would cling to their taut bodies. When we swam and played together I often worried that somebody might object, but nobody did.

It was at Sukim's that I met Diph. He invited me to be his guest at Bhai Bay, some twenty miles further south. Having nothing to do I gladly accepted. Living in Bhai Bay, I felt what life must have been like thousands of years ago. There were no signs of modern civilisation in the village: nobody had a transistor radio or had ever used electricity or motor power. It was the most basic existence, yet the standard of living was considerably higher than that of natives I was to see in other parts of Asia. Here at Bhai the women kept goats and chickens and grew vegetables. Their diet was varied and of the highest quality.

At first they did not want me to do any work, but I insisted. To live and work the way they did was what I wanted. I wore their clothes, got up with the sun like the men and joined them as they set out to sea. It was hard work and we went on until the evening, more than twelve hours a day. The work was varied and satisfying, however. Bhai Bay fishermen used all their faculties in a day's work: they repaired nets and acted as salesmen, buyers and transporters; they came on shore frequently and took long breaks for lunch which was brought hot in clay pots by the women. Diph's wife was beautiful, and seemed very happy and content. Diph was ambitious, but not in terms of progressing to a European type of existence—getting a motor for his boat, a motor scooter and so on. His ambition was directed towards excelling as a fisherman and harpoon-thrower and proving himself as a capable commander of the four boats which were his responsibility. He wanted respect and recognition from his peers.

The evenings were beautiful. I joined the unmarried men and women who danced by the fires on the beach. Some of the girls were startlingly beautiful. The dances were rather erotic, but not explicitly so; unlike the erotic dances in the North, where they take the form of simulated lovemaking, these exploited simple themes—men make harpoon-throwing gestures and the daily drama of casting the nets, re-enacted in safe surroundings. The young girls, lithe as fish, move in and out among the men, twisting their bodies with fluid agility.

There were several opportunities to take advantage of female hospitality, but it would have been all too easy, rather like stealing a book from a library. At first I thought that nobody would mind, and that it would be perfectly acceptable to take an unmarried girl—after all, that is what the popular literature about these places would have us believe, and certainly the relaxed erotic behaviour indicated that this was the case. But I was to find out that the games were only games, and to the Thais there are strict differences between these and true courtship, even though a Westerner may not perceive them immediately.

These natives were so hospitable and so devoid of self-protective cunning that I had to exercise great caution so as not to overstep the bounds. If I merely complimented a man on his harpoon I might be forced to take it as a gift even if it were essential to the owner's livelihood. I wondered how such an attitude could have developed. It certainly had much to do with the natural abundance of the land. It was impossible to starve—failing all crops, chickens and eggs, there was always fish, which was easy enough to catch. Fruit grew wild and plentiful, and crayfish were there for the taking; this bay was a paradise. The colours and sounds I associated with this community pointed toward something still beyond me.

I would have been perfectly happy to stay much longer were it not for a message from Thom calling me to join him in Bangkok. I parted from Diph with a heavy heart, knowing that I would never see him again. I left him the Afghan knife that I had been carrying since I met Fuad, and took my leave.

* * *

Next day I reached Bangkok by train. The Kuala Lumpur-Bangkok express was extremely comfortable. Through the windows of the air-conditioned compartment I watched peasants working in the paddy fields using ox-powered irrigation systems. Luscious greenery eventually gave way to jungle. Just behind the engine a machine-gun was mounted; the nervous conductor cursed the guerrillas, who would blow up the tracks and ambush the beautiful Thai trains. 'Obstructing progress,' he called it. We sped through guerrilla country, then tidy fields led to the capital. I was rather startled by the railway station: a solid nineteenth-century American mock-Hellenic structure with Ionic columns and everything, it would have been more appropriate as a national library or something like that.

Before going to Thom's I went over to the post office to wire home for some money. I had rather hoped that I would get by without having to do that. I still had a little over a hundred dollars left, which in Asia might see me through before receiving charter money for the Mauritius trip. As it was, I was not footing the bill for the repairs and I could borrow money from Thom which would later be deducted from my charter money. But with things still unclear at the boat-yard, I had for a moment lost my nerve and wanted at least to have the assurance of enough money to get back to Europe should I become ill or something. As I wired home for money I knew I was leaving myself open to reproaches so I hesitated for a long while. Finally tired of deliberation, I wired home for $400 and left the post office conscious of my first defeat.

Thom was staying at a rented bungalow. The taxi driver who took me there was rather unfriendly but I ignored his aggressive behaviour. When I arrived Thom was not there. I was let in by the cleaning woman who asked me to make myself at home. It was a small wooden house, furnished in traditional Thai style; the taste was over-feminine, but good. The house belonged, I was to find out, to Jack's Thai mistress who was away in Japan. I spent a day bathing, resting and listening to music on Thai radio—sounding more American than the American forces stations one hears across Eastern Europe.

By the time Thom arrived, it was dark.

He said he was held up by Jack, who was in town, and on whose yacht we would go to stay the following day. He spoke about the delights of Thailand until we grew tired and went to sleep.

Next day we visited the floating market some ten miles north-east. It took us almost two hours to get up river on a tiny rat-tailed *sampan*, but it was an exciting journey. Bahlia trees hung low over the river and lotus flowers floated on the river banks where colour-fully-dressed girls were doing their washing.

The market itself was a floating kaleidoscope—the stalls were actu-ally boats, all different colours; they kept changing places and created dazzling patterns. The market was a culinary delight and I was told that it went on into the night with fires, singing and dancing. Thom, however, was eager that we should spend the night in Bangkok, so we summoned a *sampan* and made our way back to the city. We stopped off at the bungalow to shower and change. A *wallah* would take our things over to Jack's yacht as we prepared for the night.

16

A Night in Bangkok

Slowly the languid evening was creeping into the streets of Bangkok. Tiny men were busy moving tables, chairs, lamps and stoves into the street, transforming the modern metropolis into an open-air restaurant. Thom and I sat in a café on the main square watching the nightfall.

'It's like this every night,' commented Thom. 'All the streets of Bangkok, hundreds of miles of them, are cluttered with hungry

Thais, most of them far happier to eat out at a pavement restaurant than in the dirty little shack they have for a home.'

There was no lull in the activity of the city as the day turned into night. On the contrary, the enveloping darkness was a signal for the bustling activity to intensify.

The streets filled with cars, big fat Mercedes with tinted glass and cigar-smoking little men inside taking their young mistresses for a night on the town. Then came thousands of Toyotas, Coronas, Mazdas, many battered and half-smashed, often covered with 'sexy' gadgets—racing mirrors, fins, huge aerials, bumpers and corny American stickers of the 'Hi, sexy' and 'Elvis lives' variety. In and out of all these cars, suicidal motorcyclists weaved their way like circus hell-riders, creating the most lethal traffic of any city in the world.

'A huge modern city, feeding off an underdeveloped ignorant population. A rampant cancer . . .' I remembered reading this passage in an Eastern European book, but the city did not seem bad to me—at least, not at first sight.

We took a taxi down the wide Americanised Silom Road and continued up Rama Boulevard. To save time the driver would cross from one boulevard to the next by driving down little-used side roads. The contrast was extraordinary. On the boulevards one felt like as though in Paris or New York. Turning into a little lane, one saw all the poverty and squalor of the East.

Other parts of Asia present the contrasts of rich and poor, healthy and sick, but within the same cultural sphere. Bangkok's contrasts are East and West, Dior versus a run-down Thai shop. The only city in the world I could possibly compare with Bangkok is Tehran, but the contrasts in Tehran are less marked: the extravagant buildings are few and far between and the squalor is less obvious. Thai architectural ostentation sometimes exceeds that of the French and the Americans—particularly grandiose are the hotels, shopping plazas, cafés and cinemas.

As we reached the bright yellow and orange lights of Siam Square I asked Thom where a little country like Thailand found the money for those buildings. He looked puzzled for he did not understand it either.

The night was pleasantly cool. We felt elated and decided to walk.

We had been through a few red-light districts together but those were no preparation for Bangkok.

'Every city has its shady parts,' said Thom, 'but Bangkok—the whole city is a brothel. Walk into any hotel, apart from Hytat Indra and a handful of others, and they accost you at the reception desk. You want a girl, two, three, a boy—it will all be added to the bill and won't be too expensive. On the streets it's even worse. Just look around.'

Most of the girls did not look like prostitutes. The few that did would walk up to us and try to chat us up, as whores do all over the world. The rest just looked invitingly, but it was not until we hit Pat Pong Road that it really started. Girls would grab men, trying to kiss them and force them into doorways or taxis. Neon signs shone everywhere. There were clubs with names like Playboy, Penthouse, Sexy, Keyhole.

We entered a modern neon-lit house called Sodom and Gomorrah. It was a multi-storey sex shopping centre full of shops, bars and discos, all selling women. Women everywhere, some standing in corners, others displayed in show-cases like chocolates in a box. Shouting women rode on the escalators. The nightclubs featured bizarre sex shows.

'Pat Pong Road apart,' Thom was to tell me, 'prostitution in Bangkok works differently from Europe. Prostitution lies at the heart of Thailand's tourist industry and it's an important part of the home economy as well as a massive currency earner. Every week jumbo jets full of tourists, mainly lower-middle-class Germans, arrive here to live out their dreams. You pick up girls in shops, cinemas, parks or museums. They aren't whores in the European sense.'

Fat, balding mechanics from Düsseldorf, hard-working French plumbers arrive to make their dreams come true. For a fee anyone can be Casanova for a week. The tourists can pick up blondes, brunettes, tall girls, blue-eyed ones, shy ones, clever ones...They fall in love, they have their ups and downs, their lovers' quarrels and all the rest. All the time Franz or Fred or Jacques is flattered, pampered and told what a great lover he is. Anything that he ever fantasised about he can have. Thai girls have few inhibitions. If the money is right, clients can have just about anything. Everything is done for 'love'. Needless to say, it is all a big fake. The girls are not tall or blonde or blue-eyed—in fact the European-looking ones are

87

boys. The sex market is too lucrative to be left to the girls alone. Dozens of Thai surgeons have specialised, and others are flown in from Singapore, to perform the operations necessary for boys to sell themselves as girls.

The picture of Bangkok that was emerging was that of a pornographic Disneyland created for the diversion of the alienated Western proletariat. Thom, however, flippant and unpredictable, had a great knack for seeing things from different perspectives. Having preached the idea of Bangkok as a brothel-city, he suddenly changed back and said how wonderful Bangkok was—city of palaces and temples, muesums and little antique shops and side-walk cafés.

'It's here beneath the slime, pure, potent and clean. Just because some guys are trying to make a few fast bucks out of it doesn't mean that it's all bad.' Thom's contagious enthusiasm made it hard for me to sulk for very long.

'Look,' he said, 'first we'll eat and drink well. We'll forget the commercialised abominations—then we'll go to taste the Thai eros as it's meant to be tasted.'

The 'legitimate indulgence' that he advocated was a visit to Suraia, a massage parlour.

'You've got to see the real thing,' he said. 'Pat Pong Road was only a perverted mutation. We've got to have a real Thai massage before the merry bunch of Thais being trained by your uncles in Eastern Europe come back and turn all the girls into factory hands.'

'Before travel industry speculators have turned them all into whores, you mean.'

After the spectacle of the massage parlours of downtown Bangkok I was somewhat sceptical, but Thom was enthusiastic and went on to describe 'the real thing' glowingly, making it seem almost a spiritual affair. He said that Thai massage was an art. You start by taking a sort of Turkish bath and when your body is thoroughly cleansed the massage begins. There is body massage and nerve massage—this is executed by supple, specially-trained girls, who massage the nerve-endings in toes, fingers and eyelids. It is all based on Yin and Yang, Zen and acupuncture, 'highly philosophical stuff' he called it. But first we were to eat.

Saratai Restaurant on Sukhumvit Road surpassed all my expectations, even though Thom had prepared me for it. There were luxurious silken cushions and heavily-ornamented gold walls. An extremely attractive Thai girl in traditional dress and make-up led us to a corner. We sank down into the soft cushions. Above us, Chinese copper lanterns studded with tiger's eye and cut glass refracted the soft light into a rainbow of colours that danced on the low, elaborate copper table. Waiters surrounded us with a screen, leaving a gap wide enough for us to see a show which the waitress told us would begin in an hour.

Thom ordered something called *khae mau son tam*, sticky rice with chopped sweet-and-sour papaws. I had a whole marinaded duck, plus a tray of savoury *hors d'oeuvres*. I thought that we had made lucky choices: the food was very good and I ate with pleasure, but Thom was disappointed and insisted that there was even better food to be found in Bangkok.

Classical Thai dancing struck me as an acquired taste. There seemed little spontaneity, fire, zest or eros in the slow, repetitive movements, and I could not bring myself to appreciate the dance. Technically there seemed nothing to it. Swing your body left, clap, clap, swing your body right, clap, clap. But there must have been subtleties, or perhaps it was simply a bad night.

There was nothing subtle in the Thai fighting show that came afterwards: superb leaps, acrobatics, karate, kendo—it was highly amusing and easy to understand. As the bill was brought, I showed obvious satisfaction with the low price of this mini banquet.

We paid and got up to leave. As we walked out I studied the elegant, affluent scene, attractive women and fat old men. Thom wondered aloud why it was that the women could look so attractive but not the men—everything was wrong with them: looks and behaviour.

'You can't judge their looks by Western standards,' I mouthed that cliché, yet I wondered why it was one found the women so attractive.

*   *   *

We went outside and took a taxi.

The taxi driver pulled up in Wild West fashion, scattering the few passers-by. We were not far from Grace Hotel, a large modern structure with a big entrance and patio; it's bright lights turned the night into daylight.

We got out of the car and Thom pulled out a fifty-baht note in payment for the agreed thirty-baht fare. As it had been a rough ride and the driver had treated us rudely we were in no mood to tip him. When the driver started the usual 'I have no change' patter, Thom asked him to wait a few moments while he changed the note at the hotel. I was rather surprised that Thom had asked him so politely: given the driver's insolence it would have been more like Thom to tell him to go to hell.

The driver was not impressed, however. He demanded that the money be given to him immediately, saying that he had no time to wait. A few passers-by stopped, and Thom turned to them and asked if they had any change. A huge, fat-faced Thai told Thom aggressively to give the driver the money. Normally in a situation like that I would have braced myself for a fight, judged distance, balanced myself and chosen my man, but no idea of a fight entered my head. We were in front of an expensive hotel, Europeans were all around us and an armed policeman was nearby.

Thom opened his mouth to explain to the fat-faced Thai that the fare was only thirty-bad. He had no time to finish the sentence. The driver, who was standing behind him, suddenly let loose a kick at Thom's kidneys, sending him reeling towards the fat Thai, who was already swinging his arm. Before I had time to register much of this I felt myself being kicked from all sides. It seemed that the whole street had jumped on us. A man selling cigarettes at a stand nearby jumped over it and joined in; another ran out of his shop in the middle of serving his customers. A street-sweeper left off sweeping and rushed towards us with his broom raised. I noticed those details yet I was completely lost and confused. It was all like a dream.

Shocked and bewildered, I saw the hotel door only a few feet away. Not thinking of Thom I covered my head with my hands and ran into the hotel. I realised that nobody was following me and I turned around. Thom was lying on the ground while they kicked him from all sides. Luckily they were too worked up to hit him effectively: they were screaming and waving their hands and generally getting in each other's way.

I looked on, immobile. What had happened to me, why didn't I run out and help Thom? The two of us had been in some tough situations. We both knew how to fight against odds. Nothing but courage and determination matters. It is not strength but ferocity of attack, resignation to injury and the assumption of invincibility that can defeat objectively superior opponents. One has to hit suddenly, and hit hard. Select the gang leader and let him have it; the rest are momentarily confused. Hit them fast, then run.

My problem was that I always found it difficult to start hitting. I stood at the door of the hotel as if paralysed. Yet in my stomach I felt anger accumulate and spread through my body. I was braced for any injury I might receive yet I still lacked the strength to strike.

I crept towards the group. Due to their wild excitement they did not notice me. By this time Thom was getting hit effectively. I had to act quickly but I seemed unable to move.

Thom groaned and spat a mouthful of blood. Suddenly an Indian woman coming out of the hotel screamed and instinctively rushed to help him. The fat-faced man downed her with one good kick in the stomach. He lifted a lead pipe to strike. He had not yet swung when I was on top of him. He had not seen me coming, had not the time to lift his hand. I caught him across the mouth, throwing my weight into the blow. I felt his jaw crack and broken teeth dug into my fist. He gave a groan as his face split and blood spurted out. The pipe fell from his hand and rolled away. The taxi-driver gaped in confusion for a few moments then suddenly reached into his car and produced a gun. By the time he turned to face me Thom had got hold of the pipe.

The driver fired once and missed. Before he had a chance to fire again Thom smashed the lead pipe across his egg-shaped skull: the man folded and collapsed without a sound.

I felt a movement behind me. I turned quickly to see a baker striking at me with a knife. Instinctively my hand shot up in protection. There was a sharp pain in my palm; I hit him with my left, but as he made to strike again Thom caught him heavily across the ribs and he fell to the ground.

Meanwhile, fat-face was feeling for the taxi driver's gun. Thom saw him, took a few steps and kicked him. He started to scream and the rest of the gang froze. I, too, had had enough. As I hit the Thai I suddenly became disgusted with myself. The four men stared at us with their mouths open. I realised that they were not thugs or gangsters used to violence—just normal Thai folk, glad for any chance to hit out at the European intruder.

Still enraged, Thom started beating them with his pipe. I became aware that something was changing in me. I stood there, helpless and pathetically vulnerable, but it did not matter. The ferocity and speed with which we retaliated had shocked the Thais. They were running away, scared and screaming. On the ground, two bakers and fat-face writhed in pain, occasionally letting out a deep groan. The taxi-driver showed no signs of life.

Savage as he looked, Thom was no longer out to kill anybody. He was now working on the taxi, smashing the windscreen and hammering the roof with his lead pipe.

Two Thai policemen finally decided to step in. They drew their guns. One fired high over Thom's head while the other approached me and mumbled something about placing us under arrest.

Suddenly I became aware of a burning pain and looked at my blood-covered hand. I was losing blood rapidly, my palm sliced open with the thumb hanging down. I felt a nauseating sensation in my stomach and looked for a place to sit down. About ten minutes later, with the siren wailing, the patrol car was taking us to the police hospital.

I was too shocked to be scared and sat passively in the car looking at the blood from my hand dripping on to the floor. Thom had come to himself and got the fat sergeant to put a rubber tube round my arm to stem the bleeding. Only as the pain increased did I become afraid. I had always suspected that there would be a price to pay for my journey—nothing is for free—yet I did not know how badly I was hurt. I had been resigned to injury ever since I left Csarda but the sight of my hand made me feel weak.

Our arrival at the police hospital was met with complete indifference. For an hour I sat in a chair by the operating theatre, watching as the staff wheeled in other victims of the Bangkok night: men with smashed skulls or torsos riddled with bullets, road accident victims screaming horribly. My predicament suddenly appeared insignificant.

An hour later we decided that I should go to a civilian hospital, but the fat sergeant grunted that we were under arrest. I got hold of the Yugoslav Embassy but they carried no weight. After an hour spent telephoning the American Embassy with Thom convincing them that I was a leading concert pianist, they arranged over the phone that I be taken to the American hospital on Rama Boulevard. We left, accompanied by the fat sergeant. By that time I had started to worry about infection.

At the hospital we were received by a Thai woman doctor, and after the ugliness of the last four hours she appeared as an angel to me. Having convinced myself that I was a pianist, I lamented about never being able to play again. She took to me warmly and created a minor emergency, waking up the staff and getting hold of the leading surgeon, Mr Shim Penam. Eventually I was sewn up and stitched together with four assistants in attendance. Apparently my wound looked a lot worse than it really was and Mr. Penam assured me that I would 'play again'.

The woman doctor tried to secure my release by keeping me in hospital but Mr. Penam put a stop to that.

'Nothing wrong with him now,' he said to the police. 'You can take him.'

* * *

There seemed to be little activity inside the one-storey police station. Our fat sergeant sat with his feet on the table, a gun in its holster slung over the chair next to his. Everybody was leaning against something—a wall, a chair, a table. The show was not put on to impress the two young foreigners: I realised immediately that it was for home consumption. It was as if each of those young men permanently watched himself in a mirror, admiring his own style and coolness. Apparently no honest motivation could induce young Thais to become good policemen. Sleek, super-sexualised uniforms, hot Harley Davidson motorbikes, high wages, pay-offs and the licence to beat up and kill were the recruiting points. Like the office girls on the street dressed up to imitate Sophia Loren, Elizabeth Taylor or Brigitte Bardot, the policemen too styled themselves on models of the years gone by. There was the shaven head of fat Kojak, scratching his skull while holding a cigarette. I recognised a Steve McQueen smile, while John Wayne's walk was a clear favourite with all. Bangkok, it seemed, was a fancy-dress party, its style copying the corny movies of the Sixties and Seventies.

In spite of the Hollywood aura, there was nobody who could speak English so we were asked to sit down and wait. My hand was bandaged neatly and in a sling, and I had received a pain-killing injection, so I felt almost indifferent to my predicament.

A slim young policeman offered me a cigarette. He pulled a packet of black gold-tipped Sobranies out of his rolled-up sleeve. In one fluid movement he produced a gold-plated Du Pont lighter and lit the cigarettes. He was being friendly, and I observed him.

Like all the policemen he wore a super-tight sleek cowboy shirt with the zip half undone and sunglasses dangling out of the front pocket. The whole uniform—all clean and neatly pressed—was covered with little zips, pocket flaps and other gimmicks. As I studied this young policeman I began to feel sorry for him. He should have been out on his father's farm, cutting cane and growing rice, fathering children and developing the nation. Yet here he was, selling his soul for a few trinkets. Like the whores and the men who attacked us, he was caught up by forces that were given birth elsewhere, bigger than he was and outside his control.

The realities of Thailand dawned on me: a naive, friendly people swept by the gale of the world; white men came, bringing luxuries, excess and corruption; then the Americans, on whose support this whole weird phenomenon depended, pulled out, leaving a corrupt government to sort out its problems.

We spent the night at the police station, for nobody who spoke English could be found. We were not locked up or pestered. People simply ignored us. In the morning an intelligent-looking middle-aged man appeared and said he was a state attorney. He seemed very serious. He sat opposite us and began to speak in a high-pitched voice.

'We do not care to press any charges against you and are not interested in details, descriptions or witnesses. However, we want you out of Thailand immediately. I might as well tell you that it's in your own interest.'

He turned to Thom. 'You, sir, have been here long enough. You should be familiar with the situation here. Should any of the men you fought with find out where you are, your lives would be in great danger. We just don't want that kind of trouble on our hands.'

'Fine, that's understood,' Thom said. 'We'll stay on an American-owned boat, Spirit of the Orient. It's anchored off Sunda Quay. We are out of your jurisdiction there, and we can look after ourselves.' The man grudgingly agreed, for he had no choice. The next day we were escorted across town in a police Land Rover and then taken in a patrol boat down the channel to the big yacht moored off Sunda Quay.

17

Vietnam Fall-out

Spirit of the Orient was a large, expensive-looking fibreglass motor cruiser. It belonged to Jack Peterson. Thom and I were expected as the police had telephoned ahead to check on Thom's proposition. As we arrived we were welcomed by four powerfully-built Americans. They helped me on to the boat. I was still feeling weak, so we all went down into the cabin for a drink. It was the first time I had run into that bunch: there is a whole colony of them in Bangkok.

Vietnam fall-out—that's what Thom called them. Tall, disillusioned men in their early thirties, most of them conservatively brought up—good, straight Americans. They wore their hair short, their handshakes were firm, their clothes pressed. Yet all those square jaws and honest eyes were just a front. Misled by their appearance, one listened to their stories of villas in Monte Carlo, dates with film stars, yachts in Hawaii; yet a careful observer would note the occasional lie or inconsistency, or the yellowish tinge in the pupils of the heroin addict.

Like the Bangkok police, they acted to impress each other rather than an audience. It was a little hard to understand at first: how was it that they could talk of their prowess for hours, knowing most of the stories to be lies? Only later did I understand that they themselves had lost the ability to distinguish truth from untruth. Some of them were once heroes: the military decorations that they wore were not fakes, but the war was now over.

For most Americans pulling out of Vietnam had meant going back home. But not for all. There were the few tough pros who had joined the army at eighteen and stayed and found themselves at thirty years old with no interests and no skills except those which they had learned in the army. They made their living in a hundred and one ways, usually taking dangerous and illegal short-term employment. They earned a few thousand dollars, spent it in a couple of weeks and scrounged from more prosperous friends. The clever ones bought themselves old cargo planes or boats and made their living that way.

One encounters them in Djibouti, Beirut, Tahiti, Taiwan—wherever there is a lack of order. Bangkok seems to be some kind of world headquarters from where they all start out and return.

Jack Peterson was not typical: he was cleverer than the rest. Lanky, fair-haired and not so young any more, he utilised his own skills and the availability of cheap labour to built yachts for gullible Americans. I could not help finding him charming. His life's interest was a book he was writing—'Peterson's Life Philosophy' he called it. It was a book of short parables. His basic idea was that the world is full of corrupt men and the only correct line of action for the good and the clever was to be even more devious and cunning than the rest. It was based on a Robin Hood principle: the rich would be fleeced. The Peterson twist was that the chief recipient of the booty would be Peterson himself, yet being a generous type he maintained that some of the spoils should be turned over to the have-nots, provided of course that they were amusing and interesting. The second part of the book was a manual, a collection of 'How to' examples divided into chapters entitled 'How to screw the Arabs—Greeks—French' and so on. There were also chapters devoted to the professions: 'How to screw the intellectual—the banker, etc'. He would always start by identifying the two principal weaknesses: 1. Some inferiority complex; 2. Some aspiration. He claimed among other things that Greeks valued unearned money, for only in acquiring without producing did one gain manhood; the French wanted money pure and simple, loved impressive titles but hated real responsibility; Arabs craved to be taken seriously, to be given responsible roles; intellectuals wanted to prove their machismo. The book made interesting reading and judging from Jack's results he had got some of his formulae right.

In spite of my awareness of their vices, I rather liked some of these fellows, and, being Thom's friend, I was quickly accepted.

'So you've got yourself a nice little scramble and a hand sling to go with it.' Frank, a huge ex-commando, laughed and gave me a slap on the back. 'One thing you learn in Bangkok is that you don't win a fight, not against the Thais. If you get beaten up and die, it's over; but any other outcome and they'll keep coming at you again and again. If it gets too tough they put a contract on you. You know how much it costs to have someone knocked off in Thailand? About a hundred dollars for a white man.'

'Seventy-five,' interrupted Jack. 'It's gone down. There's stiff competition and Kwan's mob have cut the price to an all-time low.'

'You get cut rates on family executions, provided you supply the bombs,' said Frank.

I did not know whether to believe this or not, but I was later assured that it was true.

'Well how do you survive here?' I asked in amazement.

'In two ways—you make sure you have an in with the contract gangs and the cops, and you try not to get into scrapes in town. We sow our wild oats elsewhere,' said Frank. 'Still, the taxi drivers are a bitch. Many aren't controlled by the gangs and they all carry guns. If you're cool, you don't get them roused. If not, you shoot first then run to Jib Han and try to get him to work out a deal by paying blood money or something. Look, don't worry about it. I mean take it as it comes, it's part of life. Swim downstream. Bangkok is a crazy place to have fun in. If you're gonna worry about getting beat up you'll miss out on all the fun.'

'No need to discuss impossibilities,' said Thom. 'The cops have told us we've got to split.'

'Screw the cops,' Frank exclaimed. 'Look Thom, I need you for that Persian Gulf job and you say your friend here can sail the boat for us. Besides, there's a party tonight that you can't miss. I landed that survey contract with the Malays and we're celebrating.'

'We'll stay for the party,' Thom said. 'But for the Gulf job—no way. I've told you before, it's no deal, but I've got a man for you anyway.'

I missed the rest of the conversation but saw that Frank was reassured and was smiling again.

We were joined by a rowdy, massive Georgian who, I discovered later, was the second most decorated marine in the Corps. He brought with him a basket of steaks and vegetables and ushered in two tiny Thai women whom he introduced as the greatest pair of cooks that ever swam out of Vietnam.

We ate very well. The conversation changed from business to women, to business again, but as they got more drunk it changed back to the Sixties and early Seventies and the war.

'It's always like that,' Thom said to me, 'as soon as they drink they are back fighting the war. I've listened to it for the last few months.'

I watched the animated faces. They were not memories, they were not talking of the past; to them the war is living in their hands, flying through the air, throwing invisible hand grenades. Eyes glittering, clenched teeth.

One could almost hear the rattle of the helicopter, the bark of M.15, the excited voice of the radio operator calling for an air strike. The stories were interesting, but eventually I felt superfluous, picked up a book and went out on deck to read.

It was late afternoon, the tide was going out and with it hundreds of little *sampans* going back after the day's work in the city. The *sampans*, covered with fruit and vegetables, reminded one of some Hollywood water carnival.

Seeing a white face on the deck of a yacht, many *sampans* rowed up to the 'rich man's boat' and offered their goods for sale. Some of them were floating kitchens with burning stoves and simmering pots and pans. Out of curiosity I tasted some sausages. They were so awful I had to spit it out but then had some *satay* and it was delicious.

The flower boats were the most persistent in coming. They assumed that rich people must have flowers. The flowers were rather expensive for one to buy 'just to be nice to the natives', but it was difficult refusing those friendly faces and pretty giggling girls. Having bought some half a dozen bunches I decided I should get lost and go below deck before I went bankrupt from buying those unwanted flowers. I decided to go below and get some sleep before the coming party. But I was not destined to see the party. It was as I was going down the steep yacht's companionway that I suddenly felt faint. The staircase whirled around me and I collapsed. Half dazed and groggy I remember being taken ashore and back to Rama Boulevard. I must have slept throughout most of the trip for I remembered little of it. I became fully conscious again after arrival at the hospital. My beautiful Thai doctor was there, so a bed was found and I collapsed into it, catching the glimpse of her pretty face before falling asleep again.

I was discharged the next day. I had lost a lot of blood so I had to take it easy for the next few weeks. There was no need to keep me in hospital and the doctor suggested a nursing home, but I replied that I would be perfectly all right at Dunna Bay.

18

Fitting Out

The repairs on *Andromeda* were well under way by the time I felt fit enough to make a contribution. I had spent my spare time reading up on ocean sailing and learning about navigation. Perhaps because of a guilty conscience over his sorry product or perhaps out of sympathy with Thom, with whom he loved to identify, Jack had given us not only the use of the yacht rent-free but also the freedom of the yard. Although by that time my wound had closed, it was still bandaged; but I was able to work with my left hand. Since Jack's wife allowed us to make use of the boatyard men when they had nothing to do, which was often, my chief contribution was in cajoling, threatening and bribing them to work.

Some two weeks after my telegram, my Yugoslav money finally caught up with me. There were two crisp $100 notes and a $600 air ticket voucher refundable to the payee only. That is adding insult to injury, I thought as I sent the voucher back by return mail and decided to send back the $200 as soon as I was payed in Mauritius. So much for that, I told myself, and forgot about it.

We scraped the ship inside and out. As wood is cheap and plentiful in Thailand and one of the men turned out to be a master carpenter, we decided to capitalise on our good fortune. We had the deck laid with wood and refitted the inside completely. The ferro-cement yacht was not badly damaged but there were a hundred and one little things wrong with it. The rudder was twisted and the steering cables were bent and about to break. Doors and hatches would not shut properly; screws were loose; the fresh-water tank leaked; the toilet pumps were jammed and all the plumbing was congested; the metal fittings were rusty. When the yacht was being used as a barge those details did not matter—all we needed was the sturdy ferro-cement hull and our huge Perkins diesel. The three tons of shackles had taken care of the ballast. Now, however, we were trying to turn the shell into a sailing boat.

We could not afford to do anything properly: we concentrated on things which were free or easily available in Thailand. Thom was most active, rushing around various shipyards and junkyards looking for cheap or cast off couplings, paint and wood. Everything was essentially makeshift; our work was of a cosmetic nature.

It was Thom's chief intention to make the boat look like a yacht again so that she would be attractive to potential buyers. He cared little about the way it handled and stood up to the sea.

'So what can happen? She won't sink, and there's always a wind to push us along.'

Jack would not let us have skilled workmen and, apart from the carpenter, the workers who came to help us were pretty useless. Jack gave freely as long as it did not cost him anything. I could hardly blame him—and he thought it kind enough to give us anything at all.

Our efforts culminated in the re-rigging. The masts came from a schooner that Jack had built for an American who later insisted on aluminium ones. The masts were made of strong Thai teak and were so heavy that we thought them useless, but we had no choice. Another difficulty was the rigging itself. To buy stainless steel shrouds would have cost several thousand dollars, which we could not even contemplate. The galvanized wire available in Thailand would cost about eight hundred dollars, which was still eight hundred dollars too much. Finally we settled for Thai-made wire used on telegraph poles, as Jack had got hold of tons of the stuff. I thought it was an absurd idea, but Jack assured us that he used it on all his boats, even the hundred-thousand-dollar ones. This was no great comfort. Still, he gave us four hundred feet for less than a hundred dollars.

In the course of this intensive work the weeks flew by and it did not seem long before the ship was rigged, painted, ballasted, sprayed and ready for launching—although there was no end to the things that still ought to have been done.

We still had no sails and had tried everything to get hold of some cheap ones. For a while we even contemplated buying up old sails and sail bags and making up some kind of patchwork, but we abandoned the idea. The original deal was that Jack was to give us some used ones he had kept from another boat, but he had recently sold them to a German. He had a brand new set of Cheong Lee sails straight from the maker in Hong Kong—but he wanted three thousand dollars for them. There was no way we could give him that, so after much haggling and signing of bonds and notes, he decided to let go of them and we were to pay him later with money we would get from sale or charter. We were rather pleased with the sails: they were indeed first-class and the only decent equipment we had on the boat.

Finally the day came when Jack simply said that he needed the slip free the next morning—and that was that, we had to launch her.

Launching the boat was no brief, formal occasion. I had always thought that one just cut the ropes and the ship slid into the water, but for us it was a slow and exhausting business that took the better part of a day. Inch by inch we lowered the boat, running around and balancing her, screaming at each other and at the sloppy workmen as she slowly crept towards the water. When she finally settled in the sea we tugged her with a motor boat over to Victoria Yacht Club, moored her for the night and went to sleep, exhausted.

The next day, clean-shaven and combed and wearing our best clothes, we sat at a table on the terrace of the Yacht Club, looking at *Andromeda*. She was moored to the Yacht Club pier, hardly a stone's throw from the edge of the terrace where the morning's discussion was taking place. We could hardly equate this gleaming yacht with the wreck we had pulled out only a few weeks before. She was a beautiful sight and we considered her our own. The lines were strong and masculine, and Thom had enhanced this by painting the hull black with a wide blue stripe running along the sides.

Along the stripe there were five wooden-framed portholes. The shiny mahogany deck and the gleaming brass and chromium deck-fittings, the walnut steps and the carved wooden guard-rail gave it a touch of luxury. Then there were the two sixty-foot masts and the complicated rigging. I tried to picture her at sea under full rig. I had to admit she looked pretty, and it was just too bad that the splendid sight was only an illusion. This fact disturbed me, but that day the sea was beautifully calm and blue, the wine chilled and delicious, so we forgot the problems of the boat and abandoned ourselves to the pleasures of the moment.

We had been trying out many different names, but dismissed them all. After an hour's argument I settled for simple Doves or Seagulls or Seasprays.

'I don't care any more,' I said. 'This is just a project. Why not give it a banal name?'

Thom objected. 'I'd be embarrassed to own a boat with a trite name like that, but you mentioned the word project. How about calling her "Project"?'

'Brilliant!' I exclaimed. 'Listen Thom, this will have been our third project together since we met five years ago.'

The day before the departure, the name was painted in blue letters against the black of the hull: 'Project III—Bangkok'.

The next couple of days saw a lull in activity. Thom, who had been so energetic in the business of refitting the ship, suddenly slowed down. I supposed it was fear that made both of us slow down—fear of the unknown ahead of us. I had had a taste of it in Pakistan, but it was Thom who had supplied the motivating energy. It seemed that the driving role had been passed to me. There was no reason to hang about in Victoria Bay, so I screwed up my courage and pressed for an early departure. In doing this the whole business of supplying the ship fell into my lap.

Both of us became impatient to get going—not so much because we wanted to, but because, having finally found the courage, we wanted to leave before we relapsed again into lethargy.

We never obtained all the necessary navigational instruments, or even a lifeboat. There was an old German sextant on the boat that we had used previously and had found good enough. But the journey ahead was considerably different from the one behind us. The stretch of open ocean was over three thousand miles this time, compared with the eight hundred between Jaffna and the Andamans. We would be sailing in rough seas and trade winds thousands of miles away from land. The rainy season was coming and ahead of us were currents and storms. There would not be a super-powerful Perkins to get us out of trouble, nothing but the sea and the wind.

We planned to sail in an arc in order to catch the lower trade-wind route, and we estimated that our journey would take six weeks. On that part of the ocean six weeks meant planning for ten weeks and making sure that we had enough of the bare essentials for much longer. One never knows what will happen and how long it will take. Would the mast break? Would the winds blow us into the southern polar region?

I bought Captain Duval's book on ocean sailing to get an idea as to how to supply the boat. I drew up a list of things we needed and totalled the cost: it came to such a fantastic amount that the journey seemed impossible. There were also legal fees to be paid—everyone is out to fleece a yachtsman: a fee to endorse every document concerned with the boat, an ownership registration fee, a port of registry fee, a docking fee, port taxes and mooring fees ... As a matter of principle we payed nothing throughout the journey. We would simply refuse to pay; the officials were always surprised but accepted it. 'Send the complaints to the port of registry,' we would say, knowing that the boat was not registered anywhere.

Because of marine regulations we had to have a lifeboat, fire-fighting equipment, a vermin-free certificate, a seaworthiness certificate and more. We had none of those things, so we faked them. We bought a lifeboat container with no lifeboat in it, empty fire extinguishers and so on.

Having got round the legalities of the trip, we had to plan the technicalities. Thom was getting increasingly discouraged so again I pressed on alone. For a while there seemed no solution until I ran into trader Chang. He said that he could supply everything with goods from Red China. I was sceptical, but he delivered.

Apart from the charts which we found on the boat and which were British, almost everything movable came from Red China—a new sextant, the compass, water pump, lamps, gas cookers, tinned food. We did not have cutlery so we settled for chopsticks. The ship acquired an oriental aura with all the Chinese objects and lettering.

*　　*　　*

Finally came the night before our departure. I walked along the little pier until it was late, trying to supply myself for the two month journey across the barren ocean. I drank in the sounds of the warm tropical night, the smell of *satay*, the soft movement of women's hips swaying in the twilight. That night we both drank a fair amount and settled down to an uneasy sleep.

Ever since that first night in Csarda I had been aware of an unpleasant feeling of indecision. Only now did I recognise that it was the sensation of fear, deliberately suppressed. Had I given way to it at that early stage, I would never have left. That night in Csarda I cheated and got drunk. I used a psychological trick, getting everything organised, going through the practicalities of getting my passport, visas and vaccinations while pretending that I was only joking.

The self-pretence distracted me from making a rational decision about whether or not to go. That night in Csarda it had to be a sudden decision, and therefore it was an easy one. The fear was with me when I finally fell asleep.

PART THREE

Voyage to Lotus Land

19

The Wind

We were up at 4 a.m. The sun had not yet come up as we stood calm
and collected, breathing the moist Thai air for the last time on that
morning late in May. We concentrated only on the job in hand.
Thom stood on the pier shouting instructions to me and half a dozen
deck hands who were pulling the ship out of the congested harbour.
The tide picked her up and carried her out. I ran alongside on the
shore, making sure she didn't hit the wooden planks along the
embankment; when she had finally cleared the dangerous part I took
a flying leap and jumped back onto *Project*.

The yacht glided past the anchored cargo ships. The sun peeked
above Payaies Island. We raised the small staysails and the boat slid
slowly and clumsily out and towards the western cape. Once away
from the current and with the ten-knot wind coming off the beam,
we raised the rest of the sails.

It was a thrilling and beautiful experience. The huge mainsail,
pulled up by the powerful, gleaming winch, shot up crackling and
popping like a firecracker. It swelled out immediately; we left it un-
adjusted and set about hoisting the jib. The wind was a good steady
easterly, and increased in strength as we left the land. With all sails
set we went about adjusting them; as we pulled in the big main sheet,
the large mainsail swelled out tight, as smooth as a balloon.

We sailed close-hauled and the big yacht keeled, her port rail
almost touching the water. The roar of the wind around us grew
much louder and she seemed to fly rather than sail.

'Wow,' cried Thom, 'we're bombing along at twenty knots!'

It was of course not that fast but it felt that way for we were sailing
against the wind. Apart from the excitement—and that wears off in
a few hours—beating to windward is usually considered the most
unpleasant, uncomfortable and violent of all the tacks, yet the extremely rough first three days on this tack were the only good sailing
we were ever to have on *Project*. We were seasick, naturally, but

nothing could ruin the thrill of the flying motion, the whistling of the wind and the crackling of the sail.

Three days later we hit the doldrum belt, the windless pockets surrounding the Equator. The sails emptied and the ship came to a halt. For a while it was fun: the peace and quiet of the doldrums gave us a chance to collect ourselves and readjust to normal routines. The life at 45° ceased, the noise died down and we could stand firm on two feet at last. We cooked our first proper meal and had a sound night's sleep.

Three days later it grew hot and five days later the fun stopped. The ferro-cement hull heated up and it was hot below, hotter still on deck. Too exhausted to eat or sleep, we lingered aimlessly, lying on wetted towels and looking up at the sky in hope of some activity. The sails flopped as pathetically as we did. Every now and then one of us would overcome his fear of sharks and hurl himself into the ocean, while the other kept guard with a gun held ready. One afternoon a noisy family of grey whales came to inspect us. They stayed for a few hours and although we were too exhausted to be curious or excited, we used the opportunity to swim: with all those whales we had no fear of sharks. But we were unable to relax completely, for who could trust those whales?

After seven days we began to fear that the wind would never rise; maybe we had hit a permanent pocket. It was nine days later when the wind finally picked up, an eight-knot breeze coming off the beam. We were heading due south, veering away from our planned course in the hope of catching the westerly current and the trade winds to take us comfortably to Mauritius.

Crossing the Equator we celebrated with a general splash about and finished the last bottle of whisky. The sky had changed and the nights were beautiful. I took a week of night watch and after two nights I had familiarised myself with the sky. It was easy to navigate with the Southern Cross: I simply headed straight for it.

We saw little of each other and were not particularly unhappy about the fact that the cabin was separate from the galley which was smaller but cooler. Thom established the galley as his territory. We made no formal arrangement: it just worked out that way. With Thom firmly entrenched there I preferred not to cook at all rather than have to put up with the repressed hostility that emanated from Thom while his territory was being invaded. We both had supplies

108

of books, biscuits and water and access to food storage, so the intrusions into each other's space were kept to a minimum. To this day I firmly believe that single-handed sailing is psychologically much easier than being confined in a small space with another male. The ideal situation would of course be a man and a woman. In spite of the lack of room it was surprising how much privacy it was possible to achieve. In some ways the experience was a great exercise in tolerance because I had to learn a great deal of self-control and consideration for Thom. Weeks and eventually months of poor sleeping, malnutrition and stress seemed to wear our nerves and tolerance to an inhuman level: every little habit—a cough, bad breath, belching, stretching, yawning—was magnified a hundredfold. At times we hated each other so much that I felt just a spark was necessary to provoke murder. Consequently we examined ourselves very carefully: any silly idiosyncracy, and life-long bad habit, would immediately be emphasised by the reactions of the other person. Little egoistic impulses—gobbling food, taking up too much space—none of that could be tolerated for more than a few minutes. We had to learn how to eat, sleep and even think without aggression or invasion into the private space around the other person. It was an extremely useful exercise, but very tiring. I often took double and even treble turns at the helm and preferred to sleep outside under a small canvas tent I had made for myself in the cockpit. I preferred to be on the deck alone: that was my territory, and Thom hardly ever intruded. With the sliding doors pulled tight the deck was sealed off from the rest of the boat, and the click of the Jensen door-latch would trigger off a feeling of perfect loneliness.

There was something magical about the nights so I often spent whole nights alone on deck. I would set the sails tight. To compensate for the fragile balance of the boat I would allow some play in the jib and mainsail. I would pass the main sheet around the winch next to me and wrap the end of the rope around my hand; the jib sheet I would cleat—within easy reach of my right foot for minor adjustments. Having completed all that, I would sit myself comfortably at the wheel, ready to sail the night away.

Steering the boat felt like struggling with an unruly horse. The wheel was constantly pulling and playing up, trying various tricks and going where I did not want to go. The challenge was to sniff the wind, anticipate the boat's tricks and force her to comply. With the coming of the dawn the wind, the yacht and the sea, which had all acted as a single entity, would return to their individual roles. In those moments a wonderful peace descended. The night's physical activity, painful and laborious as it was, served to exorcise the feelings of guilt and anxiety that drove me out of Europe. So just before dawn I would lash the wheel and go forward to sit and watch the glistening bow-wave.

Often during those nights I would get the strange sensation that the whole world is one living organism in which the living and the dead are all functioning parts. I was struck by the absurdity of the current idea, which I used to repeat parrot-fashion at university, to the effect that you can do whatever you like so long as you do not affect anybody else. In those starlit nights it seemed so obvious that we do all affect each other whatever we do. I felt that happiness could never be wholly self-contained, for every emotion seemed like pollen that would be picked up by the winds and carried to the ends of the earth to affect the minds of others. I'd sit there all night on the bowsprit, flying high up as the bow rose on the crest and then dropping deep deep down into the grey silent water, and I would feel as if the weights of the past were lifted from me, and my childish mistakes forgiven as memory's sounds and pictures discharged themselves into the sea.

20

The Rain on the Sea

Towards the end of the fifth week we hit the southern trade winds and bad weather. We were never again to have a quiet day on *Project*. The sky turned grey, the rain came down and the sea became hostile. With the wind from abaft, we set the sails on a broad reach. Then our troubles began: the yacht showed herself for what she really was.

'She's not a lady, she's a bitch!' Thom was to say repeatedly.

She was badly designed, badly constructed and badly balanced.

Any of those would have made her uncomfortable but all three made any kind of enjoyable sailing impossible.

The huge wooden masts made her top heavy. The sleek, narrow hull was under-ballasted. As a result any gust of wind upset her frail balance and the rolling motion would be picked up by the masts which rocked the boat violently to and fro. Once started, this rolling could last five minutes. The worst of it was that it took very little force to set the ship rolling. Wind apart, any large wave hitting the hull at a particular angle would do it. We learned that at no time could we really relax: while we slept, ate or talked there was always an uneasy expectation. A violent roll could come at any time, spilling our coffee or hurling us out of our bunks.

The ship was no good, it was obvious: all we could do with her was remove the top-heavy masts and replace them with aluminium ones, and rebalance the hull, a job that would cost thousands of dollars.

We made very slow progress. The weather was constantly bad: it rained for days at a time. The hatches were incorrectly sealed and so every time the deck went under, gallons of water poured in. Our clothes and bedding were swamped until there was not a dry piece of cloth left to wear. As the rainfall was continuous it was impossible to dry anything, so we slept in soggy bunks.

Having a fairly large supply of cooking gas, we started to use the gas as a heater and clothes-drier. Eventually we discovered that half the gas cylinders had not been filled—trader Chang had cheated us. So there we were, in the middle of the Indian Ocean, with no means of cooking.

When troubles come they come in bundles, so when I announced one day that a current had thrown us off course for Diego Garcia Thom was not surprised. We were now heading towards the cold nothingness of the South Pole, but we had had so much trouble that we were indifferent. The good news that we could still use the southern current to reach the lower trade route and sail to Mauritius that way failed to cheer us up. Any solution was at least a month's voyage away and therefore in the abstract. We were cold and wet today and tomorrow we would be the same; there was nothing to be done about it.

The weeks passed, always with the angry sky and the foaming steel-grey seas, and the same dreary routine, four cold lonely hours of watch staring into the endless grey nothingness, and then the uncooked canned meat. The desire for a hot cup of soup or a slice of bread became almost uncontrollable.

In time we learned how to trim the sails and the helm to counteract the motion of the unbalanced masts. This took great concentration and constant adjustments to the sails and the helm. I could not keep it up too long, for after two or three hours of intense concentration I collapsed exhausted, but at least on occasions we had some peace for three hours or so and a chance to raise our spirits a little. Particularly annoying was the damp feel of wet clothes; one was constantly wet, and particularly so while resting in the damp bunks.

Existential concerns and the search for meaning in life were brushed aside. Bodily desires became so strong at times that I imagined all that was necessary for happiness was a full stomach and a dry bed. I could not imagine anything more glorious than that.

About ½° south of the Equator Thom fell into the ocean. It was by sheer chance that I saw him fall in. I threw a lifebuoy which promptly sank (Chang's equipment). It took ages to bring the boat round to pick him up. Neither of us said a word as, shivering and shaking, he climbed back on board. Why the hell hadn't he tied himself, I thought—although I never took the trouble to do so either. Tying was too awkward for one had to get up constantly to readjust the sails and balance the boat. The man below hated the one on deck —he of course was 'responsible' for every roll. We were not objective enough to realise that each of us was as 'slow' as the other, and would make the same mistakes.

The worst part of it was the rain—I dreaded the hours I had to spend on deck working all the time. Every now and then I would tire and a sudden jerk would catch me unawares: the bow would dig in and I'd know what was coming; I would cleat the mainsail quickly as the boat practically overturned. I had to hang on desperately to the wheel, grasping the base with my legs and trying not to be swept away by the inevitable wave that swept across the deck. The boat went on swinging like a pendulum until, wet and exhausted, I finally steadied her again. There was no end—the rain fell ceaselessly. The slow Chinese torture of raindrops on one's head went on and on and on. One can bear suffering when one can anticipate the end, but for us the end was too far away—it was no use saying that in a month's time it would be over when every hour was unbearable.

In the beginning we had expected to get used to the motion and overcome seasickness, but it proved impossible. In the storms we were continually dizzy, continually sick: one's body cannot get used to the gales because the pattern of movement is too unpredictable. After the first week of bad weather we just gave up—but we could not stop working. The sails had to be raised and lowered, the boat had to be steered. We had no appetite but we ate, for one has to, and we threw up again, and at the same time carried on working—pulling in the ropes, tightening the screws, repairing the shrouds.

It was over two months now since we had seen the last sign of life, a Japanese fishing trawler. We could not afford to get lost for nobody else knew of our whereabouts and no one would look for us; we were no Sir Francis Chichester, with helicopters and television to keep track of our progress. We could not even say for sure where we were. As the sky was almost constantly overcast our navigational fixes were few and far between, but we hardly cared any more. We could no longer eat the cold Yungpa canned pork, for it made us sick. Our staple diet became a little flour, milk powder and honey mixed up with cold rainwater. The days were melting into each other monotonously. We stopped differentiating between day and night and simply vegetated while the ship sliced on through the water. We forgot that we had ever not been at sea.

21

Mauritius

The night was pitch black, the ship moved steadily through the thick grey water. It was a fair sea and the densely-spaced two-foot waves beat a rapid, even pulse.

Some time after midnight a patch of sky cleared, exposing a cluster of stars which seemed like a ray of hope, a promise that all would be well. Neither of us could sleep: according to our last fix we would sight the Mauritius light that night. We spent the whole night climbing up and down the mast, searching the horizon, straining our eyes. There were many false alarms—stars low on the horizon blinking rhythmically as they were veiled and unveiled by the swells of the sea. As the night started to fade we decided to go to sleep, hungry, cold and miserable. Thom went below.

I was still up as the sun cast its first rays. Barely able to keep awake, I decided to heave-to before descending to my bunk. It was while I was cleating the jib that a cluster of clouds attracted my attention. They were concentrated over a single area; the rest of the sky was perfectly clear. Suddenly I saw it : a small round blob of grey, appearing and disappearing with the swells. I did not want to make a fool of myself but I wanted so much to let out the traditional call: 'Land ahoy!' For a few moments I stared hesitantly. Well, what could it be? A whale, a ship? No, it had to be land.

At last I could contain myself no longer: I ran to the ship's bell, rang it and lived out a childhood dream, screaming, 'Land ahoy! Land ahoy!' Thom was on deck in a flash, struggling with the cord of the glasses which had got entangled on a hook; he ripped the glasses away and ran up the bowsprit. It was land all right, but what blasted land was it? Thom rushed to the charts to check if this was Mauritius. There had to be a four-second light, and the tiny Round and Flat islands before. There was no other land in that area except for Reunion and surely, I thought, we could not have been that far out in our navigation. Thom climbed the mast; through the glasses he could see St Martin, a known landmark, a huge rock balanced on top of a mountain peak.

'It is Mauritius,' he cried, and climbed down.

It was a beautiful day; we had a gentle twelve-knot wind and a current behind us. We hoisted a spinnaker and the ship sped like an arrow to her target.

The island rose out of the sea like the back of a prehistoric animal. The grey blur dissolved into patches of colour. Colours started differentiating into patterns and the shapes started to take form. First came the rugged mountain peaks, then the hump and then there it was, green and purple in the early sunshine, warm and inviting. It was a marvellous feeling. Two months with not a ship or land in sight, two months that had drained the two of us flat as a dead battery. What is it in the sight of land that can create so much excitement in the heart of a sailor? The old clichés, read many times in books, now took on a living form in our breasts. Land, forests, lakes, beaches, restaurants, hotels and people—it was all out there ahead of us, now only a few hours away, stretched out like a beautiful gift in the palm of the sea.

Thom busied himself preparing breakfast. He brought out the last of the morsels we had kept: a box of Weetabix, some milk powder and a jar of honey. We ate and sang and danced as the island became bigger and bigger. It was a glorious, welcoming day—fish jumped with mad joy, breaking the turquoise sea around them, as the purplish misty curtain rose. Houses became visible and then we saw the port with its ships. *Project III* slid in speedily.

On Mauritius the sight of a large yacht is a very welcome one to at least a hundred people who make their living from rich yachtsmen. There is a Swahili expression, *shamba*, which these islanders have adopted. It originally meant the size of a farm or house, but its modern meaning is a milking cow, or a good thing to be exploited. The fifty-five foot schooner approaching the island looked like a very good *shamba* and there was much excitement among the Creole port hustlers and ships' chandlers as to who would make it to the ship first.

The yacht was still not in the harbour as little motor boats started on their way, the people waving hands and flags.

'Look,' exclaimed Thom. 'All these boats coming out to meet us.'

We were almost in the harbour and passed the first large cargo boat which curiously enough happened to be a Yugoslav ship. I read the name:—*Admiral Zmayevich* 'Kotor'.

'Quick, the Yugoslav flag,' I shouted to Thom. We ran into the cabin and tossed things aside in our frantic search. It was among all the other flags which we had prepared; moments later we had it flying.

The few sailors who were on deck must have been quite surprised to see a yacht flying the Yugoslav flag and as *Project III* sailed past they greeted us with several loud hoots. Not knowing what was going on, another ship picked up the hoots.

Thom and I stood on deck feeling like royalty. Surrounded by little boats and hooting ships we ran up and down the deck like little schoolboys, whistling, shouting and waving.

'Watch out! You'll smash the boat,' some jealous yachtsmen were shouting from a Durban-registered yacht. But we'd show them what's what, we decided, as we went in with the full rig up, hanging on to the last moment; only as we cleared the last pier did we drop the sails in a flash, executing the manoeuvres we had practised to perfection. We reefed the sails quickly and smartly as if in a parade, turning the yacht smartly and coming to a dead stop almost perfectly level with the customs buoy; we hoisted the yellow quarantine flag and a few minutes later a blue and white pilot ship guided us to a pier. It was the end of July. We had arrived.

As the ship was docked we collapsed, tired, happy and bewildered. Dozens of men from the little boats climbed aboard. Several tugged at our sleeves, yelling. It took us at least five minutes to realise that they were speaking French patois: 'Voulliez-vous que je faissé' this or that, how much fuel do you want, can I supply you with groceries for your next journey, gas, oil, washing, dry cleaning, do you want the ship scraped, slipped?

Our defences were so low and we were so tired that we were agreeing to everything. Dazed and confused, we moved as if in a dream and before we knew what was happening the sweet-faced cocoa-coloured men were taking away all our washing, the empty gas bottles, and we had signed who knows what orders for food, parts and supplies.

By that time a large crowd had gathered on the pier. As we waited for customs clearance a boy was sent to fetch some food: fresh fruit, still warm bread, butter and eggs—things we had not seen for a long time.

When we had finished the customs formalities we did not have the strength to go on shore. We ate and collapsed into a deep sleep.

* * *

I had a beautiful dream: I was sitting on a sunny terrace in a peaceful café somewhere around the Mediterranean. It was late afternoon. Opposite me sat a gentle, long-haired girl who wore a simple light dress with one piece of jewellery, a cross on a chain round her neck. She leant forwards, breathing heavily and trying to whisper something in my ear. The cross caught a ray of sun and blinded me with a brilliant glare. I could not understand what she was whispering into my ear. Her voice became the murmur of a brook then disappeared into the distance.

The sun was streaming through the porthole as I awoke. Everything was perfectly still. The calmness and silence startled me. I opened my eyes, trying to collect myself and still not realising where I was. The strains of a cheerful calypso were blown on the wind; the words were: 'Lève-toi soleil, lève toi soleil, la nuit est bien, le jour est mieux.'

I was up in a flash. I felt good: energetic and clear-headed. I glanced at Thom who was still asleep. I jumped ashore and went into the sun.

The narrow streets were full of activity; gently, subtle-featured natives walked briskly about their business. A man needs land and people—it is no good to be alone, I mused.

I stood in brilliant sunshine on the pier, facing a large square. A row of one-storeyed white buildings sprouted signs: Moneychanger, Souvenir Shop, Restaurant. I changed some money, experiencing that pleasant Asian sensation as my $30 (nothing money) became 200 Mauritian rupees (serious money). So I walked out counting my red Mauritian rupees. I continued up a narrow street that led to a busy market-place. I could feel in my body the pulse of the market's life: there were subtly varied sounds, smells, colours, red tomatoes, yellow papayas, huge fish and a sea of flowers and vegetables of every possible colour and shape.

Ignoring the half dozen or so hustlers around me, I sat on a terrace and drank in the atmosphere. Soon I felt very hungry; I walked towards a main street, amicably declining the dozen invitations for a drink, and stopped at a place called 'The Snow White'. It was a sort of café that catered for the local office girls and young Franco-Mauritian males. The pastries looked good and there was a delicious smell of sausages coming from the kitchen. I ordered a plateful and a mountain of fresh French bread and coffee, and ate with great concentration for the next hour, being distracted occasionally by the sight of a shapely leg or a casually exposed breast.

When I had thoroughly gorged myself and was fortified with a morning shot of Green Island rum, I decided I might as well find out about sailing to Ceylon. Not that I was in any hurry to go, but as I did not want to spoil my stay in Mauritius by being preoccupied with the problem of getting to India I wanted to arrange it as soon as possible. I asked the way to the island's biggest agency, Blue Star Shipping, and entered their office on the Boulevard Royal.

The tidy clerk wore gold-rimmed spectacles, was very friendly and talkative and ready to book me a passage anywhere in the world—but he regretted there was no scheduled passenger service to Ceylon or India.

'What do you mean, no passage to India?' I asked incredulously. 'Where do you get all your natives from?'

The clerk smiled. 'That was many years ago.' He explained carefully, as if I had made a serious remark. 'Of course, if Monsieur desires we can book him on a flight to Nairobi. Monsieur is sure to find a connection to India from there.'

As I turned to leave, angry and disappointed, he remarked that there was a cargo ship, *Commandant Zamavique*, bound for Bombay later in the month; it was a Yugoslav sugar-cane carrier on its regular run.

'A Yugoslav ship?' I stopped in my tracks. 'You don't mean *Admiral Zmayevich*?'

'*Mais oui, monsieur*—that's what I said—"*Commandant Zamavique*".'

'Oh God, the French ...' I thought as I hurried towards the pier. Captain Pero greeted me with open arms and a tumbler of Slivovitz firewater.

'But of course you can come with us, brother—I'll give you a cabin to yourself. We've plenty of room—no trouble.'

There was just one problem—the ship was not due to sail for another nine weeks. On their last run they had carried zinc oxide, so they had to scrape and recoat the holds before loading the sugar cane.

'Nine weeks!' I exclaimed. 'That long?'

'What do you mean long? This is Mauritius, not the Albanian border or the salt mines. Soon you'll be wishing it was twelve weeks. Why are you so anxious to get to India anyway? Nothing but flies, dirt and beggars there. Wish I were on my way back west already.'

After meeting the officers and the crew and arranging everything for the passage to India, I walked back to *Project*. Nine weeks to wait. India kept eluding me; still, I decided to make the most of it. Having reached the boat I found Thom with a bunch of Franco-Mauritians already drunk and turning the day into a party.

22

Mañana!

So the carefree Mauritian life began. Our experience was not typical; Franco-Mauritians are a closed group, and many yachtsmen we spoke to later found them reserved and unfriendly. It must have been Thom's easy-going manner, plus the fact that he made an effort to speak in French, that accounted for his popularity.

They automatically assumed we were rich young men and no amount of explanation could convince the locals otherwise. At first we were invited by young-men-about-town but eventually Thom made himself acceptable to the grown-up set. As for me, I mixed with French and Creoles alike.

Franco-Mauritians themselves are one of the last manifestations of a phenomenon that has disappeared through the seven seas: a small, tightly-knit community, twenty thousand strong, practically owning an island whose Creole population is close to a million. Conservative, rich and arrogant, they hold on to their privileges, insisting on their historical right to their position. They argue that they are the original inhabitants and as such have special rights. The island was uninhabited when the French arrived; the Indians and Chinese were imported later on, as labour. We did not contest the situation at the time: we were guests and observers, and accepted that role.

Without realising it I was being drawn into a life of indulgence. The European life in Mauritius was something unreal: it was a dreamy existence—nobody worked, nobody had a worry in the world. It was a living anachronism—the turn-of-the-century atmosphere lingered on. The price of sugar on the world market was guaranteed by treaties. The plantations were huge, the 'natives' worked.

The men's lives were made up of hunting and fishing and entertaining. Fun life, but no culture, no serious music, thought or art, no deeper purposeful activity, at least not such as I could see, though it was physically healthy, with plenty of outdoor sports.

There were no clouds on the political sky either. Prime Minister Ramgoolan was a kindly old gentleman, whose main passions were

Sanskrit and his rose garden. The leader of the opposition was Gaetan Duval, a twenty-nine year old 'playboy' ('King Creole' he called himself) whose life's achievement was his date with Brigitte Bardot, a true story, apparently—he showed us pictures. Apart from this and his sports car and a race horse, his main interest, it seemed, was in choosing the right kind of suit for the race track. In Parliament he wore levis. The Mouvement Militant Mauricienne, the leftist party, was sweet. The leaders, a group of intelligent young men, seemed to be pushing for some kind of Titoist socialism.

The aimless, easy-going existence infected us too. Thom had taken to the island like a duck to water and showed no signs of ever wanting to leave. In due time he met a local girl, Isabelle d'Arneut, a very sweet thing who was as impressed with Thom as he was with her, so it was obvious that Thom was in no hurry to leave.

I remember one afternoon sitting alone in d'Arneut's orchard high up on a hill overlooking the sea. I tried to imagine what it would be like to live on an island like this. It seemed that there was something incomplete, something unreal about it—almost like sleeping one's life away.

Sitting there in the orchard I wondered about the nexus of yearnings and desires around which this Mauritian community crystallised. The French's were materialistic all right, but I could not sense any vibration of greed or hate as the dominating strain—unlike the rhythm of Pat Pong Road, which was an expression of shrill, green, high-pitched lust. The Mauritian aura had no barbed, ugly overtones. I could not feel the joyous elation of snow-covered Mashhad, neither could I feel any great evil in Mauritius. Rather like a waltz or whipped cream, pleasant but essentially nothing. I mentioned these thoughts to Thom and Isabelle, who was no fool; she said that she lived in tune to the rhythm of France, and visited Paris at least once a year. Once a year, I thought, did not seem to change anything, so I kept these thoughts to myself.

And so it went on this life; the races, the theatre, political talk over rum and candle-light, casinos, discotheques . . .

I had almost forgotten about the Yugoslav ship and my plan to go to India as I grew insensitive to the force that gripped me that night in Csarda. The mindless Mauritian existence was like a drug. At the time it seemed that there was no reality apart from the island. I spoke about that to an intelligent English girl who was on holiday there, but for all her perceptiveness she was a tourist: she had flown there, so she could not understand.

Two weeks had passed since she had left, and since then I had not engaged in one sensible conversation. After her departure, I began to spend an increasing amount of time on d'Arneut's plantation, vegetating. It was infectious, that island resignation.

It was late on a Thursday afternoon that reality unexpectedly knocked on my door. I was on *Project*, sitting idly on the deck enjoying afternoon tea and home-made biscuits presented by Isabelle's girlfriend. My main concern that afternoon was whether to spend the night in Chinatown in Port Louis and eat at Lim's or go out fishing with a bunch of rowdy Australians. It was in the middle of this deep dilemma that I caught sight of a blue-clad sailor and recognised the blue and white Yugoslav merchant-marine uniform. For a while I wondered why he was coming to see me, but before he had reached the jetty I knew what he was coming for: it was Thursday, the nine weeks had gone by, and the Yugoslav ship would be leaving to-morrow. He was coming to tell me that the time had come, and to help me move my things on board.

A cold feeling ran up my spine. What should I tell him—that I had changed my mind, that I was perfectly happy where I was? Should I prolong my stay in Mauritius? But *then* what? I realised instantly that if I did not use this opportunity to leave, I'd be stuck in Mauritius for an eternity—it was just the ideal place for getting stuck in. Thom had already succumbed—but then perhaps that's what he wanted. What should I do? My mind rushed back to the questions that I had been asking myself incessantly during the two years before Csarda. I had left in order to solve these dilemmas, but had managed to suppress them for these last few weeks; should I continue to ignore them? The journey that had begun in Csarda was not over. Come what may I had to leave. I heard the steward's heavy steps on the yacht's deck. I did not even let him on board. I heard myself saying in a strange muted voice as if against my will, 'Please tell the captain that I'll be there in the morning.'

The man looked at me. He wanted to say something but I had already turned my back and was on my way down into the cabin to fix myself a drink.

23

Tropical Nocturne

After centuries of practice, life in Port Louis dies with the sunset. Quickly and silently, the people disappear. The sun's orange ball slips behind the Blue Mountains and the sea turns crimson. The shadow travels across the water, over the land and up towards the citadel. As it reaches the shore, the shadow changes colour.

I sat alone outside the Phoenix Café, watching the purple curtain sweep away the day's activities and decided to make it a night to remember. I walked down the wide and stately palm-lined Boulevard Royal to the pier. As I stepped onto the yacht and looked over the city, the streets were completely empty and dark.

On the yacht there was much excitement. Radio Green Mauritius blared French pop music; Thom, with shaving foam on his face, was still half dressed, running up and down and getting ready to paint the town red.

'So what's the plan?' I enquired. 'Whose party are we going to tonight?'

'Ah, to hell with Franco-Mauritian parties,' Thom said, for he was in the middle of one of his rows with Isabelle. 'I want a break from all that playing about and polite nonsense—let's go out on the town and burn it up. Make them remember your visit.'

'So where do we go?' I asked.

'La Morne,' he said, speaking of a showy place and a hang-out of film people.

'Maybe I can pick up that Sylva what's-her-name—mind you she is getting on a bit but they've got a new stand-in I hear,' Thom said putting on a black silk shirt and arranging a falling lock of hair.

He insisted that I wear his Italian suit—just once, for this last occasion, he argued, so as 'not to embarrass him if things were to develop'.

First we'd start off together, he proposed as we set off, but if something came up we'd separate, each following his own nose. Afterwards we'd meet again and go to Sam's Disco or for a midnight sail on the yacht or as the circumstances dictated.

At La Morne it was a gala night. It had something to do with the Miss Mauritius contest. There was quite a crowd, some film people were over from the Seychelles, and with all the tourists and the regulars there was an aura of festivity about the place.. Thom vanished and I walked towards the food tables.

The evening was to start with a sumptuous buffet. Mauritian cuisine is generally poor, but the tables before me were laden with French pâtés, grilled and boiled lobster, crabs, shells, caviare—food that not even a Mauritian cook can mess up. Somewhere I found an extra large cheese plate and loaded it unashamedly with all kinds of food. I was going to drink and have a good time and wanted to do it well, without grace or finesse.

I caught a glimpse of Thom who had joined the noisy film crowd that had arrived from Europe for some *Emmanuelle* remake. I saw him in animated conversation with some cover-girl and beckoning me to come over. I hesitated for a second but then pretended I did not see him. Not my scene, I said to myself, but then perhaps it was just that I felt insecure in such company. I walked around looking for a suitable table. I wanted to avoid tables occupied by Franco-Mauritian girls—not that I had much against them—it was just that their quick Gallic wit and constant *double entendres* were too demanding for me. I decided to spend the evening alone, enjoying my food and sipping the delicious wines in peace, watching the world go by.

It was still quite early, but all the tables were taken. I walked down the crowded terrace and spotted a couple of French acquaintances. There was an attractive non-French looking girl with them. She seemed fairly friendly, the tall blonde type who looked confident enough not to keep having to prove herself. A safe enough table, I decided; I walked over towards it and was invited to join them. I was introduced and drew up a chair.

'What a curious selection of food,' the girl exclaimed jokingly, looking at my laden plate and putting on the dumb-blonde act. I looked at her relieved. It was just the conversation and the mood I was looking for—light, relaxed and unserious.

'Are you going to eat all that?' she said with a lilting sing-song accent. It was a South African voice.

'Yes. I am a growing boy,' I said and paused waiting for witty thoughts to come to me but none came so I just smiled, moved my chair around closer to her and put down between us my overladen plate.

'Looks like you have been stocking up for winter,' she added mischievously.

I looked up and smiled. Thank God, this was Anglo wit, free of constant toilet and genital innuendo that characterises the Franco talk. 'It's just that I do not know what to do with my hands,' I said, taking on this role that the circumstances prescribed, a role that I had by then rehearsed; they were other peoples' lines, but then why not: it was a one-night stand, I thought, so I took her plate and emptied some of my delicious food onto it and we both ate. I was so hungry I lay off talk and wit and let her do all the talking, which was light and refreshing like the fruity wine and the atmosphere around us.

I took pleasure in picking up the frosty bottle out of the bucket, wrapping the swan's down-soft embroidered napkin around it, listening to the clink of ice in the silver bucket that shone on the table reflecting the moon behind me. There was also the fascination of pouring the effervescent liquid, green and white bubbles bursting and climbing up the walls of the glasses, the fruity smell of crushed field flowers as I poured.

I looked at the girl, open to her easy, honest type of beauty; there was something rustic and naive about her. I asked myself if there was a clean way of sharing any more with her than this relaxed South Sea dinner; it seemed impossible so I just leaned back in my chair, thankful for the pleasant moments I was enjoying. I lit a cigar and took in the rest of the scene.

The majority of the guests had finished their dinner and the local combo began playing a lilting calypso tune. It was an attractive picture: the lantern-lit terrace by the sea, surrounded by flowers; people sitting around dimly lit tables, shadows dancing on their faces. A couple of hundred yards away lay the beach and then the wide expanse of the moonlit Indian Ocean shimmering through the palms.

The gentle breeze brought fragrant scents from the lush flower-border, which gave on to the neatest rose garden. Growing among the tables there were rich-smelling clusters of bougainvilleas that blended their scent with the sea breeze, creating a heavy aromatic cloud. Over the soft sounds of the band I could hear the breaking of the surf. It was a special occasion and people were dressed formally.

The lights were dim, the music soft, and the ladies looked elegant in long dresses. Somehow the sheer power of the surrounding magic worked on the guests, forcing them to make an effort to be graceful. The men stood erect, their shoulders straight.

I asked the South African girl for a dance. It was somewhat awkward for me prancing around to steps that I have never managed to learn—but then as we danced I collected myself while reflecting that dancing, like conversation, can be just a part of a prescribed ritual to which one mindlessly adheres. One move leads to the next in the sequence prescribed by popular literature and television. It was all so easy on the dance floor or in life so long as one stuck to patterns prescribed by society. And that night both the girl and I were playing our parts.

During the slow dances I had the chance to appraise the girl's body, subconsciously giving it marks out of ten—which were high, for she was well developed. Without thought and commitment, the mind was working out its pleasure calculus.

I was surprised how simple it was to make conversation during dinner. Making cool comments, sending the waiters about, knowing what to order and how. Yet somewhere in the middle of that mindless ritual I started to reflect; while talking of wine and music, a part of my mind stepped out of the scene and analysed it reflectively. A part of me realised that I could never have been so suave and smooth if I had been genuine; it was the lack of real involvement that made the smooth performance possible. How sad, I thought, that the less genuine one is the easier one performs. I thought of my genuine performances: when choked and confused by longing, shyness and enthusiasm, one is so gauche. Like the pathetic clown Petrushka in Stravinsky's ballet, who, while deeply in love with a beautiful ballerina, only scared and confused her with his exaggerated behaviour, while his rival, the crude Moor, uninvolved, unsubtle, but through his indifference very cool and collected, was able not only to slay Petrushka but also to win the ballerina.

An hour later we were strolling down the long empty beach—holding hands, with golden moonlight dancing on the girl's hair and bathing her bare elegant shoulders, her evening dress trailing on the sand. A pair of young people in movieland environment. The stuff of which dreams are made.

But it was not to last. In the final hour or so the girl had broken the spell. She was still too young, too naive to dance through a role imposed on her by the sexy décolleté dress and the setting. She spoke of herself seriously—not glamorising herself, not mouthing the cool lines heard from some television heroine's lips. She stopped being a television-person and she became a real person. A young secretary from Durban with problems—a sick mother, a broken heart, disappointed with her failure to win a university scholarship, she had had to save very hard to come to Mauritius and stay at expensive places and perhaps meet a young man with a yacht and steady job to offer her a secure stable existence. *Petit bourgeois* plans—but for her probably perfectly decent and acceptable. It would have been so easy for me to act out the role I had assumed—but then it was not possible any more—she had ceased being an object, she had become a human being.

She sensed a certain coolness and withdrawal overcome me. I had changed. She stood still and looked up, confused.

'I am sorry,' I said, trying to minimise the hurt. 'I do not feel well, can I take you back.'

She was a nice girl. There was not anger or malice in her eyes; just sadness. As she whispered something I could not contain myself, and tried to kiss her, this time with emotion; but she said she did not need to be escorted and slipped hurriedly into the palm grove alone.

For a while I stood, wondering what to do. Run after her? Was there anything wrong with her? But then I knew I had to press on— it was me who was not complete—I myself still did not know what I wanted. I had to go on. So I stood musing and romanticising. A sudden gust of the wind carrying sea spray brought me out of this mood. Oh hell I thought, what's all this sentimentalising, that's what comes with indulgence in analysis and philosophy. Tonight is the night to eat, drink and be merry—I'll worry about things some other time.

So what to do? Why not something silly? I looked around me and realised I was not far from the island's famous La Morne Casino. I decided to go and gamble.

*   *   *

I walked along the moonlit palms towards the casino. At the entrance, the big French doorman nodded invitingly. I shrugged my shoulders as he swung open the door.

It was a large glittering room. The decor was mid-sixties—lots of shiny metal, glass, plastic, dark walls, large mirrors and chrome.

The croupiers were cocoa-coloured young girls; dressed in long black evening dresses, they cut an elegant figure.

I changed a hundred and twenty rupees, twenty dollars' worth. The girl passed me twenty-rupee tokens/chips. If I lost—fine; if I won, so much the better. It took me forty-five minutes to lose them playing a careful game of blackjack. I counted the money I had left in my pocket, 750 rupees, 120 dollars, more. I needed sixty dollars to take me through the night before cashing a cheque that I had received as my share of the advance from a Club Méditeranée charter we had arranged. I decided to put the remaining 60 dollars' worth on red. It did not make much difference if I lost for I had decided to spend it in Mauritius anyway.

Looking around for the likeliest croupier, I saw a tall Creole girl. She stood, bored, by an empty table, mechanically spinning the large wheel and going through the standard performance as if before an invisible audience. As I walked towards the table she smiled. 'Three hundred and sixty on red' I said, for the sake of saying something and placed my money. With half of the numbers red, I had a fifty-fifty chance.

Red came up. It was so simple. I felt silly grabbing at those funny-looking chips. I looked at the girl; she had large liquid eyes and a cold uninterested look. I felt I was going to win. I glanced at the girl and said in English, 'Spin it again.' The red came up. The girl was as cold as ice. I felt she ought to have smiled so I made a rather corny remark about breaking the bank and picking her up afterwards.

There was a hint of a smile in the girl's eyes, 'I'm sorry but you'll have to break the bank before 2 a.m. for I go off at 2.15.' I felt stupid. What's all this acting cool again? I thought. I had just won 240 dollars, good money for around here; take it, and have fun.

Unable to think of any face-saving answers or gestures I picked up the chips, said 'thank you' and left the casino. A few months ago winning 240 dollars would have made me excited. But now I was indifferent. Why not go on till it becomes serious money, money that made a difference, I thought.

I returned; the girl was still there. 'En rouge,' I said simply, unwilling to back out and tossed down the chips. As the wheel spun, I regretted the gesture. Suddenly the whole scene appeared ridiculous to me. I knew I was going to lose and thought I did not care. I decided I would never gamble again.

Red came up again. I collected my 480 dollars and walked out. As I left the unpleasant feeling that had temporarily filled me vanished. I took a deep breath and suddenly the air was rich with the smell of jasmine. I had just won close to 500 dollars (including my initial stake) and the night was still young.

I walked towards a rank of old Humber taxis, still unable to shake the South African girl off my mind. I hesitated for a second before stepping up to the taxi.

'Golden Moon,' I said to the first one in the line and slid into the back.

*　　*　　*

Golden Moon is Mauritius' most famous brothel-cum-nightclub. Situated ten miles south of Port Louis, it had been one of Thom's favourite night spots. Unlike the tourist discotheques and night clubs, the Golden Moon had an atmosphere of its own. Here the Russians smashed vodka glasses and the Greek sailors danced their slow-motion dances.

As I arrived, the place was in full swing. As soon as I stepped in I was recognised by a group of Yugoslav sailors. They shouted and waved to me to join them. I acknowledged them and stopped to survey the scene. The first impression was that of a village dance hall rather than a brothel. It was a large dimly lit room with a bar on the entrance side and a Creole band at the opposite end. Along each side were metal tables and chairs. A clearing in the middle served as a dance floor. Everywhere girls sat or stood, all colours, shapes and sizes, each assuming a different attitude, some provocative, others bored, some friendly, others surly.

The customers sat divided by nationalities, as usual the Greeks and Yugoslavs on either side of the band. Germans were in the middle and the rest anonymously dispersed. The Greeks and the Yugoslavs were dominating the scene: the Greeks were the more numerous, but the Yugoslavs made up for it by increased volume. The band played a mixture of old discotheque hit songs, *Saturday Night Fever*, *Lady Bump Bump*, and the local music.

I joined the Yugoslavs. They were huge burly Dalmatians, big and friendly, loud-mouthed, open-handed, lavish spenders.

Having been slapped on the back by half a dozen heavy hands, I sat down. We drank whisky, Johnnie Walker. Good-bye to my calculated drinking; it took the twelve of us ten minutes on average to finish a bottle, so we ordered the bottles in twos to expedite the process.

In the cosmopolitan atmosphere of the Golden Moon I recognised the uniqueness of my people. One could not miss them; loud, wild, boisterous, full of life, they dominated the scene, making the rest seem stiff. The wildest dancers, the loudest singers, they were everywhere, sitting with the band or doing acrobatics on the dance floor. Perhaps the most amazing thing about them was their reckless spending. The owner told Thom that the Yugoslavs were the only people he freely allowed to smash all the glasses they wanted. 'They spend so much,' he explained, 'I like to keep them happy.'

And they did spend. The captain seemed to be the standard-bearer. His hands full of money, he periodically tottered among the band demanding that they play Yugoslav gypsy songs. He was stuffing money into their pockets, their hands, their instruments. Sometimes the band would have to stop playing for ten minutes while he taught them a particular number. But that night it was his thirtieth visit and the band could already play a fair number of Yugoslav folk tunes. Every time they began to play, one of the Yugoslavs would shower them with money and then they would grab the best-looking girls and dance madly, jumping around like horses. About two thirds of the girls sat around the Yugoslav table. I asked the manager if that was bad for business. The man laughed, 'Bad for business? The girls will make more money with a dozen Yugoslavs than with fifty Germans. Of course, the Russians would spend too, if the poor beggars had anything to spend,' he concluded. This was just the atmosphere I was looking for. I gulped my whisky straight from the bottle in Yugoslav fashion, taking up anybody's challenge. Bottle followed bottle, and the gulps became longer and more frequent. My head was spinning, but I felt no nausea or sickness, so I continued drinking, every now and then ordering hot toast and prawn sandwiches and black coffee, trying to keep the chemical processes in line.

Soon I was feeling the effect of the drink, I was perfectly conscious of everything around me, but less able to control my movements and contain my impulses.

The Yugoslav captain appeared, embraced me and said, 'Let's sing *Shining Eyes*.'

I did not know the song, but we went up to the bandstand just the same. 'Play, you mothers!' the captain shouted at the band, throwing down another handful of notes and ordering another round of Johnnie Walker bottles. He announced his song and began to croon in Croatian, *Syayne ochi*. The lights started spinning around in my head. I tried to sing but could not open my mouth, I grabbed the microphone, but nothing came out. I did not know the tune. I closed my eyes, and saw dozens of eyes, women's eyes, swimming all around me. Black eyes, blue eyes, narrow eyes, closed eyes. Shining, glittering eyes.

I felt a soft hand on my shoulder, I looked up and there were the eyes, deep violet eyes of the South African girl. A soft voice spoke. 'Would you like to dance?' she asked.

My mind was spinning, yet my legs held. I looked at the girl's eyes.

A wave of soberness swept over me. Suddenly I realised I was in a brothel. I looked at the girl. I saw a young prostitute, the eyes were brown and sad and tired and yet still there was a spark in them. She seemed very young. I asked her how old she was. 'Seventeen,' she said. She was beautiful.

We abruptly left the dancers, unconsciously pushing against a group of Greeks who were dancing arm in arm.

'Hey you!' shouted one and grabbed the hem of my jacket. Without thinking I pushed him away violently. I never quite realised what happened next. They came from everywhere, the whole Greek ship crew threw themselves at me: feet, fists, enraged, grinning faces. It did not hurt.

I heard the girl scream as the Yugoslavs jumped like tigers.

In the next few moments I was free. Around me Yugoslavs and Greeks were smashing bottles over each others' heads. Nothing hurt, nothing felt broken. My nose was bleeding, Thom's suit was torn. The girl had run off and nobody seemed to be paying any attention. I'd had enough and decided to leave. I got up, walked to the door and stepped out into the night. The moon was huge and hung low and yellow as I stood by the ocean listening to the surf and letting the breeze revive me. I walked for a while along the beach then took off my clothes and stepped into the water.

The sea was calm and warm. It felt good just to be on my back, eyes closed, drifting, waiting.

Some time later, I opened my eyes and saw the moon. For a moment it stood still but as the wind returned, it spun in a circle and disappeared. Pictures flashed in my head.

It seemed as if I had been in the water for eternity when I was startled by the sound of many men's voices. I rolled over on my stomach and I looked towards the beach.

Somewhere, further down on the beach, there were fires burning; the fishermen were working, pulling out their nets. I decided to join them and swam back towards where I had left my clothes. It took a while to find them for the water had carried me quite far but when I returned the fishermen were still at work. I greeted them and they greeted me in return; I stood and observed them. Shiny, glistening, brown bodies worked in tune with each other tugging at the ropes, pulling out the nets. All the men shared in a common movement. It seemed as if they were all one body moving to a rhythm with the net and the sea. There seemed so much power and joy in this shared togetherness of movement. I wanted to participate in this movement, this togetherness of goal and effort. Without a word I joined them, took a place alongside the rope and melted into their movement. Heave ho—or *Atna Ayay* as they said. It was strenuous work yet every half hour or so we were rewarded by the sight of a full net as the glittering moonlight played across thousands of twinkling fish. Having pulled out one net we'd move over to the next and so it went on—heave ho, *Atna Ayay*. It took two more hours and when we had finished I had made up my mind. I'd considered my obligations to Thom. I had other ways of fulfilling them apart from continuing with this meaningless existence or making a living by chartering a boat.

I asked the fishermen if they could row me over to the yacht club pier.

We approached the *Project* as the tide was beginning to turn. I climbed aboard. Thom was there still asleep. I took off the wet silk suit, put on my old clothes and picked up my few books.

On the galley table, I left a note. 'Sorry about the suit. Off to India as planned. You will manage without me—will write. Good luck, B.'

Having written that I returned to the waiting fisherman's boat.

A few hours later dawn had broken and the Yugoslav ship *Admiral*

131

Zmayevich was being piloted through the channel and out towards the sea.

The captain must have been very surprised to see a man in a native fishing boat energetically waving a flag while trying to cut him off. It took him some time to recognise the Yugoslav flag, get the message and finally stop. After twenty minutes or so, I was climbing up the hurriedly lowered ship's ladder.

As I swung over the side, I saw the curious face of the Yugoslav captain twist into a smile. 'So it's India for you after all,' he said. 'Well, welcome aboard.' I waved goodbye to the fishermen and cast a last look towards the port. *Project* was still there and visible. Thom would soon be getting up. The ship was out of the channel now, heading swiftly north-east.

I found a secluded spot on the bow where I could watch the waves. Behind me Mauritius sank into the ocean.

24

Passage to India

I had a hard time adjusting to this voyage. I lacked no comfort, with a cabin of my own and regular meals in the officers' mess.

There was every opportunity for me to make a holiday out of the trip—a billiards room, a library, games room. The sailors would say how lucky I was to be free to enjoy myself all day. But I did not enjoy myself. It felt disconcerting to have somebody else in the driver's seat.

For the first few days I had an uncontrollable urge to take command of things and check the ship's position and make sure everything was going right. Being friendly with Captain Pero I had access to the bridge. I kept looking over the charts and feeling that something was going wrong, convinced that we were straying off course—it was absurd, naturally. I dared not voice my fears to anybody, but on the third day, I would not contain myself. I went up to the bridge and demanded as politely as possible to be allowed to check the navigation—'just out of interest'. The smiling captain let me look over the log book. It made no sense to me at all. There were no stars, no elevations—just a row of meaningless symbols and figures. I asked for a sextant but everybody smiled and the captain said, 'I hope you don't ask for a magnetised horseshoe and a windbeacon. This is the twentieth century—we aren't star-gazing astrologers.'

I did not trust that computerised information. The bleeping of satellites, electronic and radio beacons. I wanted to take control, for I could not imagine that things could work without my active participation. It felt wrong to me, this modern sailor's life. It was so abstract. Everything on the ship was constructed to make one believe oneself still on land. It was all abstract technical work, pressing buttons, watching little red and green lights go up and then interpreting them and making adjustments—like making love through an interpreter. At the time all I wanted was to identify with the crew, to be actively involved in the voyage. But it was impossible—slowly I was resigned to my passive role. I spent increasing amounts of time up in the bows, watching the sea below me. Here there was a positive movement I could understand.

I did not let the negativity get me down. For a couple of days I raced around the ship trying to find a secluded corner, a location where I felt positive and energetic.

Given the normal European situation I could have easily handled the steady roar of the ship's engine and the incessant ship's vibration—I would have not even noticed. But having worked so hard to sensitize myself I was in no mood to start withdrawing again.

I found an unexpected solution, a safe haven. It was the wooden lifeboat hanging over the side. Connected to the ship only by the ropes, it participated only in the natural roll of the ship and it was swayed by the sea, yet it was completely independent of the mechanical motion and the motorised vibration.

On the ship's side of the lifeboat there was canvas canopy so that, once inside, the view of the ship was blocked by the grey canvas, and all one saw was the wood of the boat and of course the open view of the sea.

The discovery delighted me—I found a way of slipping in unseen by anybody, for I did not want them to think me odd.

Apart from at night when I slept in my cabin, I spent practically my whole day in the lifeboat. I moved in my books, blankets and even a borrowed cassette player—bottles of wine and glasses.

As the lifeboat was suspended over the lower half-deck there would be nobody who'd come around or hear even the loudest music playing. I built myself quite a nest with a canvas windbreak, a sunshield, all equipped for comfort.

The trip took a new dimension. Again there was just the sea and me, yet this time I had no worry; there were no sails that would fly out of control. I could day-dream aimlessly. I even drank wine, something that on *Project* we could rarely do for fear of making a slight but important mistake.

I'd stretch along my makeshift blanket-upholstered 'easy chair', pour myself a glass of wine and put on a Beethoven tape. Somehow the Seventh Symphony seemed most appropriate to the mood. Unlike the green sea of the voyage to Thailand and unlike the steel-grey sea of the Mauritius trip, this time the sea was a dazzling blue.

Under an intense bluish haze the sea merged with the sky, unconfined by a horizon, and the music swelled out over it. The colour tones seemed to harmonise with Beethoven's music, sometimes dying away, then becoming a clear pure single strain, then building up to a thunderous explosion of sound and colour. It was on this trip that I noticed the changes in mood and shape of the ocean and the sky which were independent of weather.

The weather and the time of day set the basic colour but within the same colour there is a spectrum of shades which changes geographically.

I had missed this change of mood of the sea and sky when on *Project*—perhaps because the trip was so slow that the changes were imperceptible, perhaps because of concentration on the tasks at hand.

As my suspended basket skimmed away from the region of Africa to the Indian continent the basic sky and sea pitch toned down continuously. The sunsets were less dramatic, less nervous, the sea vibration was more regular, deeper, more serious and sombre. The frequencies were steadier and the patterns more predictable. Yet there was a dark new touch of the sinister and macabre in the sunsets. The sky grew heavier, more mature, blander, yet concealing more violence.

PART FOUR

The Length
and Breadth of India

25

The Fragrance of India

We were still many miles away when I caught a whiff of India in the air. It was not a smell, nothing so concrete—we were still too far away. Perhaps it was simply the knowledge that she lay there somewhere behind that horizon.

I became aware of something stirring within me. I perceived a new tug and felt that I was no longer drifting or fluttering like a leaf carried by the wind. It was as if I was diving directly like an eagle plummeting straight to its target. It was not my own will any more that carried me forward, rather an acceptance of the gravitational pull of the continent ahead. The night before arrival I fell asleep around midnight expecting to sight India sometime around noon the next day and to dock in Bombay in the late afternoon.

Early in the morning as I lay sleeping the captain received a radio message that the port of Bombay was full and he was to dock at Ratnagiri instead.

It was around four in the morning that the ship's engines stopped and the big ship dropped anchor just outside the port. I did not wake up immediately but slowly became aware that something unusual was happening. It took a while to figure out that the ship was still.

I lay motionless trying to figure out why the engines were silent. It did not occur to me that we had arrived in India. The first rays of sunshine had only just started to filter through. I glanced at the porthole: the glass was covered with condensation from the thick blanket of morning mist that hung outside. I lay back in a half-conscious state, trying to come to grips with the new sensation of stillness. The cabin was getting lighter and I heard the sounds of land coming from the outside.

I sprang to the window and wiped furiously at the misted-up glass. The wind momentarily tore through the fog letting me catch a brief glimpse of land. I stared at the moving cloud of fog, my heart thumping. A few yards away, hidden by the last wisps of the morning fog, throbbed India. I felt a surge of energy, grabbed the bedsheet and, wrapping it round my waist, I ran out of the cabin and up on deck. The heavy aromatic smell of India hit me like a sack: jasmine, incense, cow dung, *frangipani*, curry powder, the air was almost tangible—nothing like it on earth. I ran to the bulwarks and as the fog suddenly lifted, there it was, India.

The copper-red land was framed by swaying luscious greenery. A long column of red-turbaned coolies crept by. Their dark shiny bodies moving in unison as their column snaked along. They were carrying goods from the port to the railway station on the other side of the estuary.

The busy little port was full of oxen, chickens, dogs and men walking around the machinery.

Standing in the station, the little blue and yellow railway engine was painted with pictures of the Indian pantheon of gods—it looked like a gypsy caravan as it puffed out clouds of whitish smoke.

Little children ran around giggling, some stopping to pee in the gutter.

An old man squatted over a pan fanning the flames. So many unrelated things going at the same time. I could hardly wait to dip into this cauldron. I ran around the ship nervously waiting for the sailors to lower the boat.

But we had to wait a long time before being given quarantine release and finally allowed on shore.

I used the time to collect myself, to take leave of the crew and say my good-byes to the captain, thanking him for his hospitality.

It was already late afternoon when, clean-shaven and wearing a recently-bought pair of jeans, I sat in the dinghy as we pulled away towards the shore. Fifteen minutes later, I finally stepped on to Indian soil.

The smell had become so intense it coloured the perception of everything around me. We were still in the restricted area so there was no army of vendors and hustlers to descend on us. We were being given a chance to catch our breath before stepping into real India. Not being a sailor and subject to the maritime immigration procedures, I left the group of sailors and walked across the empty no-man's-land towards the customs and immigration building. The splendidly dressed sentries looked as if they had stepped out of a fairy tale. Nowhere else in the world have I seen a regular police force carrying lances and sabres and wearing ostentatious red turbans with fan-like tops. They greeted me with friendly smiling faces, displaying themselves and parading like proud peacocks to show the visitor from the Yugoslav ship that they were real. It was already late at night before I had received all my shots and had gone through the formalities before being allowed to step into the country. I walked out of the restricted area and towards the station. The port was already empty. The workers had gone home. I ate my first curry at the empty station restaurant as I listened to the big black steam-engine building up steam for its night's journey north.

My plan was to continue north-west to Amritsar, for I wanted to start my tour from that traditional gateway and work my way south in due course. From the sleepy station-master, I bought a ticket for the sleeper and boarded the train. I had still not quite 'recovered my legs' and was feeling very tired as the train whistled and moved off. I pulled down the shades and collapsed into deep sleep.

*　　*　　*

I was awoken late next day by the conductor. 'Gwalior junction, sahib. Gwalior junction, change trains here for Amritsar quickly, quickly,' he spoke excitedly as I got up and out of the train still half asleep. I dashed across to the bright green train on the other side. It was impossible to board it—this was India and the train was packed to overflowing. Tired and dazed I rushed up and down looking for a likely window to repeat my Pakistani trick, but the Indians have taken care of such bright ideas: all windows were barricaded with strong iron beams.

The train was just about to leave when I heard someone crying in English 'over here, over here.' I rushed up to a blue car which for some reason had no bars on the windows. There was a bunch of laughing Europeans leaning out of the windows extending hands to help me climb in. Pulled up by them, I finally scrambled in as the train moved off.

It was a second-plus-class compartment and a reserved one at that. They had reserved half the seats and squeezed me in. I joined them in conversation. There were three of them, all overlanders from England. They had also just arrived in India and Amritsar was to be their first stop. They were as excited about their arrival as I was and glad to have somebody with whom to share their feelings. For them as well as for myself Amritsar was to be the beginning of the Indian experience. I looked out of the window to see where I was.

It was close to noon and the hot sun burned on the golden flat fields of the Punjab which stretched into the distance. So this is indeed India, I kept repeating to myself as I watched the new scenery, the heavy oxen with tiny dark peasants—and the bright ochre landscape. All four of us were laughing, joking and jumping around like excited schoolboys. As we spoke well of India, the many English-speaking Indian passengers tolerated our noisy behaviour.

John had already been to India five times; he had played in what became quite a famous pop group but left as big business took them over. Bearded, long haired, smiling and relaxed, he had the kind of manner that puts everyone at ease.

Roger, the radical intellectual, had left his teaching position at Sussex University over some policy dispute.

Bob was a cockney type who had a comical mop of long hair. As we spoke, the ochre fields flashed past, and by the time we were in the region of Amritsar we suddenly found ourselves surrounded by an expanse of green fields. As the train passed a group of smiling schoolgirls dressed in blue and white, John exclaimed, 'Isn't it fantastic—these vibes—can you feel them, hey can everybody feel them?'

Roger remarked that there were no vibes, only his emotional reactions to the relaxed expression on peoples' faces, which were of genetic origin, and so on.

I agreed, but also felt something more. 'Yes, I feel it every time,' continued John, turning inquisitively to the giggling Bob who was sitting on top of a pile of baskets.

'Yeah, I felt it too. Wow, all those green lawns, everybody driving on the left, Indians everywhere, man it's just like being in London again.'

Even the Indian behind us laughed. A tall bearded Sikh, he broke into our conversation and asked us to spend the night in his home. Before I had a chance to accept John interrupted. 'We appreciate your offer,' he said, and suggested that we visit him the next day. 'The first night in India,' he said, 'we must sleep at the Golden Temple.' He had made this journey five times before, and spending the first night at the temple had become an initiation ceremony—like carrying the bride across the threshold or taking your shoes off and washing your feet before entering a temple.

I did not protest and the man, being a Sikh, was glad of John's enthusiasm for the Golden Temple, so he invited us to come the next day. As we stepped off the train, I felt as if I had been in India before.

The small square in front of the railway station was jammed with rickshaws, and as we hauled the luggage off the train the Indian experience started. There must have been five or six men pulling at my sleeve and shouting in my ear. I identified three of them as rickshaw drivers but was too overwhelmed to comprehend what was being asked.

Nearby a loudspeaker blared some love song. The voice of the station announcer drowned the music while he himself was being drowned by the whistle of the train. A few yards away a cow was munching vegetables off a stall. The stall holder turned around and started screaming at the cow but would not hit it to make it move away. Aha, Holy Cow! I thought. Women were everywhere.

The evening breeze brought the aromatic smell of curry. I became aware of the five people tugging at my sleeves who were joined by a powerful-voiced *puri wallah* who kept trying to pass me a palm leaf of some aromatic food. My senses were drowned. A European mind trained to concentrate on only a few select stimuli cannot cope with these situations. The scene before me was a picture of frenzied, uncoordinated confusion, as if somebody had just kicked an anthill or knocked over a beehive. One felt as if a disaster such as a bomb explosion in a railway station was just about to happen or had just happened and everybody was hysterically rushing about doing wrong things at the wrong time getting in each other's way. But then one looked at people's faces more closely and realised this was just business as usual.

Lost and confused, I did not know where to look, what to listen to. Somebody could have stolen all my property, if I'd had any, and I'd hardly have noticed. It all lasted only about ten minutes—by that time my eye caught John. He was calm and unmolested; the locals sensed he was an old hand.

He gave instructions to the drivers and said, 'Let's go.'

Ten minutes later we were out of the city centre and being carried by rickshaws through a spotlessly clean park. After we reached an amber pond we stopped and paid the drivers.

It was a cool secluded spot; the leafy trees hung low and glistened in the warm late-afternoon sun. We put the bags on the ground and

141

rested. I almost fell asleep but was animated by the splashing of the water and the shouts of Bob and Roger who were already swimming. After we had washed and dressed ourselves, John produced a bag of delicious *samosa*. We ate, slept a little and, as the night started to fall, decided to leave for the temple.

26

In the Land of the Turbaned Sikhs

It was very dark. The six-rupee rickshaw ride took almost half an hour. We could hardly see the buildings and the streets, but we were in town. Only a few streets were lit, but in the unlit streets the vivid, unseen pulse of life could be felt even more distinctly. India's warm life crept into my bones, it took possession of my sinews. During the ride we said nothing, just took in the surroundings.

As we cleared the last corner of the dark street we were dazzled by the temple, or rather its huge walls; it burst on us like a firework. After the weeks I had spent in lands characterised by low mud and brick houses, this monumental architecture gave the impression of being titanic. From everywhere there came the low-keyed religious music which charged the warm night with spirituality.

A throng of tall, turbaned Sikhs were washing their feet and preparing to enter. Outside the temple stood the ostentatiously peacock-feathered guards. The four of us deposited our shoes, washed our feet, covered our heads and walked in. As we passed the large gate the music became quite loud. We faced a large, oblong, basin of water, surrounded on all sides by white marbled walls and colonnades covered with ornaments. In spite of the music, the expanse of still water radiated calmness and the whole place was wrapped in tranquillity. Men and women and whole families walked around the large basin, moving softly. Their voices were hushed, their face muscles relaxed.

'Do you feel it?' John put his favourite question.

'Feel what?' asked Bob

'The Sikhs believe that this lake emits the cosmic *prana*, the life energy, the fine primal matter of which even thoughts are made. They come and walk here in order to recharge their bodies with *prana*, their celestial nourishment which, according to their belief, vanquishes doubt, sickness and even death.'

There was indeed something contagious in the air, an all-prevailing mood of tranquillity. In the centre of the pool there was a white marble shrine covered with golden ornaments and connected to the rest of the temple by a long white bridge packed with devout Sikhs walking to and fro.

We went to the shrine and were given food prepared by the Holy Men, spiritual food. In the sanctuary a group of men were chanting from the *Granth Sahib*, the Sikhs' holy book which is kept here.

As we strolled along the shore we could see bearded, intelligent-looking scholarly Sikhs sitting in glass enclosures and turning the pages of the holy books. Everywhere there were paintings of scenes of the life of Guru Nanak, the founder of the Sikh religion.

I lay down on a marble bench and looked at the dark sky. The moon was already up and I watched it turn the bluish water to glowing gold. I felt tired and joined John and Bob who were going to sleep. One of the sabre bearers handed us three thick straw mats and showed us towards a covered marble porch. As I lay there, my ears filled with soft music, the smell of jasmine in the air, I thought how marvellous to be alive, to be here, to hear and see. Then sleep came.

*　　*　　*

Next day we went over to visit Mr Singh. He was a tall, loud, opinionated man, but you couldn't help liking him for his charm, which came through as soon as he opened the door of his bungalow.

'Ah my friends, so you have seen the Golden Temple? It is certainly the most beautiful building in the world. The Taj Mahal of course is more famous, as a Ford car is more famous than a Rolls Royce. You see, we Sikhs do not believe in boasting and publicity, so the world is unaware of the architectural grandeur of our Golden Temple.' Mr Singh went on explaining the wonders of the Sikh world, his favourite statement being 'I do not like to boast', or 'Sikhs are very modest people'.

In fact, as I was to learn, he was a typical Sikh. Tall, arrogant, boastful yet friendly and charming, and more generous than some of his Hindu brothers.

'Yes my friends, the Punjab is India's most vital part. Sikhs lead and staff the Indian Army, it is Sikh policemen who keep law and order, and it is the Sikhs who do all the driving and the heavy jobs that will lead India to its inevitable greatness. You see, we Sikhs were created to be the leaders of India. Hindus, they are weak, tepid, placid, so our Guru Nanak created a religion for lions. We are all called Singh—Lion—for our great Guru turned us into a warrior race. The Hindu can have their non-violence and the rest of it, for they've got us to look after them. Did you know that the Punjab is going to overtake Western Europe in terms of standard of living and production in five years? Look.' Mr Singh produced a copy of a local newspaper and its headlines confirmed his statement.

They were a friendly, happy family: two healthy looking boys, one eleven, the other thirteen; a pretty giggling girl of nine; even the wife showed herself. We were joined for dinner by Mr Singh's brother, who was versed in the holy scripture and almost as ostentatious as his brother, but educated and intelligent.

The meal was good, but in spite of Mr Singh's assurance that there was no cooking like Punjabi cooking, I found it a little heavy. After the dinner we retired to a comfortable lounge; judging from the furniture Mr Singh, a retired army officer, had obviously done very well for himself. We settled down to sweets and philosophical discussion. This time the brother took the lead, and the rest of the family kept a respectful silence.

'I would like to prepare you for your Indian experience,' he said. 'Now is the right time to catch you. I would like to communicate something to you, explain a few things, for I'd be happy to help a few visitors perceive our land in the proper way,' he said while folding his legs in the oriental manner. He continued, 'It is so easy to misunderstand the behaviour and the situations you will encounter. You see, the European mind is incapable of anticipating the degree of diversity that characterises Indian things. Generalisations about the Hindu religion and racial characteristics break down on encounter. You will discover this,' he said, regarding us sympathetically.

'Indians,' he continued, 'seem to be polytheistic and monotheistic. They seem to worship God as an abstract idea, yet they seem idolatrous. You will run into Indians who are honest and correct to such

144

an unusual degree that you will drop all your defences and fears about your property and safety, only to encounter the most cunning thieves, liars and confidence tricksters.'

This seemed to me a little high-flown, but I realised it was just the man's style of speaking.

'Indians,' he said, 'will appear to you as extremely honest or extremely dishonest, they are light skinned or darker than some African Negro tribes. All visitors speak of diversity and indeed many writers, as well as historians, have claimed that there has never been such an entity as an Indian nation—it is only a collection of races living in that geographical area. Yet we are a nation,' said Mr Singh emphatically, 'we are a nation even if defined negatively. What we share is that we differ from the rest of the world, differ in unique ways which unite us.'

'East is East and West is West and never the twain shall meet' he said, 'but then you see,' Mr Singh explained, 'Kipling was only speaking about India. What he really meant was World is World and India is India and never shall the twain meet.'

I was intrigued by this for I was not sure if I shared this opinion—still I did not comment and let Mr Singh continue.

'Yes she is different for India behaves essentially differently from the rest of the world.

'The whole world seeks happiness and the non-Indian world equates happiness with the maximum amount of physical goods for the minimum amount of work. The world equates happiness with consumption. In India our happiness is to be found in doing the work; we fulfil ourselves in performing the duty of work, *Dharma*; the fruit and the consumption is immaterial, at least in theory. This is so,' he added, somewhat apologetically.

As I was to find out, the Indians are inexhaustible talkers and can go on endlessly. Not that what they say is not interesting or un-important, but they have this capacity to go on forever—with time one learns to halt them but this being my first encounter with this phenomenon, I just listened, remaining the last person until late at night while my friends and the rest of the family were already at supper. It was not until the *mamah* of the house came to my rescue that I finally left.

The next day I took my leave. I would love to have stayed, for I had quite taken to the Singh brothers, as well as to John, Bob and

Roger, but I was anxious to get into Hindu India as soon as possible. I took a train to Delhi.

27

Alice in Wonderland

Indian train journeys, rather like the Indian experience in general, remind one of Alice's travels in Wonderland. In Europe two and two are four, dogs chase cats, one eats when one is hungry, wears warm clothes when it is cold, animals obey man and there is some kind of order and logic to which the mind accustoms itself.

One travels around the world and sees more or less everybody else being governed by similar logic and rules.

India operates on different laws, laws that the European mind cannot grasp. Drop a glass in Europe and it falls down—in India it may fly up.

A train ride in India is one of the best ways of falling down the rabbit hole, the tunnel of Alice. White rabbits turn up dressed in frock coats, pulling out watches and saying they are late; turtles walk by, wearing gold-rimmed spectacles. Crazy, nonsensical things happen.

The splendid, uniformed, first-class-carriage attendant appeared, 'Pardon me, sir, may I kindly be seeing your ticket?'

'Oh, I do not have one,' I answered with a smile. 'I was not having the time to get one.'

'In that case, sir, may I kindly be enjoining you to purchase one from the Officer in Charge,' meaning himself. The Railway Officials generally modelled their behaviour on the very Pukka Victorian English Gentleman.

I had no intention of paying over twice the price of the normal fare just for the privilege of first-class travel. Yet second-class was, as usual, impossible to get into. Masses of people hanging like bats out of the windows and doors and crouching like brown beetles on the roofs.

I managed to talk the immaculate conductor into selling me a berth in a reserved sleeper—this is only marginally more expensive than the ordinary fare, but practically impossible to get. It involved listening to the man's problems with his mother-in-law, which in India take epic proportions, and sitting patiently while the man showed me a genuine Tamil Wedding Dance, but it was worth it.

The train berths in India are booked days or weeks in advance. Companies allocate reservations to their employees, as we do with opera seats in Eastern Europe. There is no passage between carriages on Indian trains. I had to stay in the first class until the next stop, so I decided to enjoy it. It was a very comfortable house on wheels, with beds and deep upholstered easy chairs. I walked into a large bathroom, took off my clothes and enjoyed a luxurious shower. When I came out I joined a man with two daughters sitting in one of the compartments. He wore a well-cut English suit and was tall with a light complexion. These people were of a different world from the India of the fields and streets.

The Indian élite distinguish themselves in speech, physique, and upbringing. They are a different species. Generally unseen, they remained in their chauffeured cars or clean carriages with tinted windows. It is a part of India that the average tourist rarely sees.

I engaged the man in conversation. He was a banker on his way down to Calcutta where he wanted to enrol his two daughters at the University. They were beautiful, tall, long-limbed and graceful with sparkling white teeth and silky hair neatly combed; their conversation was polite and amusing.

It was in the second class, however, that the Indian experience was at its height : hens, old men, babies, jugglers, singers, people cooking in corners on open fires; boastful soldiers, bossy policemen, arrogant Sikhs. Outside, hanging on the window-bars were grinning beggars, idiots and children. And then came the stations; Indian train journeys usually being two- or three-day affairs, stations assumed the significance of a port to a sailor. The train rolled in very slowly, a mass of vendors and beggars descending on it. Little brown men carried large bowls of steaming drinks that came in all the colours of the rainbow. The train turned instantly into a restaurant. Plates, cups and food materialised; fifteen minutes later the train rolled out and as the dozens of vendors ran alongside, hundreds of empty cups and

147

saucers were hurriedly hurled back to them. I never saw anybody cheat and retain any crockery.

A day later came Delhi, and the biggest railway station I had ever seen—it was built by the British. The atmosphere and the architecture transported one back to the days of the Raj. Rich people, poor people, red turbaned coolies, ran around like ants. There was shouting and excitement.

Life ... for me the sight was too exhausting. As I got off the train the accumulated energy of all that bustling activity made me dizzy. I dropped onto a bench, lay down and closed my eyes.

I still could not handle India. I paid a coolie to take my luggage. I collapsed onto the seat of a rickshaw and asked to be taken to the six-rupee-a-day Venus Hotel in Old Delhi. For three days I vegetated, never leaving the hotel room.

Europeans usually dislike Old Delhi. They are offended by the continual harassment of the pushers, black marketeers, pimps and beggars, but in India you have to learn to accept these things. The slums of an Indian city have much to offer a receptive visitor. Far more vital than the somewhat antiseptic New Delhi, the old city pulsates with life and passion. The sheer force and vitality of its people shakes tourists like an electric current.

A few days later I ventured out and immersed myself in this Mad Hatter's tea party. For a whole week I bathed in the warmth of Old Delhi's life, wandering aimlessly through her streets looking for the biggest mobs, the most crowded restaurants.

I learnt the city's rythm and moved with the crowds; mornings were spent with the commuters at the famous Indian Coffee House and as they dispersed I hurried to join the crowds in front of the Post Office, then to Rodney's café, then to dinner at Kumar's.

After that it was the movies. Of course I did not understand a word, but it did not matter. It was amazing to observe the Indian film-star hero, strutting like a bear across the screen wearing pin-striped trousers, polka-dot yellow and purple silk shirt, enormous bow tie. These amazing outfits would be worn in unexpected combinations—tweed jackets with bowlers, pointed shoes for respectable family men, Oxford brogues for dashing young rascals. Most unusual was the head gear: golfing caps, night caps and other ridiculous garments. Music was an equally absurd mixture of orientalised Hungarian csárdás and *High Noon* or *Magnificent Seven* themes played on *sitars* or electric guitars; then there'd be bits of orientalised operatic clichés—with Carmen's song a clear favourite, all others drowned in a sea of indigenous sounds. The story lines themselves were in keeping with the music. A single plot would manage to combine cowboys and red Indians, musketeers, Roman gladiators, as well as hippies, Kung Fu and the whole pandemonium of Indian gods and goddesses. Indian films are the theatre of the absurd and once one accepts this, one is open to enjoy it.

Ridiculous as it may seem, the Indian cinema has its essentials straight. It is free of destructive violence and unclean sentiments. In Indian cinema, husbands love wives, children obey parents—gods are in heaven and the bad are where they belong. Heroes are positive and heroines are good and they can dance too. The overall effect, unintellectual as it may be, is to convey clearly a sentiment rather than a message. Absurd as they are, these films are not unrealistic in the early Hollywood happy end sense. The boy does not always get the girl and people do die and suffer and lose their health and riches and there is evil, mental and physical. Yet throughout the performance— good remains good. Gods stay in heaven minding their own business and so does everybody else.

After the movies it was back to Rodney's and girl-watching. Indian girls are the greatest flirts in the world. Their flirtation stays within bounds, but they make an art out of it. They must have the world's most sensuous contours—round firm shapes like ripe melons. They walk with downcast eyes, modest expression and body movement that radiates motherhood and humility. Theirs was not a call to the lustful element of the erotic soul, it was a call for conception, the plea of those swaying hips, moonlike and perfect, their movement attuned to some greater universal truth. These women were quite unlike the teasing high-pitched flirts of Bangkok.

And then came 10 o'clock and they'd be gone as suddenly as they came—slowly the pimps and black-marketeers would creep out of their holes promising the seven heavens, whispering of hidden delights. Sometime after midnight, as the last crowds were disappearing from the late movies in Patna Avenue, I felt stuck with nowhere to go. I had to return to the solitude of my room and sleep.

A week later I had had enough of Delhi, I had to go on. But where to? Anywhere. Like a good tourist I decided to visit Agra and the Taj Mahal. Three more days in Delhi and I left.

I took a train, preparing myself for another journey. 'See the Taj by moonlight', the prospectus read, so I arrived just after sunset.

28

The Taj Mahal by Moonlight

I must have arrived at the emptiest part of the dead season, I thought, or perhaps the train had stopped at an unscheduled stop or at the wrong station. I was the only European on the platform.

'To the Taj Mahal,' I said to the rickshaw driver and off he went. We rode through barren nothingness for an hour, and then we reached the river. That was the end of the road and the driver wanted his money. 'But where is the Taj?' I said. 'I want to go to the Taj.'

'Here river—here end road. Taj there,' the driver said, pointing to an enormous wall across the river. Since there was no bridge across anyway I saw no sense in arguing with the man so I paid him off and watched him leave.

I took off my clothes and swam across to the monumental wall. It stood there looking 100 feet tall and extending all around. There was no Taj. There was no door either, and nobody about, not even a house in sight.

Perhaps there are two Taj Mahals and I've come to the wrong one. Or perhaps this is really the great wall of China, I thought humorously to keep up my spirits. In any case, there had to be a door somewhere, I decided, and started to walk. There was no end in sight so I kept jumping over the eroded red earth. After half an hour I came to a corner and turned it with great expectations; but beyond the corner there was still nothing to see but the endless wall, and there was no road. I carried on walking and my spirits fell. An hour later I finally came to the front side and realised that I had approached the monument from the back. At last I arrived at the gate— an enormous one, but locked up and nobody there. I turned around and noticed a village: it could not have been Agra. There were just little scattered houses which seemed empty. Nobody was about. It seemed unbelievable: where were all the tourists and the hotels?

I walked towards the village looking for a lighted house. I finally found an open shop where English was spoken. The man said 'Taj locked up—dead season—tourists away—hotel in Agra.'

'Where Agra?'

'There.' The man pointed down the road—Agra must have been very far away for I saw nothing.

'Maybe Taj open tomorrow,' the man said fatalistically. 'No tourists—no business—lock up.'

By that time I was furious; only yesterday in Delhi the girl in the tourist office had been going on about the Taj by moonlight. I would not accept it. I was still new to India. I bought some chocolate, a ten-rupee torch, and was off, determined to rectify this injustice and see the Taj. I went back to the wall and started to plod round it again.

There was no road and it was tough going but eventually I reached the river again.

I knew where I was going: about five yards west of the corner I had previously spotted a small opening in the wall. I reached the spot. It was there, the opening the size of a trap door, and situated just above the water level. It was closed by wooden boards. I tried them. They were rotten.

Normally the door would have been hidden by a brick projection, an arch that looped along the bottom of the wall, but this section had fallen down perhaps decades ago; it seemed obvious that nobody ever checked and perhaps nobody knew about it.

I decided to break open the hatch. After all, the Indians advertise the Taj by moonlight all over the world—I had come a long way for this and was not going to be cheated. It took me ten minutes to break the wooden boards open by swinging from a low hanging branch and kicking with my boots. Since nobody was likely to come along I made all the noise I wanted.

Having kicked the loose planks away, I switched on the torch and looked inside. The torch threw a shaft of light deep inside the wall—it became apparent that the wall was at least thirty feet thick, containing rooms, corridors and staircases.

This was probably some secret entrance—it was not just a hole but a door to a passage. There were narrow steps leading down and a spiral staircase going up. I climbed in. I tried the steps first. After a few minutes I heard the splashing of water—the stairs led to an inside lake or reservoir and as far as I could tell there were things swimming in it.

I was surrounded by darkness with only the pencil shaft of the torch to illuminate the way. I made my way back as quickly as possible, slipping and bumping my head against the low ceiling. I wanted to get out quickly and go back to the river, yet when I reached the opening I did not leave: I don't know what made me change my mind but I decided to get in at any cost.

I turned back and looked around. There was a staircase going up; I took it and it led to a series of low corridors—I had to bend very low to pass. I walked down one of them and came to a dead end. The other seemed to carry on indefinitely. It was in the third that I suddenly fell into a hole. For a split second I assumed that I had had it, but the hole was only a few feet deep. By that time I was frantically determined to get in—I realised that I could not remember where I had come from any more, but I did not care. If it comes to the worst, I thought, I shall wait for the daylight and tourists. It did not occur to me that day or night might not make any difference in the passages inside the thick wall.

By that time my torch was getting weaker so I switched it off and used it only in places where I was uncertain.

I got down on my knees and crawled. After about half an hour I decided to give up trying to strike lucky and sat down to work out a system. I was not too scared: I forced myself to believe that I could get back any time I wanted to and that my only real concern was to continue.

A half hour later I finally gave up and decided to get back to the river—I had nothing but the sounds of water to guide me and by that time I was becoming scared. I realised that these passages might cave in and that I could fall through or run into snakes and who knows what.

I stumbled back onto the stairs that led to the hole in the wall. For some reason there was no moonlight coming through. I walked to the crevice and I noticed that someone had closed it and a shudder of fear ran through me. I had scarcely had time to collect myself when I realised that this was a much larger door and therefore not the one I had used to come in. I banged on it to see how thick the wood was and realised with satisfaction that I would be able to kick through it. It took just one kick to open it.

I almost stepped through and down a fifty-foot drop but I was held back by what I saw. The sight before me was truly miraculous.

Bathed in the moonlight, glowing like a jewel, the pale monument to conjugal love seemed to be floating in the milky effervescence. I had confused the directions and had made my way to the inside of the wall.

The shock of having almost fallen down a fifty-foot drop wore off immediately for the sight was so compelling. I stepped on to the ledge, got hold of a rail and swung myself over on to an inside balcony, and sat down to admire the view. For a long time I sat there, fascinated.

After an hour or so I finally decided to make my way down. It was not easy. Although the wall was rough and full of holes and projections, the stones and bricks were often loose and I had to take great care. Once I finally touched ground it took a while for me to collect myself. When I did, the Taj was mine. Alone in the huge garden, without a soul in sight, I walked along the beautiful paths.

It was a warm night. I took off my clothes and bathed in the silvery fountain. The difficulties and strains of getting through had somehow numbed my twentieth-century mentality and, with no disturbing influences in sight, I felt myself adopting the role of a seventeenth-century mogul. Perhaps it was because of the architecture, which bore the thoughts and emotions of its own time. As I bathed I felt a slow relaxed emptying of the mind. Time slowed down. I tried to feel what it was like to be a Mogul Shah, to sit in the moonlight meditating on conjugal love. Who was the woman that he loved so much? I closed my eyes and visualised her—a delicate Indian woman with sensuous hips and wide eyes smiling self-consciously. Were there ghosts? I wondered afterwards. Could my vision have been inspired by something outside my imagination? Surfeited with fantasy, I stretched out on the white marble and fell asleep.

In the morning I was woken up by the sunlight and the sound of the gates opening. I slipped out as the first visitors came in. I did not want to linger or see the Taj ever again. The presence of tourists could only ruin the experience that was sealed in me. Knowing India, I hoped that the door at the back would stay open for a long time to come—perhaps long enough for my descendants to repeat the experience many times.

29

Calcutta: City of Kali

The next eight weeks were spent in frantic rushing about. I wanted to be everywhere at the same time so I kept jumping trains, changing buses. I went west to Bengal then down to Ceylon, up north into Nepal and back again west.

And finally one day in Calcutta, completely exhausted, I found myself settling down to catch my breath, taking a cheap room in notorious Kalighat. Kalighat is Calcutta's district of temples and brothels. Opposite my house there was the Kali temple—that very 'infamous' one where they regularly carry out the blood sacrifices to the cruel goddess Kali, depicted as a frenzied woman with a necklace of skulls around her neck dancing on top of her dead husband. Kali-kuta is her city and so is the whole of Bengal.

I stayed in the penthouse room of a *chai khan* and had the roof to myself. From my roof garden I could observe the gory goings on at the Kali temple as well as the activities of the Bazaar in front and of the brothel next door. Just over the river there was also the daily burning of the bodies of the homeless. In order to secure a room I found myself paying a month's rent in advance—but it was only $8 anyway. Originally my plan was to stay only a few days but, as it happened in Herat, my energy suddenly ebbed. I felt lifeless and, with the rent paid anyway, I just stayed put. I stayed close to my penthouse as if afraid to go further than a few yards from my base. Consequently what I know of Calcutta is Kalighat—but what a place to know ! There were the whores, if one could use such a harsh-sounding label for these unfortunate children. So unlike their European counterparts or the flashy Thai fun girls. There was no aura of the corruption or depravity that hangs so heavily over the Pat Pong road. I wondered about the spirit in which these consummations took place. I could not sense the disharmonies that emanate from similar activities elsewhere. And these girls, they looked so clean and innocent. At sunset, they prayed as fervently as anybody, eyes shining with religious zeal. And they were children, many of them perhaps 13 to 15 years old. There were, of course, other whores in India—the horrible fat whores and their Chinese and Anglo-Indian pimps that accost tourists—but not so these innocent children, many of them strikingly pretty.

Even the customers were reverent and modest. Shy little peasants from the interior, skinny and bewildered, clutching their sweaty rupees and giving them to Mahabuba, the fat mother-like madam who sat at the entrance, big and solid like some mythical Buddhist statue.

I could not imagine the gods dealing too harshly with these children. Life itself was harsh enough, for it does not take long before they are out joining the countless corpses that meet the arrival of every new day in Calcutta, lying in the gutter waiting for the city garbage collectors to take them over the river to be burned. For Calcutta, as many say, is 'hell on earth'. Yet I stayed put as if petrified in my roof-top garden overlooking the blood-stained *lingam*, the huge stone penis of eternal Siva, the shrine of Kali. I watched the beggars and the frenzied Bihari transvestites prostrating themselves in the streets, smashing their heads on the stone floor, worshipping the harvest. And yet I could not find Calcutta horrible. At times I was almost afraid at finding myself thinking that, from a higher perspective, even the life of a rickshaw-man may be richer and more meaningful than that of the multinational executive or a Comecon factory director. So I melted into the crowds at the Bazaar, becoming absorbed into it, losing myself in it.

It was in a Kali temple, while looking at the naked breasts of some goddess bursting like ripe grapefruits, that I realised that I could look at all those erotic scenes with new eyes, free of lust, seeing only certain features—fertility, spring, sun and moon. And suddenly all those erect phalluses and naked buttocks and breasts that Indians worship—the blood and gory details—all fell into place. They were shocking only for as long as one found them shocking.

Indian temples abound with picturesque scenes of debauchery and all sorts of evils, yet there is no lust, no horror. Somehow by some sleight of hand the devout discharge their evil sentiments, peel them off into those statues, as if the temples and all that is in and around them absorbed all the negative emotions of the people who come to pray. It was in the temples that one felt that separation between lust and eros, pleasure and exhilaration.

A curious thing about India is that bazaars and temples are regularly side by side, and here in Kalighat there were also the brothels as a further enrichment. In India the boundaries between all kinds of things are hard to determine. The temples do not have clear limits. I thought I could tell whether a place was a souvenir shop or a little temple by looking at the age of a building. A shop tended to look of recent origin and makeshift, yet it had all the deities and trappings of a small temple. A priest's domain tended to be of stone and to be a little heavier on the holy images and incences. But it was not easy to tell: the life of the temple and of the bazaar spilled over, each into the other.

Only in the beginning did I find the phenomenon ironic. Eventually one learnt to understand. It is not that religion is profane in India. The distinction between secular and religious hardly makes sense in Hinduism. The priests, the Brahmins, are simply men; they have no need to feign holiness all the time. When the time comes for being holy and serious they become so and are treated with due respect. Yet the same man shows a different side of himself when engaged in a transaction, and is treated as an equal by hard-bargaining fellow-traders.

Mundane things are holy in India and vice versa. Eating, sleeping, making love, birth, all these are still regarded as sacred mysteries. The ability to comprehend the apparently ridiculous, to overcome the shock of seeing the unusual did not come instantly. The willingness to understand came only much later. For a long time I tended to focus on the bizarre, the unusual, seeing almost nothing else.

The European mind works that way; so does the popular Western press. A baby born with two heads or a bizarre traffic accident is bigger news in London or Paris than a major world political event. Yet in contrast, the West also hides the bizarre, hides the deformed, isolates him in hospital wards, in old peoples' homes, sweeps him under the carpet, pretends he is happy in his comfortable ward. In India the aged, the dying, the deformed, the cripple is out there, a participating member of society. Yet a newcomer, unused to the shock, sees nothing else but the deformed, the macabre.

I tried to analyse the psychology behind the phenomenon, and it appeared to me that the beggar, the deformed, the fakirs and *sadhus* were really high priests in some highly sophisticated national catharsis. The 'average', the 'normal' Indian is extremely clean, yet in the street one sees people defecating practically wherever one looks. To a perceptive observer it appears obvious that the deformed, the beggars, the defecators revel in their depravity. The defecating is not, as the guides to India would have us believe, some rare but acceptable custom; it seems more likely that it is done in order to shock.

This seems to be the case with much that is bizarre and macabre in India; it is purposely put on public display. Why? Perhaps the depraved through their depravity have a social function and duty, a *dharma* equal to that of sacrificial virgins or heroes sacrificing their lives for the good of their country. With their depravity the sacrificial minority ward off the 'evil eye' and procure virtue and health for others by reminding them that everything is God's gift and we are all his children.

It is in such a way that even the most deprived has something to be proud of in this crazy Indian reversal; the more deprived, the more macabre the better. Later I was to notice that the holier a town was, the higher the incidence of depravity. In Calcutta I was still far from attaining the attitude that made me eventually accept India. My moods alternated. At times I was enthusiastic and happy to be there only to grow sad and depressed about India and everything Indian.

Sometimes I thought I could not take it anymore; it was as if I felt some heavy oppression pulling me down. Before coming to India I feared that perhaps, once there, I would not be able to sense the country's hidden charge. It is there all right, yet, having lifted the lid, I recoiled. I recoiled not because it was bad, not because Europeans could not understand it: I simply lacked courage to dive and sink into it. At times I'd try to immerse myself into the well of India and let the waters close over my head, but I still held my European breath, still held a piece of rope to pull myself out. I had no courage to exhale, to let go of the rope and sink deep, to dissolve my will to be, my will to conquer and dominate. It is the lack of will that seemed to me to make Indians different from the rest of the world: they seem to have surrendered their will to something deeper, they are not fighting, not restricting, not searching. This is what India seemed to demand—submission, letting go, no fight, no struggle, no desire. The Indian air seemed heavy like a stone and death-oriented.

But then the Indians had a way of cutting through this gloom as if by magic. I'd walk down some hideous Calcutta street despairing over the state of humanity when some Indian beggar might stop me with a worried look and ask a barrage of questions. At first I would think he was just begging, but on a few occasions a passer-by would stop and translate. The beggar was actually asking me why the white Sahib looked so sad, and could he help. Some of these beggars would be such jokers and clowns that I could not but laugh at the absurdity of my own Western self-righteous pity disguised as benevolence.

It seemed farcical that I was upsetting these people by being depressed about their 'depravity'. In this curious way I realised how cruel pity can be. By 'pitying' our lame and our blind in Europe we really isolate and humiliate them. One learned to view things in this perspective and realised that the great majority of Indians are neither lame, nor blind, nor defecators on the street. I suddenly realised that India was only perceived as macabre by the unclean perception of the observer. The macabre receded and assumed normal proportions as I opened up to the normal everyday people. Some were serious, some sombre, others funny.

Quite often I had to stop to ask direct questions or the like. Most of the time these questions would be answered in the expected manner, yet sometimes most unusual answers were given. A question asked in Delhi, such as how to get to Calcutta, might produce an answer such as 'Take the Indian Ocean liner', or 'There are five Air India jets taking off every hour from the main square'. Or 'Calcutta? Take the first left then right then walk for a *farsak* or so.' One either gets irritated to the verge of hysteria, or more likely one learns to accept it and be at peace with it.

*   *   *

I left Calcutta to start my mad rush around India again. Up to Patna by train, down the Ganges by boat, west to Mysore, east to Bengal— it went on and on, this crazy rush, until one day I realised in Benares that I was behaving no differently to the perennial American tourist in Europe dashing from the Eiffel Tower to the Colosseum via Tower Bridge. So now I had been everywhere in India. Almost three months had passed and I realised that I had not been to India at all.

Better pick one city square, one café, or one village and take a few months and then at least I would have seen and experienced something Indian, and that would be something to remember.

I figured it would take me about a year to get the deeper feeling of India in a city so I opted for a village or a small town. I also needed peace and quiet and a library to get on with some reading, so a small town became a natural choice.

An Englishman recommended a small village south of Madras. Before leaving, I collected the mail at the Benares Poste Restante. There were a score of letters. I read all of them. As the train rattled over the Ganges bridge I opened the window and threw the package of them into the water. Somewhere below, the water carried away the colourful pieces of paper.

I had no plans, no ideas and very little money; that was exactly how I wanted it. I was so tired of goals and plans and schedules. I was in India, India was *now*, I felt warm and relaxed. The train rolled on.

PART FIVE

Puri, the Holy City

30

Puri

Undisturbed by a cloud in the stillness of a windless day, the sun was scorching the earth below, as I walked out of the low white and green railway station. In the distance the Bay of Bengal stretched smooth and still like oil. The few passengers that arrived had disappeared and I stood in front of the gates alone. There was not even the usual rush of rickshaw drivers and coolies. The only person visible was a young boy frying smokey *samosas* in a huge black iron pan. So this was Puri, the holy magical Puri, the seat of learning and inspiration that fed all the major religions of the world. It certainly had no such aura around its railway station. Perhaps it would have been better if I'd continued to Madras, I thought, as I looked around for a rickshaw.

I walked over to the *samosa* boy and asked for a rickshaw; the boy disappeared into a courtyard and a minute later reappeared, followed by a skinny-legged man pulling a battered rickshaw.

'Santhana Hotel,' I said, mentioning the 'in' place of Puri. By now I had stopped bargaining. I had learnt the fair price for most things. For services I would add fifty per cent extra to allow for my being a foreigner, and would simply state what I was willing to pay. Usually it was accepted. By that time I had already some knowledge of Hindi which I learnt unsystematically simply by writing down and memorising most common words and phrases.

'Acha,' the man said and we set off down the dry mud road, leaving behind us a cloud of dust.

I had been heading for Madras, but after three days of rail travel I'd had enough. A German pastor had told me about Puri, a town where Indian *rishis* claim Jesus received his religious education. A Dutch girl spoke of a magnificent beach, and by the time the train stopped there I had decided to see the place.

The air was thick and dense, the sky overcast with an orange halo, the ocean mist and the dust were dimming the sunlight, bathing the city in a strange, mysterious glow. Puri, to an Indian, is a holy city.

It is a city of temples, *gurus*, *ashrams*, *yogis* and beggars. It is one of the four holy Indian cities that fulfils for Indians the role that Mecca does for Muslims, or Jerusalem for Jews and Christians.

Indians believe that even the dust which hangs in the air in Puri has magical revitalising properties, and they flock to Puri for purification, inspiration and comfort.

It has always been a holy town, a shrine even to the aboriginal, atavistic, dark-skinned, pre-Aryan population. Different cultures attribute different causes to the spiritual halo that surrounds the city. It is either the holy rain, the holy forest, Lord Jaganath or the holy sea, the holy this or the holy that. Religion and superstition aside, there is no doubt that geography and climate have produced a unique package of light, smell and colour at this spot. It inspires the visitor to meditate. Around it imaginative Indian minds have created a mystique, a folklore.

Today, the original natural aura that embalms the area is augmented by the thousands who believe fervently in the holiness of the place. The collective expression in those devout faces affects a visitor, regardless of his religious background (or lack of it). Even at night when you do not see the temples and the faces, you experience the darkest, blackest, moonless sky, when the ocean alone gives off a phosphorescent glow, emitting songs, whispers and cries that penetrate every nook and cranny.

It was at night that this consciousness about Puri first visited me. Having slept the whole afternoon I awoke around eleven o'clock and felt the absolute blackness of the night. I could sense the sound of the ocean, even before my ears had registered it.

I lay on my bed, staring at nothing, while life and consciousness surged through my body. Then I jerked the mosquito net away, wrapped a towel around myself and walked downstairs. Everyone was asleep, the lights were out and only the cook was up preparing *chappatis* for the next day. The flames of the flickering fire danced on his earnest face. I felt hungry and walked silently towards him. Softly, as if sensing my tranquility and not wanting to disturb it, the cook passed me some half dozen thick steaming *chappatis*. I took them and walked out through the door.

Outside was complete darkness, only the glow of the surf breaking on the long beach. I ate the *chappatis* and walked towards the sea. It seemed so close, as if the house were on the beach, yet it took a long time to reach it. I dropped the towel and swam in the warm salty water. I swam a long way out, feeling the strong current pulling me parallel to the shore and towards the city. There were no stars in the sky, nothing visible, just the touch and the smell of the water around me—I swam back to the shore half an hour later and walked along the beach to where my towel lay.

Walking through the palpable thick darkness, I felt how small and isolated and frail a human being is, surrounded by the immensity and mystery of the cosmos. It was a very different feeling from the one you get on starry nights in the Alps as you walk from a cosy wine-bar back to your chalet, warmed by the wine and music, when you look up to the stars and think of the infinity above. No, the Puri feeling is different. You feel the infinity, not the external infinity of the light and the stars, but the hidden, unseen, unheard infinity. You register nothing but know intuitively that above you, below you, around you is reality, life. You feel the pulse of your heart, the warmth of the circulating blood. You feel the sensation of walking on your feet, yet you see no ground. Sane Indians believe that there is no world outside of man, that the whole cosmos is only our projection of the reality that is within us. Zoroastrians on the other hand say that there are no individuals. Persons are not single entities but simply points of contact, occasions, meeting places, where different forces—ghosts, forms and moods—met and combined. As I walked alone that night either interpretation seemed equally possible and so were hundreds more and there was no need even to bother looking for the right one.

*　　*　　*

The following day, I woke up feeling refreshed, strong and hungry. After a large breakfast of fruit, curd and milk I set off to walk into town, barefooted and wearing loose, light Indian trousers and a shirt. It felt good walking barefoot and I remembered Plato saying that men who cover their heads and feet can never think like philosophers.

I was directed towards the Grand Road, which entered from the west side of town. It was a wide road with houses on both sides and a row of stalls in front of the houses, giving the impression of a huge market. The stalls were laden with fruit, clothes, *saris*, vegetables, tools and holy pictures. The wide street was crowded with people, rickshaws, beggars, slow majestic cows. As I approached a square at one end of the Grand Road the beggars grew in number. The end of the street was filled with beggars, lining both sides. They sat or lay next to each other in allotted circles, leaving not an inch of space unoccupied. The unclean ones marked their little patches by placing their bowls on them when they left. I was surprised to see another European who stopped me and gave some advice as to how to deal with beggars. I listened to him and left for the main square.

In the middle of the square a red-turbaned policeman stood on a pedestal, directing the traffic. There was no real traffic, of course, for in Puri there are only a handful of cars, but he stood there, well fed, tall and arrogant, his thick legs protruding from his enormously wide khaki shorts. In heavy boots with a twirling moustache, he looked more like a general than a traffic cop. The traffic he was so busy directing consisted of rickshaws, cows and pedestrians. He whistled, shouted and waved his hands but nobody took any notice and he did not seem to mind.

On the west side of the entrance to the temple of Lord Jaganath was a row of 'bakery' stalls. A group of colourfully-dressed young Indians were busy rolling *chappatis* and *samosa*, *chiangis*, *piagis* and all kinds of pastries, most of them to be deep fried in the handy stoves.

Food stalls appear to be everywhere in India and particularly in Puri, where any free space seemed to contain at least one Indian cooking or frying something. Outside the temples poorer pilgrims lived on the ground. Living, cooking, dying and being born, all took place on the street for countless millions who have no home—only a particular spot at the roadside.

On the eastern side of a large fountain there was a group of children. They were gathered around the story-teller, a clown whose face was painted red and black and who was covered in feathers. He told stories, gesticulating and making faces, occasionally letting out a shrill scream. Here and there one could catch sight of a passing Holy Man. There were orange-clad *sadhus* walking about with tridents and alms bowls. An elephant that came by, carrying logs in his trunk, seemed the most calm and composed creature in the street. As the elephant reached the square, he was spotted by a group of monkeys that hang on to the tops of stalls and houses. They broke into some kind of mocking chorus. Feeling over-awed by multiple sensations, I walked towards the ocean.

31

The House on the Seashore

Some time later, while walking on the beach I ran into the European again. His name was Florian. He was a painter from Munich and had made his home in Puri. He invited me to his house for a meal.

His house turned out to be an empty mansion—he only used two rooms on the ground floor.

He seemed very fussy about preparing his food, using only the clean vegetables and cutting them up very carefully. I asked him if he was taking such elaborate procedure for fear of disease, but he told me it had all to do with spiritual charges carried by the food. *Tama, raja* and *sattva* he called it. *Tama* is concentrated in rather stale food, particularly institutional food cooked by indifferent nervous people, or by machines. *Tama* means darkness. Tamastic foods fill the mind with dark negative inertia, blocking out activity. Some foods were particularly *tama*-prone: pork, beef, pungent-smelling and greasy foods. *Raja* is the dynamic charge that takes readily to fish and lean meat. It inspires activity but is also a source of anger, lust and frustration. *Sattva* is the godly element that enters the food through the love the cook feels for the person he is cooking for. It takes best to milk, etc.

Florian went on for a while but I wanted to talk about a place to stay, so I interrupted and asked about the house I saw last night.

'Ah,' Florian smiled, 'that house is empty but it is haunted.' He spoke half mockingly, so I could not judge whether he was telling the truth. I told him that I was sure no ghost would bother me, and asked him if it could be rented. It was not, Florian said, since nobody but the housekeeper wants to live there—but I was likely to get it even for free. I wondered how it was that the housekeeper dared to live there. Florian explained that he was a poor untouchable, a Tamil from Madras, an unwanted stranger here. The owner wanted somebody to live in the house.

The heavy, yellow house was turning gold as the last rays of the afternoon sun bade it farewell. I stood outside concentrating on the beautiful sight. A monumental, heavy, colonial structure, with a large terrace and porch on the seaward side. Only about fifty yards from the sea, it stood tall and erect on the yellow sand, alone like a meditative *sadhu*.

I opened the gate set in the high wall, making much noise as I did so. Inside, naked save for the strip of tattered cloth around his hips, stood a skinny black man who looked at me smilingly.

'Where is the boss?' I asked in Hindi, then in English.

The man did not understand but said almost pleadingly, 'You want live here?'

'Yes,' I said.

'Come. Come.' The room he showed me must have once been very beautiful. Large, with alcoves and wide windows, high ceiling, completely empty and clean. The wooden window shades were shut and as my skinny *chowkidar* threw them open, the light and sea breeze flooded in. The sea seemed almost to reach the terrace. On the shore one could see small, skinny fishermen, loin cloths around their waists, naked bodies glistening in the sun.

I was overjoyed. 'I come,' I said.

It was fun, setting up house in that strange town. I decided I was going to stay a long time. I did not think for how long. I had no thought of leaving, only of setting up house.

In the morning I went to the merchant from whom Florian bought his goods. The shop, a low mud building had a straw roof. The merchant was a sombre, sulking, fat man whose function seemed to be to sit motionless by the large iron money box and watch while his son did the work.

The boy was quick and intelligent, but like his father and mother and the whole family, fat.

I needed many things—a stove, cooking utensils, straw mats, kerosene lamps, candles, knives, cups and plates. I took time examining the lamps to make sure they worked, and checking that no plates were broken. It was all ridiculously cheap, most of the things were made from clay, including the stove. In Asia one lives practically for peanuts—one arrives with 100 or 200 dollars and they are worth a thousand or more dollars: one can live on a dollar a day.

Having piled all my purchases into a rickshaw, I moved on to Gurta the Grocer. He was thin and nimble and he and his family worked intently. Seated in the centre of the store, the goods piled high around them yet all in easy reach, they moved with a speed that amazed the eye.

The boy served the customers. Sugar, *ghee*, matches, flour, rice—he had all these things in hand the moment one mentioned them. It was fun going to this grocer; he sent out warm, friendly feelings and at the end of every purchase smiled and handed out sweets.

I moved on to buy wood, cloth, a lock and chain. I bargained, not just for fun, but because I had many things to buy and the cost would mount up.

It was already night when I set off for the house; the rickshaw followed with my treasures. I felt very excited. The house was just outside the city and I walked the last stretch along the beach in darkness with only the glowing house as guide.

To make the house more lived-in I took with me two stray puppies, one black and white spotted, the other yellow. All I had to do to win them was to be nice and give them some food, and they never left. And so began my new life. I had already owned a horse; now I was a householder.

There was something almost magical in those long walks from the town to the house. Puri does not spread out but ends sharply in a small cluster of brightly-lit shops. I would return at nightfall laden with shopping. Leaving behind the Indian holidaymaker-pilgrims, the bustling activity, the sound of singing from the tea shops, I would come to a stone monument adorned with skulls and then suddenly there was the pitch darkness, the beach, the surf and the lonely walk to the empty, silent house. Sometimes there were small fires in front of houses on the beach and clouds of incense. The superstitious fishermen were worshipping their god of the sea. Swimming around their little boats they often moved among sharks, yet they would not be attacked if the god of the sea were appeased.

So at night they built little sand castles and shrines, just next to the sea. They placed holy images to face the sea, lit fires and incense and left fruit and flowers as offerings. The tide came in and washed the offerings away in the night. These dwindling fires were a comforting sight. I would also make an offering of fruit. I was not too worried about sharks, but offering the fruit to the sea seemed the right thing to do and I was charmed by the idea of making the offering.

While walking those last hundred yards or so to my house I would get the Lord of the Manor feeling, and it would occur to me how beautiful it was to be able to live so simply. When I opened the gate, my dogs would bark in joyous welcome. I would light a candle and walk down the long corridor to my room. The housekeeper's family would be sleeping. I'd open the doors towards the sea and a light breeze from the ocean would fill the room.

The kerosene stove was useless so in one tiny room I made a wood fire. I soon learnt to roll and make *chappatis* and my diet was hot milk and *chura*—squashed rice mixed with dates and bananas. Meat was awkward to cook and hard to get, so I ate none. I would take the food out onto the porch, place a lantern next to me and enjoy a simple meal. Then I'd lie on the porch to think, sometimes to sing. Competing with the constant howl of the wind would soon make me hoarse. Then came the last swim of the day, the warm water comforting to my naked body.

I had bought a lot of books on Indian history and religion and the prospect of reading those would pull me away from the sea. At first it was difficult to read by candle light but I got used to it and my eyes did not seem to trouble me. It was difficult to sleep in the house. The doors banged, the wind whistled. There were constant unintelligible groans and whispers from the 'ghosts'. Real sleep came only very late when the wind had calmed and the rats retired. Next day I would be woken by the fishermen as they came up on to the porch to talk, sleep or repair nets. I did not swim in the morning; it was nicer to walk into the courtyard and splash myself with cold water in buckets from the well. I loved the mornings: the nights were mysterious, macabre, yet fascinating, but the mornings were carefree. The back of the house, with its tall concrete wall, gave security and isolation: here there was no howling wind, but stillness and warm sunshine.

After washing I felt famished. I would walk to my room where Janekee, the caretaker's wife, would bring me delicious hot *chappatis* as only she knew how to make, tea, fresh mangoes and oranges.

At about ten I would feel strong enough to face the ocean. I'd take a book, a sarong, and set off down the beach for the long walk to the river. It took an hour to reach but it was worth it. There I would be completely alone; nobody but animals ever came there. The sea was calmer, cooler. My days followed no specific pattern: I would read and sleep under the shade of the pine trees, or lie looking and thinking of the sea or the river. I did not eat because it was time for a meal, I simply ate when I was hungry, the Indian way. Not that I deliberately sought to imitate them. I just drifted into it.

The first day I moved into the house I was very eager to play house, to make tables and chairs, a bed and a bench on the terrace. It was easy: there was wood around and I could borrow the necessary hammer and nails. Yet the enthusiasm wore off. I thought of all the poor millions in India who have no house, no home but a street corner and not even a mat or newspaper to sleep on. You are aware of how poor they are, but it is not simply a matter of poverty. A broke European could, within a day, gather enough mud, wood and palm leaves to make a house, but all that takes effort and initiative, and property weighs on you. Will rain wash the house down, will somebody break into it, is the roof leaking? Many an Indian does not even bother to find a rug or a piece of newspaper to put under his head as he sleeps, for even the owning of a mat means trouble and responsibility. You simply feel tired and you sleep.

This attitude came automatically and easily. I liked the house but I had no bed, no favourite corner, no attachment. I would read in the big room upstairs for it was cooler and when I felt tired would stretch out and fall asleep there and then. Bed, chairs, tables did not seem worth the effort. I sat on bricks, and tables were wooden boxes. It was enough to have next to nothing in order to be happy. I looked at the beautiful ocean; the house itself was beautiful and charged with the spirit of the craftsmen who had made it with care. It was altogether a luxurious life.

Some evenings I'd wander barefoot through the streets of Puri. I'd steal out wearing Indian clothes, the flowing cotton robes. Deep-tanned by the sun, I'd slink through the streets in the dark night, melting into shadows, becoming indistinguishable from the natives. I'd walk softly through the busy streets, absorbing the sounds of the night—the squeak of wheels, the noises of the smithy at his anvil. And then it was back to the lonely house and the long, eventless, endless Indian days and nights which rolled slowly—as if there had never been any other life.

Was I happy or sad? Whatever it was, it was good, it was intense and I was open to it. It was a happy-sad feeling; it was good, yet so different from pleasure. I scarcely experienced pleasure, as such, in India. That is why I was so aware of it in the few moments when I felt it. I would suddenly experience pleasure on the occasions when

171

I'd feel like a millionaire after changing dollars into rupees. There was pleasure on the rare occasions when I'd go to Santhana's Restaurant and stuff myself with greasy meat curries, spicy foods, liquor, sending the whole family scurrying about for a few miserable bucks, calling me Sahib, bowing and bringing me everything they had. That was pleasure so similar in texture and feeling to the inevitable anxiety that came when I wondered what I would do on returning to Europe. Would I have my thesis accepted? Would I get good enough recommendations to earn a place in a big institution? The sensations accompanying these thoughts were very similar to the prickling taste of curry and the tingle I felt when I'd looked at girlie magazines that Ayub the Muslim cook had brought over from Goa. After a week or so of visiting Santhana's I gave up forever. How much better the happy-sad life I led alone in my big house. So I stayed put and lived.

32

The Girl

A few weeks after settling into my house I decided to visit Herr Florian. I was rather looking forward to talking to him again and wondered why I had not gone to see him earlier.

It was late afternoon as I reached the house and climbed the few steps to the shabby porch. The door of his room was open. I was just about to knock when I was startled by the sound of a girl's voice accompanied by a sitar. Deciding not to disturb her, I quietly turned back and sat down on the porch. The girl hummed a plaintive, melodious folk song. I tried to imagine what the words could be—probably something to do with a young girl's heart broken. Her voice was high, soft and trembling and sounded French. I imagined a fishing village in Brittany, a fisherman's daughter singing her mournful song. How melodramatic I thought, and smiled. The singing stopped and I could only hear the oriental sound of the sitar. I walked in and said hello. She was the only person there. A slender figure seated on the floor, her back against the wall. I could not see her face; her head was bent over the sitar and all I could see was a heavy, luxuriant curtain of hair. It must have been chestnut brown in colour but now it was unkempt and covered with dust: it hung in disarray over her shoulders, and seemed to breathe a wild life of its own. A cheap *sari* was pulled up over her knees. Her outstretched legs were long and lithe and covered with mosquito bites and patches of mud. Her bare feet were bruised and covered with dried blood.

The girl lifted her eyes slowly and said hello without animation; she fixed a bored lack-lustre gaze on me. As she examined me a certain nervousness seemed to come over her and disturb her languid composure. I stood transfixed by her deep green eyes, and did not have time to take in the rest of her face. As my look descended to her full, sensuous mouth, the girl lifted her hand, covering her face as if in shame or fear.

Embarrassed by her gesture, she opened her mouth as if she were only trying to cover a yawn.

'You must be looking for Mr Florian.' Her voice, now nervous and shy, was obviously French. Before letting me reply she was on her feet and continued, 'Actually, I was just leaving ... I'm late ... it's quite late ... I must meet someone ... please excuse me.' She gathered up her things nervously. She had difficulty in closing the sitar case, but when I offered to help her she declined and hurried to the door.

'Actually I was walking towards the town,' I said and asked her if she was going in that direction.

'No, no, it's all right, I'm not going that way,' she said.

'I'm sorry to see you go. Do you come here often?'

'Yes, often,' she said, 'almost every day. I will be here tomorrow.'

I watched her walk away. There was a contradiction in the sight of the little girl with her uncombed hair and tattered *sari*, walking proudly, as if unaware of her shabby appearance. I asked myself had I offended her. The story of her having to leave was obviously untrue. I could not even quite remember what she looked like.

Herr Florian bustled in cheerfully twenty minutes later.

'Were you expecting a girl?' I asked. 'Yes, a French girl, Michelle.' The old man told me that he had met her in town a few hours earlier and she had said that she was coming over here and would wait till he came. 'We are supposed to be having a party tonight. She was to

173

bring her sitar and would sing for us—she has a beautiful voice you know,' he added.

'Yes, I heard it, it was very pleasing.'

'Oh she was here then,' Florian exclaimed. 'Why did she leave? Did she say she was coming back?' I described the incident, and how I felt I had offended her. Herr Florian smiled with satisfaction. 'No my dear boy, you didn't offend her, she was just embarrassed. I'm glad that she was.'

I did not quite understand; Florian spoke on as if to himself. 'She lets herself go; dirty, unkempt, she ignores her looks. It's all that living with Dietrich that does it. He's no good for her at all. Not that he's a bad chap. I told him what I thought of their liaison and he agreed, but he said it was her idea from the start and she's the one who does not want to go back to Europe.' 'Who is Dietrich?' I asked.

'He is an architect from Hamburg, very successful, very hip,' Florian answered. 'He has a wife and children and a respectable position in Hamburg. He is thirty-six years old and has the best of both worlds.'

I wondered what he meant, so Florian explained that Dietrich was very business-like for eight months in the year, building concrete slums for the workers on expensive government contracts; the other four months he would spend in India, living the life of a romantic idealist. He'd been doing it for several years now. This year he brought Michelle with him; he found her at Sylt in Germany. She was working there during her school holidays.

We were interrupted by a knock at the door as two newcomers, Mark and James, appeared banging their *tabla*. They were followed by a pale, lanky American girl carrying a guitar.

Mark slung a sack on the floor. 'Got the goodies here' he said. 'Look, Kashmiri brandy, Punjab whisky and Star beer,' he announced as he pulled one bottle after another out of the sack. 'And here is the best *bhang* in Puri.' Since they seemed to be about to have a party I said that I would bring *paratha* and *samosa* from Puri. I went to fetch it.

Half an hour later I came back just in time to join them for a hot lobster supper that James had brought in an earthenware pot.

'*Kankra* for all,' he said as he tipped them on the tray of *paratha* and *samosa* that was already steaming on the table.

Mark had brought his pet cobra which he assured everybody was harmless since he milked her every two days. He did some cobra charming but nobody really cared for his act and finally he put his snake away in a pot.

We all ate. The lobsters were good, the *paratha* crisp and hot. After we had all eaten we sang *mantras* and folk songs.

* * *

During the dinner James mentioned that he'd heard that Georg was in town. At first there was much excitement at the mention of Georg's name but when the singing began the subject was forgotten.

Florian walked out and sat on the terrace. I had already heard Georg's name mentioned several times. I decided to ask Florian who he was and silently followed him on to the terrace.

'Please tell me about Georg,' I asked.

Florian asked me to sit down and began to tell me about Georg's life.

'Georg,' he told me, 'is an Indian in all but his genes.' His father was a highly educated Greek, who taught philosophy at Freiburg University. He had left Europe to live and teach in India. That was in the last century—India was still holy, magical India. The Maharajahs held sway. He was received by the Maharajah of Orissa, himself an educated man. Like Georg's father, he held that there was only one great philosophy and that Plato was its greatest representative in the West, and it was the same philosophy that was carried by the Vedas and Rishis of India. Santhana he called it, from *santhana dharma*, eternal duty. In post-classical times, Florian said, European philosophy was separated from religion, politics and economics, and had become a sterile game of marbles for intellectuals only. In India it lived on. Georg himself grew up in India with a firm Platonic background, yet he was essentially an Eastern thinker.'

The story intrigued me. 'So this Georg is living here. I've heard people mention him but I always thought Benares would have been a more likely choice; why Puri?'

'Puri, my dear boy, is one of the world's rare cities, charged with the concentrated energy of thousands who believe it to be holy. This town is surrounded by desert and jungle—walk west and you run into cobra and scorpion, walk east and there is the ocean. You may find it macabre, you may loathe its oppressive atmosphere, but there is magic in all those beggars, cripples, fakirs and holy men. There is

175

the magic of intense desire. This may all sound too mystical for you, you have not been here long enough. You have yet to feel the magical charge of Puri. Benares, Jerusalem, Mecca, those are turning into tourist packages, but Puri stays pure. Its macabre charge repels the tourist, hippie and adventurers, few can take it, it scares them away. Anyway, as I said, you will see.'

'Is Georg in Puri now?' I asked.

Herr Florian said simply, 'Yes.'

Before I had a chance to ask more questions, he got up and walked back to join the party. I remained seated on the ground.

The others seemed absorbed in themselves and the good time they were having. They had all eaten well and were now relaxed, lying about on the straw mats. All, except Herr Florian and two Divine Light Americans, drank *bhang*. They would like to have smoked hash instead but Herr Florian did not approve of it. The American girl sang and recited poetry. I sat absorbed in thought.

An hour later somebody wondered why Michelle and Dietrich were still not there, so James decided to go and fetch them. Some twenty minutes later Michelle walked in.

Her hair was now clean and shone in the light of the candles. On her feet there were silver-spangled Greek sandals. Her long legs were now washed and free of bandages. She wore a clean and simple green cotton dress. My eyes fastened on her full, sensuous mouth. The reddish lips looked like soft buds. Long silky lashes covered her downcast eyes. In the Indian fashion she wore a single precious stone on one side of her thin nose.

I noticed that her breasts were still those of a young girl and her hips somewhat narrow, but her face was lovely and she carried herself with grace. So clean and fresh amid the dirty Indian surroundings, she looked almost unreal.

There were exclamations of surprise at her appearance but James' cat call was cut short by a sharp glance from Herr Florian.

She stood at the door confused and embarrassed—behind her stood a tall, energetic man in his thirties, dressed like what he took to be an artist, and looking out of place. The girl looked at us almost pleadingly; it was a search for approval, like a little girl washing her hands before lunch and holding them out for inspection. I felt that she wanted me to walk up to her and do something, yet I sat motionless. I was embarrassed and did not know what to do. After a minute's silence she quietly walked up to me, like a child going to its parent. She sat down on the floor, resting her chin on her knees, she tilted her head and looked at me. I said 'hello' in a matter-of-fact voice; Dietrich, still standing at the door, relaxed. She sat there, still child-like, and answered 'hello' with an air of expectation.

Herr Florian saved me from further embarrassment. He spoke gaily to Michelle: 'How good of you to come; we can hardly wait for you to sing,' and he offered her food. 'First have some lobster, have some-thing to drink, both of you.' He motioned them both to the table.

She refused to sing any Indian songs, saying she did not have the inner understanding. She sang French songs, sad lilting Breton songs of the sea, storms and drowned lovers. Having finished her songs she returned to me like a child coming to play. 'I would like to talk to you. What do you do?' she asked. 'I am a student.' 'A student,' she echoed. 'Are you a good person?'

I was becoming embarrassed again so I asked her what she did, in an abrupt but not unfriendly way. She sighed. 'Nothing, I just live with my parents. They are artists—that is my mother is, my father does not work—we live in Paris. I don't like Paris.'

She spoke of Aix, where she came from, and Avignon—she had a grandmother in Avignon and as a child had wanted to stay there with her forever.

'I discovered life in Avignon,' she said. 'The fields spoke to me, the red poppies, the bees, the ancient walks. They taught me I was a woman, they promised me life; but then my parents moved to Paris.'

She never had boyfriends at school she said.

I looked at her and imagined her in different surroundings.

'Do you go out much in Paris?' I asked, trying to maintain a casual tone of voice.

'No.'

It turned out she had been to a discotheque only twice in her life.

'Yes, once in Portofino, with all those touristy Italians in tight trousers with layers of flab hanging over their belts. I felt like a cow at a market. It was different in Paris—degenerate and decadent. I had to take a shower after I left.'

She had had enough, she had left home. She wanted to learn German so she got a job in a de luxe hotel in Sylt, where she met Dietrich. He was very handsome; oh, she knew he was married. No, he never lied. He was very exciting with all his stories of India, Thai-

land and Bangkok brothels. They were lovers before they came to
Puri...

As she talked we were joined by Dietrich who turned out to be
quite a pleasant chap. Normally I would have taken to such a fellow,
for one could learn from him. But I disliked his friendly tone, I did
not like the way he looked at Michelle, I did not like him being there
at all. I tolerated his presence for a while but finally I got up abruptly,
excused myself and went out. Once out, I was glad I had left. I could
never cope with confused situations; intellectually, yes; in literature,
yes—but not in practice.

33

In Search of a Common Rhythm

After that day I stopped visiting Florian. I did not want to see
Michelle again. I spent my time increasingly alone with my dogs at
my secluded river estuary, making friends with the animals, bathing
in the cool water. Nights, I'd go over to Tukuri the Tailor, an Indian
who ran some kind of saloon, the Indian equivalent to Florian's place.
There were pretty Bengali girls there and one did things that one
does with Indian girls: we discussed Tagore's poetry, played chess
and giggled nervously, but it was fun and there were always lots of
people around, and sometimes fellows would play sitars; some were
very good, and the girls danced. Tukuri had his *tabla* shows and the
days went by.

It was some ten days after the party that I saw Michelle again. It
was night and I had just left Tukuri's. I paced along Lakshmi Boulevard, wearing loose, silken Indian robes, feeling the cool night air. It
was the evenings that made southern living so attractive: the north-
ern world would die at seven and the southern world wake up. It
was in the evenings that one was farthest from European reality—all
was sensation, just the feel of the sand under one's feet, the occasional hammer-taps from the smith's shops, the light, the fires.

The smell of fried *piagi* reminded me that I was hungry, so I bought some straight out of the frying pan and had a cup of tea; I sat down on a stone and took in the Puri evening.

I was about to order some *samosa* when I noticed Michelle walking from the direction of the Lux. Her clothes were disarrayed and her manner distraught. She did not notice me, so I hesitated a second as to what to do; but then her eyes were on me, so I got up and approached her.

'What's the matter?' I asked, noticing the tears in her eyes. She made an effort to appear calm. I took her elbow and said, 'I was just about to walk in the Jogoda Gardens; do you want to come for a walk?' She did not reply but followed me to the gates a few yards away. They were locked. 'So much the better,' I said. 'We'll jump the wall at the back and have the garden to ourselves.'

A few minutes later we were sitting on a marble bench under the luxuriant willow trees. Michelle had collected herself and was throwing little pebbles into the pond in front of us, breaking the image of the moon.

It was very peaceful and dark in the garden. The crickets and other night musicians must have taken the night off. Only occasionally the wind would blow some strains of the harmonium playing the Jogudar evening *puja*.

I stopped asking her what was the matter and assumed it had to do with Dietrich and that it was all over. I was glad it had happened, naturally; she had taken her own decision and was not pressured by me.

'You know,' she began hesitantly, 'I don't believe much in all this ideal man, ideal woman talk, this myth of perfect love, this lie, thrown at us by poets and priests. You see,' she said, 'I went with Dietrich because he was around at the time. I gave to him an equal proportion of myself to that which he gave to me of himself. I have no obligation to be loyal and faithful with him. Indeed, as soon as I could find somebody more suitable than Dietrich then I would enter into a different kind of liaison. A person, any person,' she said, 'needs to have relationships with other people, many other people. I need men to talk to, to love. No one man can satisfy one woman completely and permanently. A woman needs different kinds of loving by different men. So why be restrictive, jealous or possessive? Love the one you are with and open yourself to life as much as possible.' She looked as if expecting a comment but when I remained silent, she continued to speak.

'A man, too, needs more than one woman to satisfy his emotional and sexual needs,' she said, 'so why restrict each other? Can we not free ourselves from our possessiveness, our fear, and liberate our minds and bodies and all live a better and more fulfilling life?'

The girl was, by this time, panting. Her eyes were open and large. She looked at me with a look of a child who had broken an expensive china plate.

I felt the emotion that made her body heave. I was by then very sad. Everything was more complicated than I had assumed. For a second a thought flashed in my head: how about saying I agree with her ideas. I heard myself saying in spite of my real feelings, in a cold voice, half mockingly, 'Yes, you are perfectly right, as a matter of fact I was just going to suggest to Dietrich ...'

Tears appeared in her eyes. She must have sensed I was not being honest but then I thought I would hurt her even more if I told her what I thought.

I realised my mistake. Michelle was on her feet. It was no use hiding the sobs now—she burst into tears and darted away.

I wanted to run after her, to comfort her and assure her that her intuition was much better than any ideas, but then I thought, who am I to tell what her intuition was. I may well have been wrong. It seemed futile. I heard her waking up the watchman, the noise of the gates being unlocked.

I walked back into the night wondering if Michelle could be right. In a way it was true that nothing permanent can take a definite shape. All is just a hint, a moment, a promise. Even beauty: every woman is beautiful for a moment at least, when through a movement, gesture or expression she suddenly captures something. Yes, beauty was no single person's possession; it was fragmented, so why perceive beauty only in that which is yours according to some piece of paper. Why not live like Michelle, think like Michelle—love all women? I bent and picked up a tiny white flower that the wind had blown from some shrine. I looked at the delicate thing, so infinitely complex. I looked yet more closely at the patterns, colours, compounds within that single flower.

Yes, Michelle may have been right. But it was not a matter for changeable opinions and philosophies, but for some deeper perception.

34

Tantric Initiation

Four days later Michelle and I met again at Florian's.

Her day was spent between visits to Baba and Herr Florian. Baba she would see at sunrise and sunset. It was a daily ritual. Herr Florian she squeezed in between; it was Baba that really mattered to her.

The few Westerners in Puri spoke more often of Baba than of Georg. Many went to see him regularly but Michelle was his most ardent follower. Baba was a *sadhu*, a *sanyasi*, who lived just outside Puri. Michelle had proposed that I join her in her sunset *puja* at Baba's. We set off walking on the inland side of Puri. The ocean side had bigger buildings; it was stately and spacious and had a promenade atmosphere, with people taking leisurely strolls in the sea breeze. The other side was how I imagined 'typical' India to look. There was no wind and no feeling of ocean, there were luscious trees and bushes, mud huts, shrines, temples, the song of tropical birds, monkeys running over the roofs of houses, sacred cows and an occasional working elephant.

The roads were muddy and dirty, yet welcoming.

It was a long walk and we continued in silence. Baba lived about fifteen minutes outside the town, along the river. I expected a small house, or even a hut, but there was none. Baba lived under a tree. He never moved from there, day or night. Always within a radius of perhaps ten feet he went through all the actions of living.

There was a small clearing before the tree, which was covered with straw mats brought by a small group of Indian men, women and children, who sat around in silence. There were two other Europeans.

Between Baba and the people there was a wooden stand, hiding the lower part of his body. On either side of him were fires with cooking utensils.

As the flames leapt, I glimpsed the beautiful face of a dark Indian, in his forties. The features were finely drawn; he had a high forehead, large fleshy nose and lips, and soft, relaxed eyes. It was the face of a sensualist—fiery, full of life, not the face of a monk or a thinker. His rich hair hung down to the ground and his beard merged with the beads at his waist. He was slight and moved like a cat.

The man used the erotic in him, he smiled at women and smiled suggestively.

In a long insinuating look, his eyes penetrated Michelle. A Tantric, I thought, as my mind rushed to remember what I had heard of them. Worshippers of *lingam* and *yoni*, male and female organs, some of them attain union with God through sexual union with specially trained women, skilled in the arts of love—the intention being to drive the *Kundalini* power within to the peak of excitement and at the moment of climax to turn the full force of accumulated sensual power inwards towards the 'Godhead' inside.

The more macabre rites involved sitting on top of mutilated corpses on moonless nights and exposing themselves to all kinds of horrors in order to convert their fear and anxiety into a union with God.

Michelle confirmed my thoughts. 'He is a Tantric *sadhu* Baba,' she said. 'In *yoga* one attains union with God through many means— *Raja-yoga*, the way of exercise and austerity, *bhakti* through the love of God, *jnana* through philosophy. *Tantra* is the way of the ecstatic sensualist.'

While we talked, more people had come, mostly Indians, one carrying a small harmonium, and three others carrying large *tabla* drums.

'You are to relax to the sound of the drum,' Michelle told me. 'The drumming will empty your head of thought. The rest of the people will join in later in a song. When you feel ready, that is when your body absorbs the song, not your mind; then you can join in too. The drumming and the music will progress in such a way as to free you of anxiety. God cannot enter into a thinking head; the object is to dissolve your consciousness in music, in the smell of incense, the palms, the flowers. You are to lose your intellectual consciousness and become the beat of the *tabla* drum, the cloud of hashish, the ray of the moon. When you have achieved this state, then God will enter you.' Michelle seemed to believe all she was saying.

A half-naked Brahmin appeared and silence fell upon the group. He made a few signs on the ground, picked up some mud and powder and made a paste in his palm. With the paste he proceeded to paint a sign on the forehead of all present. A huge *chilum* was presented and filled with *charas* and topped with a chunk of burning charcoal. Baba took several large puffs and more *chilums* were lit and passed around. A thick cloud of smoke enveloped the group. The deep, slow, rhythm of the *tabla* broke the silence.

The moon glittered in the lazy river; the scents of incense and flowers, holy oils, palms and earth hung heavily in the warm air.

I lifted my eyes and caught sight of the moon through palm leaves. It was magical. I held back for a second, and refused the *chilum* as did a few of the Indians. The rest of it was all right: I dropped my guard and was absorbed into the atmosphere. The drums sounded soothing and relaxing.

The cry of a tropical bird pierced the air. I heard the drumming more distinctly.

I felt the girl touch my hand. 'Tonight is my night,' she whispered softly, her hot breath in my ear. My heart thumped. 'I am being initiated into *tantra*. I am glad you are here with me.'

I squeezed her hand and felt her against my shoulder, warm and throbbing. I let go of her hand; she leaned against me, closed her eyes, her body heaving. The drums grew louder. As the beat grew slower my mind flew back to the night in the Jogoda Gardens and the questions I left unanswered. Had I betrayed something deeper in myself in order to uphold some abstract law, the expression of a culture which time had overtaken? And this girl here, who lived for the moment, was she truer to the male/female rhythm of which both of us were just individual manifestations? I did not know. In this Indian night with the drums rumbling, Michelle seemed closer to something that I had still no notion of—yet was it right, this rhythm she was in tune with? If only I could become still enough to feel that pulse. Yet I could not.

I was brought back to India by the sound of men's voices. They were singing now, humming softly. A cloud passed over the moon. There was a flutter of activity—seven fires were prepared and lit around Baba. They must symbolise the seven *chakras* I thought, the seven centres along the spine and the brain, receptive and productive of *Kundalini*, the power of the serpent, the dark glowing sexual energy transferred to that of god-charged *Prana*.

Harmoniums joined in. There must have been something in that mournful wailing sound that reduced the power to think. It felt so much simpler to listen, to become the music.

Everyone was chanting now and the drumming assumed a definite repetitive pattern. I recognised the tune of the *Hare Rama mantra*;

slowly they sang it, over and over, *Hare Rama, Hare Rama, Rama, Rama, Hare, Hare*. The words were so simple you had no need to think for yourself. When they came to *Hare Krishna* I found myself singing along. On it went, endlessly, for well over an hour, or perhaps three—who could tell?

Chilums were passed around more frequently. The beat gradually accelerated. The four initiates were called by Baba to step forward. They did so. A semi-circle of seven other *Sadhus* formed behind Baba with the initiates standing at the focus.

The orange-clad *Sadhus* settled into lotus postures and the initiates prostrated themselves before the parapet. A large silver dish containing some burning fluid was placed on top of the parapet, and the flames shot up, illuminating Baba's face which assumed a sinister, almost violent air. His eyes were bulging and saliva dripped down his massive black beard.

Cymbals were passed around and we all started to beat to the rhythm. I fixed my gaze upon the children; they seemed the most fascinating. Little girls, perhaps four years old, they sat with closed eyes and heads uplifted, singing with so much zeal and devotion that it was contagious.

The oil-covered body of the Brahmin shimmered as he walked around the fires, throwing herbs and liquid on them, making them periodically flare up. The singing built up to a crescendo. It became so fast it seemed impossible to pronounce the words properly, yet the Indians managed. Then the music came to a sudden stop as if rehearsed; only the drums rumbled on.

The initiates were asked to present their offerings to the *guru*: five kinds of fruit and an unspecified amount of money from each, according to his means. The pile of money before Baba seemed quite impressive and I was startled to see Michelle throw down a bundle of blue 100-rupee notes.

The drumming slowed down and died and the harmonium resumed its gentle tune. Baba spoke in Bengali and a Brahmin interpreted for Michelle. I was close enough to hear him.

'I will cause the seven holy *chakras* of your body to glow,' the Brahmin repeated in English. 'I will light a fire in myself and pass it into your spine, waking up the dormant *Kundalini* of your bodies. May it dissolve your personality, your ego, until all of you becomes the fire itself, merging with the eternal flame of God. It will surge up your spine lighting one *chakra* after another until it reaches your head, lighting your life with wisdom and knowledge. Look at me.' Baba spoke loudly for the first time. 'You will see light emerge from my body.' He placed his hands on his forehead and stroked downwards towards his navel. 'Do you see the bluish-white light stream out of my body?' There was no reply.

'Surely you see the light, the bright bluish light—concentrate on the light, feel my light warm you.'

There was a gasp in the audience. I leaned over to James, grabbed him by the arm and said, 'What is it?'

'The light!' he said, excitedly.

Baba cupped his hands together and said, 'Do you see the white ball of holy *Kundalini* fire in my hands?'

'Yes,' cried the audience.

'Do you see it?' I asked Gérard.

'Yes, I can see it.'

I did not see it. Each of the initiates was asked to come up to Baba. He placed his palms on their heads and whispered to them, in a low voice. He touched their eyes, ears and noses and then manipulated their spines. Having received this treatment they all returned to their original lotus positions.

'I will light up the *Kundalini* power in you now.'

The seven flames shot up simultaneously as some liquid was poured on them.

'Feel the warmth of awakening *Kundalini* in you. See the light enter your spine. Do you feel the first *chakra* glow?' he asked them.

Most of them answered, yes; he called again to the few who hesitated, and massaged their spines until they all stated that the fire was lit, warm and bright, moving up their spines to their heads.

Silence fell onto the group. The fires had died down, but the moon shone bright. They all meditated for about half an hour. Baba continued murmuring to himself and smoking *ganja*, and then seemed to fall into some kind of trance.

The silence was broken when he said softly, 'Now we will eat.'

Gently and slowly the people assumed comfortable positions, relaxed smiles animating their faces.

Women brought thick, creamy, sugary tea, and hot rice and *dhal* served on palm leaves; a large jar of sweets was passed around. It all tasted very good.

Michelle was gay and relaxed. 'Did you feel it—wasn't it wonderful? Did you meet God?'

'Yes, I felt very good for a long while,' I admitted. 'I found the *puja* very beautiful. The ceremony disturbed me a little.'

'Oh, don't spoil it for me—I won't even discuss it. You'd be like Dietrich—you are just closed, shut up. I won't even ask you whether you saw the light.'

'Did you?' I asked.

She braced herself. 'You heard me answer "yes", do you think I would lie? I know what you're thinking, but try not to think.'

We walked back to my house together and in silence.

*   *   *

Ours was a relationship that never took off, at least not on the level one would have expected. But then I knew it had to end before even starting, for I've been through this before, getting involved with a person with whom I fundamentally disagreed. Michelle would sit in the house for hours absorbed in silence and then she'd suddenly burst into tears and run up to me, sobbing. I'd try to comfort her but did not know how; she could not easily be comforted and somehow there was never a question of physical contact between us. It seemed inappropriate. She'd shy away from it, content to lean, sobbing, against me. At times she'd relax, particularly in the evenings. We would eat, and then she'd take her *sitar*, walk over to the french windows, open the doors to the sea, and sing while the fishermen were lighting their little fires.

I never discovered what it was that bothered her. I felt I ought to do something to comfort her. She went on about feeling ashamed and she was sorry—but I never really understood her and there seemed nothing for me to do. I felt she wanted me to open up and talk to her about my own views—but then I felt who was I, a fellow from a different society, to tell her about ideas which were so different from hers that she might laugh at them? She came from a different background and may well have considered mine as backward. Our differences were more than philosophical. Poetically or philosophically I could even sympathise with her ideas. But people do not live by their ideas and philosophies and I'd had my share of mistakes and was not going to make any more.

35

A Walk Along the Beach

The day after Michelle left I woke up bitterly depressed. I had no wish to remain in Puri any longer. At the time it seemed there was nothing to hold me there, so I decided to go to Konarak, the famous black temple that Lawrence once called the world's most splendid monument to the dark erotic gods. I wanted to leave right away and force myself to forget all about the last few days. I woke before sunset and had not the patience or inclination to wait for the bus service to begin. Besides, due to the swamps between Puri and Konarak, which was only 40 kilometres away, the roundabout bus journey took four hours, so I decided to walk.

I would have asked the way to Konarak but remembered reading that it was built on the beach, so I could just walk along the beach till I came to it. Forty kilometres would be about seven hours' walking I reckoned, and decided to take a bottle of water with me.

The day was breaking and the sun had just torn through the mist. As I cleared the last houses of Puri, the fishermen were beginning to emerge from their huts. I walked briskly, greeting the men as I passed by. It was like walking on a beautiful luxurious carpet. The wet, silken sand felt warm and soft under my feet. I knew that there weren't any villages before Konarak and the feeling of elation animated my step. It was cool and pleasant and the gentle morning breeze played on my only piece of clothing, an orange *sarong*, loosely wrapped around my waist.

The sun, still quite low, cast a long shadow ahead, over the miles of beautiful empty beach. Warm blood charged my body with the force of life and exuberance; my lungs drew in gallons of fresh air. It felt good to abandon myself to sensation of muscle, air and sand. So I began to run.

I realised that I had learned how to dissolve all thought. Like waggling one's ears, one cannot imagine how it is done, but once achieved, one can repeat it effortlessly, again and again. It was during the tantric initiation, for the first time, I had let my thoughts roam completely uncontrolled, like letting horses out to pasture. I ran for about an hour then, pleasantly exhausted, I splashed into the ocean. As the cool water closed around me, my thoughts slowly returned. New vistas were opening. Not the *charas* or L.S.D. or *ganja*, not even meditation, a simple thing like an early morning run along the beach could mean so much.

It was getting hot; I took off the *sarong*, wet it, rolled it into a turban to cool my head and continued to walk.

There were literally thousands of reddish crabs all along the beach. I never came too close to them for as soon as I was within ten feet they would disappear into their holes, so as I walked I watched the constant spectacle of the carpet of crabs opening and closing before and after me.

To my left there was a green jungle, assuring me of shade and comfort. As I walked steadily fatigue overcame me. I wanted to walk into the trees and rest there, but my limbs felt like lead. Too tired to walk, I slowly lowered myself onto the hot sand, oblivious of the heat, stretched out, and as I lay there, half awake half asleep, a strange feeling came over me. It was as if my body were literally mutating, as if a fire were entering it. The molten sun poured like honey over my body. Warm and gentle it shone but did not burn for I was already well tanned.

About an hour later I was awake again. It was strange to be happy for such periods of time. In Europe happiness came in waves, one felt it coming. The climax would come, then slowly dissipate, giving way to boredom and some kind of guilt-feeling which one banished by working. Yet here I was, not working, but feeling perfectly happy for hours at a time. I drank the water in the bottle and continued. The hours melted into each other. I became hungry a few times and was lucky enough to find coconuts which I smashed open on the rocks.

It was probably sometime around noon that I must have walked past Konarak; I had no idea of it then. The monumental temple was built on the beach, so I assumed that it would be impossible to miss it—so impossible that it never occurred to me to look for it.

Of course, I did not realise that the place was built on what was a beach centuries ago. The ocean had since receded for about five miles and the jungle had filled the gap.

So I walked on, absorbed. Not until I ran into Chagie swamp, thirty kilometres later, did it even occur to me that something might be wrong. I also had no idea there were any swamps. Chagie did not look like a swamp.

All I saw was a river running into the ocean. The water was only inches deep and the river deposited its mud miles into the sea, making a stretch of water too shallow to swim in. Not that it bothered me. I paused for a second and tried to guess the time; it looked like late afternoon. I had certainly covered well over forty kilometres, I thought, so how was it that I had not arrived? Since it was Tukuri who told me that the distance was 40 kilometres, I assumed he must have meant 40 miles. He would not talk in kilometres. The idea that Konarak might have disappeared was so remote that it never entered my head. If I did not reach it I had simply not walked far enough, so I set off across the muddy river.

It was heavy going for my feet would sink and I had to drag them out, all very tedious and tiring; it took me over half an hour to get close to the other shore. My feet were sinking deeper and the mud was becoming very sticky.

It suddenly occurred to me that I was in a swamp so I decided to go back. Yet it was not easy. I was all right where I was, but a move forward or backward seemed to cause me to sink deeper. Yet I did not panic—somehow the thought of dying in such a ridiculous way seemed too abstract. If only there was something to grab hold of. I was quite close to the other side yet too far to reach for the low-hanging trees. I found that 'bicycling' in place made one come up yet with nothing to grab hold of one hardly profited. I tried to roll across the surface but it would not do—so I just hung about occasionally 'bicycling' as the hours drifted by. With the nightfall came the deliverance. As the rising moon broke up the blackness of the night, the tide came in. When the water came up to my chest I was able to swim and reach the river bank.

Finally back on solid ground, I fell asleep immediately, exhausted.

36

The Dogs and the Crocodile

I slept well, and when the first warm rays of sunshine woke me I felt refreshed and happy. I assessed my position. I had left Puri before the fishermen were up, so it must have been around five in the morning; I reached the swamp shortly before sunset having walked very fast the whole day, so I must have covered about fifty miles.

There did not seem to be any point in continuing to look for Konarak. I knew that there were no cities on the beach after Konarak. Crossing the river and walking back to Puri again was out of the question. So I would have to go into the jungle and sooner or later run into the Puri-Bhubaneshwar Road. It was only speculation about the road, but I realised with satisfaction that my predicament was not bothering me. Perhaps this was just what I was looking for—something to take all my concentration.

Would it be better to be sitting in an air-conditioned car on the highway? Not if you were unhappy in it. Such simple and obvious platitudes, already heard a million times, acquired a new dimension for me. It is not where you are that matters—all that matters is that you are happy and satisfied, with a clear conscience that you are not doing harm to anybody, and that is how I wanted to feel. I was lost, it could take days to get anywhere, but so what? I set off up the river. My surroundings changed rapidly. Sparse pine trees were replaced by thick groves. A few hours later the growth was so thick that I could advance only with difficulty.

I was quite hungry: there were some unrecognisable yellow fruits growing on the shrubs but I was afraid to eat them, so I walked on. Occasionally, a snake or a lizard would rustle by, but they looked harmless. Several hours later it occurred to me that maybe I should climb a tree and try to see where I was.

I broke through the top branches and suddenly entered warm sunshine. I could see nothing but a sea of trees. I scanned carefully all around me—I could no longer see the ocean, just the endless carpet of green and the river glistening and shining like a snake. Then my eye caught something—a trace of smoke, a small bluish cloud, perhaps a mile or two ahead. I saw no house but there seemed to be a clearing near the river.

I was amazed. This was just like a fairy tale. I wondered who I would find—Doctor Livingstone, a Holy Man, or a witch.

As I approached the hut I was greeted by the friendly bark of several dogs. There were four of them, wagging their tails. They ran up to me energetically and joyfully. I was happy to encounter some friendship at last. Their quick, agile movements and sheer boisterousness made them akin in behaviour to Western dogs, yet I realised that they were essentially Indian.

European dogs of that variety jump all over the visitors, playing and barking. That is the problem with European dogs: they take all kinds of liberties. They may be friendly but they are ill-mannered and disrespectful. These well-disposed Indian dogs were far better mannered. The four of them stood around me, bowing and shaking their heads, shy and reserved. They obviously wanted to jump all over me and play, but patiently waited for an invitation, while indicating their eagerness with wagging tails.

'Hop-a!' I exclaimed, and slapped my knee. The next minute the five of us were rolling on the ground wrestling, shrieking, barking and laughing, hands and paws and tails all intermixed in a rolling whirl.

Having thoroughly exhausted myself with the dogs I sat down and waited. About an hour went by and it was getting very hot. Playing with the dogs had made me sweaty and thirsty so I decided to go for a swim. The water that flowed by the hut was only a rather shallow stream. As the water was very clean I thought it might be used as drinking water and I ought not to swim in it. As it did not look as if the owner of the hut would be back before night, I had plenty of time to kill.

I decided to walk back to the main river, which lay maybe half a mile away. The four dogs ran with me. Two of them were quite large for Indian dogs. All four were dirty, and shaggy. Asian dogs are never of any recognisable breed, but a mixture of all breeds imaginable. They fall into two basic categories, the larger, fatter ones that tend to be of the 'old yeller' variety, and the shorter ones, black with spots of various colours. These dogs fell neatly into those two categories.

Half an hour later I was by the river. I looked at the lush vegetation. The ancient dark grey baobab trees that had no leaves growing on their thick intertwined branches, looked like long-armed witches joining their limbs in a macabre dance. I took the plunge—the water was pleasant and refreshing. Too tired to swim I let myself drift. The dogs, barking, ran parallel to me on the river bank. I drifted to a beautiful spot, a tiny golden beach with a sort of acacia bending over and offering delicious cool shade. I swam out of the water, lay down and dozed off.

I knew that there were snakes and quicksands and tigers and crocodiles in India, yet if one worried about such things one would never do anything. An apparent carelessness can be almost like a shield which protects one like an invisible halo. At all events I was able to fall asleep on the shore of this crocodile-infested river in India, my mind somewhere in Europe, dreaming.

*　　*　　*

The eight-foot crocodile must have been more curious than hungry, judging from the still uneaten pieces left on the bank not too far from where I slept. He was probably attracted and intrigued by the harmless looking white body that lay immobile on the beach. Inaudible to the dogs, the ugly beast had crept out of the water about fifty yards upstream from where I was lying, for the dogs did not notice him. Either instinctively, or by chance, the beast judged the wind direction and moved downwind, thus reducing the possibility of detection by sound or smell.

Somewhere deeper in the jungle the dogs lay in thick shade. It was noon and there was a lull of jungle activity for birds, bees, and the dogs, who lay immobile, panting in the heat, their tongues hanging out. It was hard to reconstruct what alerted them. Did the crocodile step on something or was it merely the smell? The crocodile was within thirty yards of me when the dogs sprang to life. Savagely, violently, they flew at the creature, barking furiously and baring their teeth. I was immediately awakened. I glanced around and saw the ugly, mechanical-looking beast stop in its tracks, lift its head as if amazed or disturbed from a deep thought. It turned to face the dogs, its huge tail curling. In the next instant the dogs were on top of it.

The thick tail of the beast flashed like a whip, there was a loud crack of bones being broken and the shattered remains of the small dark dog flew about twenty feet before crashing into a tree. There was something majestic, uplifting and beautiful about the attack of the dogs. I watched them, fascinated. They had saved me, I was free to run off any time, but I was humbled and enthralled by the magnificence of the attack. The fate of the little dog made absolutely no difference to the other three. There was not a trace of fear in them. They were doing a job, they were fulfilling their duty. Their nature, their *dharma*.

Quick as lightning, they flashed around the huge beast, snapping at its legs, its neck, hurling themselves at it. The crocodile's head spun lunging and twisting like some complicated machine—the huge ugly jaws opening and shutting like a mechanical trap. Watching the fight, my mind slipped away from reality—I saw no longer the crocodile, but a mechanical death machine. I saw the war between the spirit of the machine and that of man. The beast was all shell and exterior, and the snapping jaws, so strong outwardly yet all soft and pulpy inside. It became a symbol for the dominant force of our culture and for all the men who set their hopes and aspirations to its rhythm.

The dogs on the other hand had no shell—they were soft, vulnerable and warm. All they were was spirit—flashing, lunging, twisting, with a deadly resignation. It was all happening too quickly for me to register every detail of the battle. I heard the dogs' teeth digging into the beast and I heard the cracking noises, yet I was not sure whether it was the jaws of the dogs or the skin of the crocodile that was cracking.

The beast was covered in blood, partiularly around its legs, but it was hard to say whose blood it was. There was a hideous snap of jaws as the huge mouth closed itself around the large yellow dog, the friendly one, the first one to greet me. Blood shot out both sides of the beast's mouth and as it shook its head, the head and tail of the dog dropped off and the beast spat out the rest of the gnawed body. The other small dog used his chance, and as the crocodile lifted his head while spitting out the body, the dog dug into the exposed neck. I doubted the effectiveness of any of their bites, but the crocodile was hurt for its body shook in the reflex of pain. Still it was obvious that the dogs had no chance.

I had somewhat collected myself and tried to call them back, to save the remaining two, but it was hopeless—the dogs were being true to their duty.

Looking at those dogs I was humbled. A realisation flashed through me: *Santhana Dharma*, the meaning of life, to be true to your obligation to the world around you. An hour earlier those dogs were playing, teasing, relaxed, friendly, innocent, chasing the bees and running after a stick. They may have lived like that all the time— playing, sleeping, eating the food provided for them, but the time came when their services were called upon, and they were faithful. They gave all they had. Their aim in that battle was not survival, for to have run away from the crocodile they would have ceased being true dogs. They could never have had the right to eat other peoples' bread and sleep and play again. A true dog must somehow understand this. It is not a matter of thought—dogs do not think—but a real dog will not evade his duty in order to survive. His first impulse is to do his *dharma*, as for self-preservation, the gods would take care of that. This was the message of the dogs. They were going to die, but not in vain, for they were teaching a human being—giving him a message.

It was sad to have to watch them all get killed, for obviously there was no getting them away from the beast. But then, suddenly, a glimmer of hope, a surprise, one of the dogs must have caught an artery, some exposed part of the crocodile. The ugly reptile was shaking, obviously in pain. The ferocity of the dogs was truly gigantic. It was their ferocity, their absolute determination to win, that changed the logical conclusion of the battle, changed their defeat into unexpected victory.

The ugly reptile turned round; one of his eyes was bleeding, his neck was pulsating, blood was splattering him. He was no more concerned with fighting but was on the run, thinking of his life, driven by the desire for survival. However, the dogs over-reached themselves. Crazed by anger, they ran after the crocodile. Overcome by blind rage, the dogs threw themselves into the water. This was no longer their *dharma*. Their duty was already fulfilled.

As the water turned red and the mangled pieces of the two dogs broke the surface I turned away to walk toward the hut.

37

Little Baba

I reached the clearing near the hut. The doors were now open. I
called but there was no answer. I walked in. Nobody was there. The
hut was cool, dry, clean and neat, like a doll's house. There was a
floor-level wooden bed, a large table and no chairs, but leopard and
antelope furs lay scattered casually over the straw matting on the
floor.

In a corner was a simple wood stove, still warm, and next to it
cooking utensils, clay pots and pans. On the shelves nearby was food:
lentils, split peas, rice, *chura*, fruit. The pictures of Indian deities
covering the walls and the tell-tale leopard skin rugs on the floor
suggested that this was a *sadhu's* home.

It was obvious that the man had recently left and might return
soon. Rather than be found inside I went out and decided to wait for
him there. I was greeted by a goat that I had not noticed before. I
sat down.

Only a few minutes later I felt a hand softly squeeze my shoulder.
I turned round to meet the gaze of a frail young *sadhu* with a warm
friendly countenance. His face was finely drawn, delicate and sensitive, with taut, glistening skin and smiling relaxed eyes. It was the
face of a seventeen-year-old boy, but I felt he must be older. His
luxurious hair grew waist-long, well groomed and glistening. He had
silky eyelashes like a woman's. His movements made him look as if
he was gliding or dancing. The orange robe of the *sadhu* completely
covered his body, but one could imagine it being frail.

He looked at me in silence for a while, then disappeared into the
hut. I also said nothing. I felt no need to talk, especially about the
dogs; it seemed that all was obvious and no explanations were
desired.

Sometime later the boy-man emerged out of the hut carrying a
steaming pot of hot goat's milk, *chura* and fruit. He had never stopped smiling.

For seven days I lived with the *sadhu*. We never spoke, yet I could feel communication between us. There was a bond: my ideas, energies and movements were being picked up and analysed by the boyman. I was being drained, as if my experiences had all been melted into fluid and poured over the *sadhu*. It was not an unpleasant experience. I needed to give whatever was being drawn out of me, rather as a cow needs to be milked. In return the *sadhu* poured peace into me and made me forget the unpleasant memories.

I could not really say what kind of communication took place between us. Perhaps the simple act of observing the perfectly relaxed face and movement of the *sadhu* was so different from anything or anybody I had ever seen, that it was enough to bring about corresponding sensations and changes in me.

I never saw him read a book and would not have been surprised if he had been illiterate, had never heard of Europe or seen a Westerner in his life.

It is an Indian habit to place the worn-out sandals of a *sadhu* under some holy picture or shrine. The little Baba did the same with his, and judging from the size of the smallest he must have been living in the hut since he was a child. I wondered if he ever left his hut for long.

His day would start shortly before the sun was up. The little Baba never went through the motions of waking up: he'd lift himself up and slide on to the floor—rather like somebody who had been lying awake for a long time.

Four days after I arrived I woke up an hour or so before sunrise. There was no hint of the morning yet and the little Baba lay motionless. Wanting to fetch some water, I passed by his bed and was startled by the open eyes of a man who looked like a corpse. I passed my hand in front of his gazing eyes to see if he would react, but he did not. I returned to my bed somewhat amazed.

Half an hour later the jungle slowly woke up. First came the calling of the birds and then a hundred and one sounds I could not identify. At least twenty minutes before sunrise the jungle was already alive.

The goat and the *sadhu* always woke up simultaneously; perhaps it was only a coincidence, but as the goat bleated the *sadhu* rose.

We'd begin the day by washing ourselves. The mist hung low over the water and the air was dense and warm. It felt wonderfully cool and refreshing to step into the river. I swam, while Baba stood still and periodically submerged and crouched under the water. As he finished the morning's washing ritual, Baba would place himself in the lotus position on a tiger skin placed on a tree stump just above the river. He would position himself carefully and slowly, yet always in time to catch the first ray of the emerging sun, which would light up his silken, smooth complexion and dance over his shiny hair, smooth and glossy, like the scales of some tropical fish. By that time he would be motionless and remained so for several hours.

I tried to do as he did but an hour later my body would ache. I had to occupy myself collecting fruits and shelling nuts. There was no other work.

At no time did I feel bored or restless. With the work done, I watched the jungle life around me.

There is something unique in living in direct contact with nature, getting up with the sun, going to sleep with the sun, swimming with the current; there are rhythms and pulses that nature sends out. You feel in harmony with the earth, the birds, rabbits and snakes. Man consistently tries to overcome nature, to isolate himself from the heat and the cold, day and night, creating artificial heat and light, and a life rhythm alien to nature's pulse.

Here in the jungle I felt like a flat battery being recharged, the warm juices of life re-entering. Desires and longings slowly returned. I wondered about the meaning of life for the little *sadhu*. Apparently, all he did was sleep, eat and meditate, but he gave significance to his modest existence by making all his activities a ritual.

Having finished his morning's meditation, the *sadhu* set about tidying his hut. He picked up his orange sheet, descended to the river to wash it slowly and ceremoniously. With equal care and significance he washed all his garments and accessories which were, of course, very few.

Cooking was the most involved ritual of all. He inspected literally every grain of rice and every lentil he ate, meticulously washing every particle that was to be consumed. Before lighting the fire he seemed to bless the wood and the pots, as well as the food. Cooking itself consisted of well rehearsed, beautifully-executed movements, practised to perfection. His pots and pans were so arranged as to be within his reach. He stood in one place, feet immobile, arms working as if in a dance. With the flick of a juggler he would transfer water and lentils from one pot to another, a stream of flying liquid stretching like a rainbow.

It must have taken him years to work himself to such perfection and it was beautiful to watch him. I am always fascinated by skilful cooks tossing up and catching pancakes, but I could not compare Baba with those. Baba slowed everything down: even the flying water seemed to move in slow motion, accompanied by a murmured prayer. It took two hours to prepare a modest meal of boiled vegetables and rice.

It was strang how many messages nature could give. I could listen for an hour to the song of the wind rustling in palm trees. The branches told different stories: the rigid song of a withered branch spoke of dying, old age and peace. The young, vibrant, supple ones emitted high pitched whispers, restless, nervous exuberance. The insects busy, determined and, underlying everything, life in all its forms—creatures being born, dying, sad and happy. A dying cockroach lying on his back, immobile save for the one wing nervously fluttering and the pathetic clawing of his legs. I looked only at the cockroach and saw death, yet the ants around him saw food. My eye then took in the whole scene and saw only life.

The seven days spent with Baba might well have been seven years. Everything slowed down and it seemed I had been there all my life. Yet one day I left.

I had walked for four hours when it occurred to me that my leaving might have been a mistake. It was for no particular reason that I had left. The morning was cool and soothing, there was the reassuring presence of the river on my left. I strolled, aimlessly involved in the song of the birds and the changing scenery of the jungle around me.

I had not deliberated about leaving: one moment I was looking for fruit, the next moment I was leaving.

There seemed to be no need to say good-bye and the idea never entered my mind. I was leaving and now I was four hours under way before I had second thoughts. Would it have been better to stay, was there not much to learn? Had I accomplished anything by staying there? Ought I not to have discovered more about the little Baba and his way of life?

To turn back would require a thought-out decision, a decision to stay. I was walking in the opposite direction, away from decisions.

38

Father Maryan

'If you want to know you will have to learn how not to think.'

This Indian-sounding statement startled me. It was not the sort of statement I expected from Father Maryan—but then I really knew very little of what to expect from him.

I had been back in Puri for five days. It was late in the afternoon and we were sitting in the shade of a bamboo-covered terrace. Father Maryan was still in his white robe as the service had only just ended; I wore a *sarong* and a T-shirt.

We were drinking tea—not sweet milky Anglo-Indian tea, but the tea I grew up on. Served in tall glasses, the pale yellow liquid tasted of cinnamon. A cube of brown sugar added just the right amount of sweetness to cover the acidity of the juice of the whole lemon.

Meagre by European standards the meal appeared to me luxurious. The sturdy table was covered with clean white linen and bore a bowl of Polish biscuits and a single flower in a vase.

Relaxed, cross-legged in the straw easy chair, I luxuriated in the soothing sight—the green lawn, the clean walls, clean teapot, clean face of the good-natured priest.

Father Maryan began to speak, 'Yes, all thought, all philosophy, all is vanity. The mystery of God, the mystery of truth are all beyond words. Call it feeling, call it intuition or faith; those who have known it understand it but those who don't—oh well!'

He lifted his clean hand and held it indeterminately in mid-air. 'But you have not come here to talk about religion have you? Well, never mind, you do not have to humour me. It's good to have your company and hear you talk of your experience of India, of a kind which is, of course, denied to me.'

I had met Father Maryan several days previously.

Having walked from the *Sadhu's* home to the small hamlet of Kotanjal, I tried to find out about buses to Puri. There was no kind of public transport out of Kotanjal but I was told that the priest from

Puri made regular visits in a parish Land Rover and was due to come soon.

I took to him quickly. Being Polish he could speak to me in Croatian, and was of course close to me culturally and, in some ways, emotionally, but it was for the simplicity, and good-heartedness of that energetic man that I liked him most. Devoid of priestly haughtiness or assumed holiness, he radiated warmth and generosity.

I first saw him as he was washing and dressing the sores of the cholera-stricken victims among the outcasts who lived in a cave near the village. The fact that I was afraid to help him did not seem to upset him. After I had voiced the opinion that I considered Christian missionary work to be cultural imperialism, Father Maryan stopped asking me for help. Nevertheless, my comments made no difference to our relationship. Without having to discuss God or religion we shared so many common interests that we had no lack of subjects to discuss.

It took three days to drive to Puri. Father Maryan had to make many detours and stops in the course of his work. In spite of the greasy, battered Land Rover and the marshy roads, it was a pleasant trip.

We spoke of the food we missed, of music, opera, ballet. Sometimes waiting for the tide to recede in order to cross a river, we played cards—'Snap' or 'Black Peter' and other games remembered from my childhood. Occasionally, when tired or in a bad mood, I would reel off my grievances against dogmatic religion and priesthood, missionaries, neo-colonialism and so on. After the first two days I gave up, partly because the man took everything so good-naturedly that I felt silly, and partly because there were more interesting things to talk about.

Since our arrival in Puri I had visited Father Maryan frequently. I usually came at about four, while the Mass was going on. I would then browse through Father Maryan's library, leafing through books and magazines, and feel as if I were back at home.

By the time the service was finished the housekeeper would already have brought out the tea and there was always clean European food set for me. I had begun to enjoy these little delicacies very much.

That afternoon I was particularly anxious to talk to Father Maryan as I had found out that he knew Georg. Having led the conversation to the subject of philosophy, I casually indicated an interest in meeting Georg. Rather than answer me directly, Father Maryan began a monologue about the futility of philosophy. It was a contrast to our usual conversation, which dealt with philosophy as a serious subject.

'Well,' Father Maryan continued; 'I suppose you are startled to hear me speak this way, but I well remember your conversation on our way back from Kotanjal. Didn't you say that the happiest days you have spent in India were the thought-free days of your visit to the *sadhu*? Did you not, yourself, say that thought wearied you, and left you dry, empty and depressed?' Yet he said he could arrange for me to meet Georg.

*　　*　　*

Meeting with Georg was a disappointment but then Georg began by telling me that talking to him was going to be a disappointment.

He was a small, jovial-looking man. There was nothing particularly striking about him except for his eyes which somehow seemed slow, tranquil and serene, or perhaps only tired.

The meeting had not been arranged. It was not possible for me to visit Georg at his dwelling at the *Ashram* since no outsiders were ever allowed in.

That afternoon I was sitting in the garden as usual, waiting for the Mass to finish and Father Maryan to join me. There was a man sitting at the table already. He was an undistinguished looking fellow. Indeed I had seen him at Father Maryan's several times before and had even spoken to him without having been introduced. As Father Maryan appeared he simply stated, 'This is Georg.'

The man smiled and nodded. I did not even have a chance to be surprised—the situation was so ordinary and normal that it inhibited any excitement. Georg himself was absorbed in tasting the Polish cookies and seemed to derive much pleasure from the simple tea.

He spoke absent-mindedly. It was hard to follow what he said for he would comment on the taste of the tea with the same seriousness (or lack of it) with which he would talk about the meaning of life. To me he appeared somewhat senile, perhaps even imbecile. His talk was spiced with riddles.

'Everybody is so busy looking for a meaning to life, nobody has time to find it.'

He spoke of the futility of philosophy as a guide to life. Wisdom, he said, is knowing what do, knowing how to live, it is not the skill to juggle words. For some reason he became serious. He looked at me and there was a spark of enthusiasm, warmth, perhaps even love, in his eyes.

'I am sorry, if I sound supercilious or negative to you. I assume you wanted to see me in order to learn from me, but I doubt whether anything worth communicating can be communicated—verbally that is.'

I was somewhat frustrated and disappointed. As he was about to leave I ran after him and asked if he could arrange for me to learn meditation with somebody he deemed serious. Georg said he would gladly find someone, but he could not guarantee that the man would be serious. He was not even sure of himself he said, and left.

I was rather surprised with my sudden decision to learn yoga. But it seemed a unique opportunity.

39

The Ashram

The Ramakrishna Mission headquarters in Puri are housed in a large and well built colonial-style house. Untypically of India the gates are oiled, the latches work and the patio is clean.

I was taken up to the *Swami* by two novices in clean clothes. As we walked through a well-stocked library I caught a glimpse of the whole group of young novices. Looking rather alike, with shaven heads and clean orange robes, they seemed busy and hard-working. There was something un-Indian in their firm handshakes and decisive movements. Given a normal Indian library one expected to see men sleeping or squatting, lying, elbows on tables, scratching, yawning, coughing and behaving the way many Indians behave. This group reminded one more of a business school library than a school of meditative monks.

Swami Sivananda was a quick, energetic man looking more like a leader and administrator than a monk. He told me that he was not a great believer in *yoga* and meditation as a solution for Europeans and their moral and psychological problems. Indeed he had very little good to say for the famous Westerners who have traditionally represented Hindu thought in the West: melancholics, he called them. Schopenhauer, Hermann Hesse, the hippies, and today's do-it-yourself salvationists—they were all melancholics, he kept repeating. The object of yoga was not to deny life and joy. The trouble, he went on to explain, was that there are subtle sociological and psychological differences between the Westerner and Easterner. The symbols and concepts as well as the breathing and other techniques in *yoga* were developed around the Indian body and mind, dependent on Indian climate, and food, etc. These can of course be modified for the Westerner, but one has to be sensible, reasonable and patient. In principle, he was against the admission of Westerners into the *Ashram*, but in view of Georg's recommendation, he'd allow me to join an *Ashram* of a related order, provided that I promised to observe good taste and discretion should I find other people doing things that I disapproved of. In short, he told me not to criticise loudly and to keep my ideas to myself. To this I agreed.

*　*　*

The *Ashram* lay on the quiet, western side of Puri. It was surrounded by a cluster of other *Ashrams*, and thus isolated from outside noise. Enclosed by a thick ten-foot-high concrete wall, a huge garden offered complete solitude and peace.

It was a strange feeling entering the *Ashram* for the first time. I was in the town—a quiet part, yet still the town. I faced the large wall but did not sense the atmosphere beyond the walls. A small narrow door opened. I entered a tiny enclosed courtyard, a garden within a garden. This served as a kind of decompression chamber. Surrounded by the high walls I inspected the cubicle of space, concrete floor, concrete walls, not a plant or a flower, just a wooden bench and the blue patch of sky above. A few minutes later a feeling of relaxed peace descended. All thoughts of the town faded. Then a zig-zag passage and I entered a Garden of Eden.

I saw a luxuriant lush expanse, a sea of flowers with heavy aromatic scents, a kaleidoscope of colour. Clusters of bougainvillea, dahlias and chrysanthemums looked like low-lying green and lilac clouds. Marigolds and cannas swayed gently in the breeze, my mind itself absorbed in the silent dance.

The noises were few yet distinct—the hum of a bumble bee, the occasional cry of a bird, the murmur of the water trickling down a tiny waterfall. There was no building in sight. The *Ashram* seemed to be a garden.

My escort placed his palms together in prayer-like motion, bowed to me and left. There seemed nothing to do, so I sat on a stone and waited.

Half an hour later a half-naked Brahmin motioned me to follow him. He never spoke, so I followed him, treating him with silent respect. Actually, the Brahmin was a deaf and dumb kind of idiot who served as a cook and odd-job man. It took me about an hour before I figured that out and found somebody responsible.

Having been given a meal of milk and fruit, I was shown to the showers. My clothes and possessions were taken away and on emerging from the shower I found a clean soft white robe. This pleased me. I thought of Plato writing how a thinker should always wear loose, comfortable clothes and never cover his head or wear anything on his feet but sandals. I was then taken up to a man they called the Manager. He had a face typical of a certain type of high-class Brahmin: a bird-of-prey profile, high proud forehead, sharp penetrating eyes, an arrogant air. His beak-like nose was slightly screwed up as if offended by an unpleasant smell; his fleshy lips suggested avarice, yet he kept them pursed, making them seem thin and contemptuous. He explained to me the rules of the house. Up before sunrise, no smoking, no tea, coffee or other intoxicants, food to be restricted to fruits, nuts, roots and milk. Otherwise there were no rules or duties. The house routine was two hours' meditation at sunrise, an hour at noon, two hours at sunset—a discussion class between five and seven and the night *Puja*. One was free to engage or not to engage in all or none of this. He told me that I was not to start with my lessons until I had lived there at least two weeks and had shown myself suitable. So he concluded and took me to my room.

It was a small, whitewashed cell, containing a bare wooden bed, with a mosquito net over it, a table, a bench, a jug of water and a thick candle. I settled down to the austere life.

For the first few days I drank large quantities of milk and yoghourt, and gorged myself on cheese, nuts, dates, dried figs, and honey. 'God's gifts to man.' Nobody held it against me, indeed nobody checked to see how much food each consumes. There were no set meals: milk, honey and nuts are kept in the kitchen, and anybody was free to walk in and help himself at will. Fruit, roots and nuts grew in the garden. They were so full of protein and energy, that one could almost ignore the raisins, honey, yoghurt and cheese.

I did not go hungry at all. One can hardly imagine the quantity of fruit and nut variety. Of course, that sort of a diet is readily available and cheap only in India. I asked the Manager what sort of food God intended for Eskimos, to which he replied that nobody is meant to live in uncongenial places. The Eskimos, he said, should go back to China. Overpopulation and the corresponding problems that came with it is man's doing, not God's.

There is no doubt that this diet has a unique effect. The usual Indian vegetarian diet with its emphasis on floury, greasy pancakes and spices is a burden on the stomach and consequently on the mind. This diet only confirmed what I heard from Mr Singh about Indian diversity. Greasy, starchy, spicy food is typical of only part of India— the opposite diet is equally typical for another part.

After a week of this diet the complexion clears and tightens to give the skin new radiant freshness, the eyes widen, pouches and blood lines disappear. The hair thickens, and increases in richness and colour. Headaches, tension, nervousness disappear. It is hard of course, to pin-point how much these changes have to do with food and how much with the luxuriant relaxed atmosphere of the garden, regular, uninterrupted sleep and lack of concern for the outside world.

There were about a dozen men in the Ashram apart from the Manager, the cook and the servants. Most of them were Bengalis; fine-featured, delicate men. They spoke softly and moved with grace. All seemed in good health but were characterised by a certain lack of energy and vitality. Two of them were different from the rest.

First there was Sivaram, a small supple-bodied man who moved with the ease and grace of a leopard. In many ways he reminded me of the forest Baba—there was something animal, something too sensual in his movements. For some reason I felt a repugnance for the man yet I was ashamed to feel it. He had something reptilian, yet not in a dangerous or poisonous sense. It was more the way he came and went, unseen, completely at ease. I could not imagine that he had any thoughts and ideas. He lived like an animal born to meditate, to take walks, bask in the sun and eat. His face radiated peace, satisfaction and love. He seemed to love everything and everyone, always ready to oblige, kind and gentle. In many ways he was a child. A cross look from the Manager was enough to make this fifty-year-old man cry. Even the unkind looks that I sometimes, unwittingly, gave him seemed to upset him.

Then there was Chitta Baba. I liked him very much. He was a maths Professor, and retreated into the *Ashram* regularly. He, too, had a kind and gentle face but there was nothing animal or reptilian about it. He was rather large and physically clumsy. He worked hard at his job and was proud of his wife and children, whose photos he often showed me. I spent many hours talking to him, and he lent me several books dealing with *yoga*, Indian religion and philosophy. We discussed many topics together—war, socialism, friendship, loyalty. The man was Indian through and through and had a passionate love for his land and spoke of its customs, history and tradition in such warm and glowing terms that he transmitted his enthusiasm to me. I was a good listener. I felt that regardless of one's background or preconceived ideas about India, no one could fail to develop a great appreciation for Indian culture, and my love at first sight for India had by that time matured and taken roots.

40

Santhana

One week after my arrival I still had not taken part in any activities and had not been invited to join in the meditation. Much to my surprise, I was told that before my practical instruction began I was to be prepared theoretically by Georg who had decided to undertake the task himself.

Our first discussion took place on the eighth day of my stay in the *Ashram*.

It was sometime after sunset. Georg had just come out of the meditation room; his eyes were swimming, hazy and diffused, but his mind was clear. We sat down on the stone steps leading down to the sanctuary. The night was cool and pleasant and George spoke for a long time. I rarely interrupted, but simply relaxed and listened to his long discourse.

He spoke about what he called *Santhana Dharma*—the philosophy beyond philosophy he called it, the unchanging eternal message which can never be verbalised. It was instituted some thousands of years ago, he said, by the writers of the *Upanishads*, was carried across Asia to reach the shores of Greece, and entered into the spirit carried by Plato's hidden doctrines and the Academy; finally it took material form in the Middle East, was frozen into dogma by Augustine, and was imperfectly continued through Aquinas. Today it is the sentiment behind the ideology of liberation, yet it is widely misunderstood, for it is believed that technology or social engineering can solve the problems of our human condition.

At other times Georg was always guarded, spoke in riddles and broken disconnected sentences. Yet tonight he was relaxed and peaceful; he narrated his thoughts—simply and continuously. Listening to him was easy, like hearing a story.

He spoke about life being a struggle between two sentiments, the real and the unreal, the pure and the mixed. The real sentiments, he said, were love, happiness, elation, pity, compassion, joy, sorrow; and their opposites were lust, pleasure, anger, anxiety, arrogance and similar. I was surprised to see him combine happiness and sorrow and call them one and the same and altogether different from pleasure and anxiety. Should not happiness and pleasure be grouped together I asked, for were they not both good and opposed to anxiety and sorrow which are bad.

But no, quite definitely not, Georg was to argue. Sorrow and happiness are both equally good and necessary, he said, whereas lustful pleasure and anxiety were two sides of the same sentiment, both equally evil and altogether wrong.

I could to some extent understand what he was saying, for I remembered the moments of intense happiness being so similar to sadness, so I did not contest his argument.

As it grew darker and peace spread over the garden, Georg went on to speak of the great teachers. 'All were simply incarnations of the *Santhana* sentiment—the eternal unchanging *logos*,' he said. It was for that reason, he explained, that no great teacher leaves behind him a dogma or a formula. No, he argued, all they leave behind them is a sentiment around which various ideologies, communities and institutions materialise. I found myself agreeing with most of what he was saying, but not with everything. I could not tell whether I was holding back through dissent or through misunderstanding. Nevertheless I kept quiet and listened as he went on to argue that around one and the same sentiment, hostile and incompatible ideologies were just as likely to materialise as compatible ideas can crystallise around incompatible sentiments. To accept an idea, he said, does not mean to accept the physical personality of the leading protagonist or the philosophy as elaborated—it means to accept the underlying message. To accept Christ did not not mean to accept the name of Christ or Christ's written message, but the sentiment of Christ, even if one called it something else. So it is with any message or idea, he explained —all there is fixed is the *Santhana* element, eternal and unchanging. Plato called it *logos*: the word, vibration and idea that pervades all reality.

It is this duty to be what you are that Leibnitz called *Philosophia Perennis*, and Spinoza, *Veritas Eterna*. But for all verbalisations and philosophy aside, Georg was to conclude that in practice *Santhana* is summed up by saying that to live means to create good sentiments and avoid bad ones. This was his final formula.

For the next two weeks we met practically every day and spoke and argued for hours on end. Often I'd get tired of conversation and I'd get up impatiently and would leave Georg to walk around the garden.

Unlike the conversation, the garden was so alive it inspired a longing for and appreciation of the beautiful and sensuous. At night its heavy scents and soft contours were particularly pronounced. The sensuousness of the setting was enhanced by the sound of the *mantras* carried on the wind from nearby Radir *Ashram*.

Two weeks of conversations passed and we were again at the beginning.

Our conversations were going around in circles, then finally one evening just before sunset in the middle of a dialogue about essence, I could no longer contain myself. I interrupted Georg and said excitedly:

'Can you ever stop just repeating yourself saying the same thing over and over again? All you've managed to tell me was that the only wisdom is the practical wisdom of knowing what one needs and what one should do, and thus living the good and avoiding the bad sentiments—and we started this whole series of discussions by observing that such was the case!'

In an angry voice, almost shouting, I told him that the question was not 'what' but 'how': 'How does one know what one needs? How does one know what to do? Just tell me, simply tell me. How?' I looked up at him and met his serious, relaxed gaze.

His silence was the answer and I stopped talking, suddenly realising the absurdity of my question. By that time it was already getting dark so we just sat in silence as the sensuous Puri night slowly began to embrace us. Time slowed down and after a while I got up to leave, but Georg stretched out his hand and held me back, motioning me to sit. I wondered why I sat next to him—but I did so just the same.

A while later I had a feeling as if Georg had been telling me something—as if there were communication between us. I looked at him but he seemed distant and absorbed. I closed my eyes and felt the life of the garden again.

*   *   *

I found it particularly difficult to sleep that night. The unanswered question raged on. I lay with my eyes closed, brain working furiously, questing, analysing. As usual I lay flat and exhausted under the mosquito net on my barren bed, candle flickering, watching the moths, shadows on the ceiling, yet that night I finally found a temporary release.

I felt myself falling into some kind of mindless stupor, then as I lay there I felt a sudden urge to record what I had been talking about with Georg, to organise it. I got up, found a pen, drew up a chair and began to write, oblivious to the aggressive mosquitos, forgetting to wrap myself with the net. I must have been writing for the best part of the night, for when I woke up the next day I found some fifty handwritten pages scattered all around. It was late as I slipped out of bed. I was about to walk out and to join the *Puja* when my eyes fell on the scattered pages again. I decided to glance quickly through a few of the pages before going out, so I sat down and began to read. I glanced at the first sentence, which read, 'Nothing is good or bad in itself.' I recognised the old cliché and assumed that the rest of the text would be of the same quality. I would have left now, but when

I read to the end of the first page with some sort of concentration, I suddenly felt some hidden attraction to the text I had written, which kept me glued to my chair. Afterwards, when I had looked at the text objectively and analytically, I could not find one sentence that I had not heard before, that I had not at some time thought or heard others speak. Yet at that time, I found the text startling. Having read it once, I broke up the text so as to analyse it sentence by sentence, yet the meaning was suddenly lost—it died. I read the text over and over again and it meant nothing any more.

The text consisted for the most part of incoherent assertions, with occasionally a complicated sentence like this: 'Being itself is a second derivative of becoming, which itself is a function $\frac{dy}{dx}$ of existing. Man has no existence, for to exist is to be scattered as potentiality. Man really is only as a non-existing locus, a function outlined by the curve drawn through all the points, the rare instances when a particular man has functioned in harmony to the *logos*, the deeper reality'. The first time I read that text, these incoherent sentences were somehow attuned to my mood to create a message—yet without the wider context it was lost. The more I struggled to grasp the context again, the more frustrated I became. I realised that the task was futile, at least given my present mood and circumstances. Having made a last attempt to read the sentences, this time backwards, I finally gave up, put the papers away and walked out into the sunshine.

That day I resolved to talk no more of philosophy, no more to read or think. I told Georg about my resolution and he smiled and agreed and said I was progressing—and so I was. I spent the day working around the *Ashram*, repairing the furniture, digging the garden.

That night a wonderful and untroubled sleep finally came.

41

The Lotus

I had been in the *Ashram* for three weeks when *Swami* Bramananda finally appeared. I was exercising in the garden when the Manager told me that there was somebody in the meditation room whom I should see. It was noon and I was hot and sweaty so I took a quick shower, changed into a clean robe and left for the meditation room.

There were several new faces there, all dressed in long orange robes and wearing the traditional garland around their necks. A bird-like man was talking in a high, even, voice. As the men came from different parts of the country they spoke English. The bird-like man was explaining a sentence in the *Gita*.

Bramananda was not singled out by a prominent position yet I, who had never seen him, immediately recognised the leader. It was not his voice, movement, or posture, yet somehow he stood out in a striking manner. His appearance would have commanded immediate attention anywhere. Tall and erect, he reminded one of a Greek statue. His features, large, and clear-cut, were charged with expression. A pair of big, warm, intelligent and perceptive eyes were topped by neat black eyebrows. He had one of the noblest faces I had seen. His hair was jet black, his complexion was such that he could have come from a European country. Yet he did not look like any European I had ever seen. Indeed, by looking at him I realised something about Europeans I had not been aware of. His face was that of a *relaxed* European, which made one realise how tense European faces are.

He had shoulder-length hair, which he brushed neatly away from his high philosopher's forehead. Were it not for the white in his beard, one might have assumed him to be in his forties; as it was, I judged him to be in his late fifties. Actually, he was over eighty. A permanent smile hovered on his face although there was an air of authority about him. He did not address me until the other man had finished, but meanwhile the large piercing eyes fixed themselves on me.

'You are too tired and thirsty to think. Sit down. Anand, bring our young visitor some water.'

The voice was soft, a Bengali voice, rather out of keeping with his impressive appearance. I expected his voice to match the powerful face and body, yet it was soft, lilting, rather effeminate, I thought.

The water arrived, I was extremely thirsty. I had forgotten to drink after the exercise, so I drank one large glass and a second was brought.

'Now, tell us why it is that you do not agree with Arjuna's answer?'

My mind raced. Could he read my thoughts? How did he know of my being familiar with this passage in the *Bhagavad Gita* and the fact that I disagreed with that particular answer? Probably my facial expression betrayed me. Or could he read my thoughts? No, I rejected the possibility. Still, I was impressed. I stated my case.

The expression in the black eyes was blank. There was no agreement or disagreement in them. The same question was put to the Brahmin next to me. He quoted much Sanskrit and was rather boring. After three or four interpretations Bramananda finally lifted his hand. His gestures were rather over-dramatic, I thought.

'And what does Bramananda think?' The soft voice filled the room.

His gesture, manner of speech and reference to himself in the third person struck me as rather conceited—not that I would have judged anybody else as severely. This man, however, was meant to be a saint, even a god incarnate to some. He looked the part all right, but his speech, as well as its content, seemed on a lower level.

Bramananda finally delivered his interpretation. In spite of the build-up, this interpretation did not strike me as obviously more enlightened. Despite a certain disappointment to me there was still something compelling about the man. It was as if we shared some hidden understanding or friendship, invisible to the others. I had no doubt that he would immediately accept me and teach me.

I was correct in this assumption. Over the next few weeks Bramananda's time was at my disposal. At times it was quite embarrassing. The people in the Ashram longed for a glance, or a word, from their guru, in the way that an impassioned lover longs for a glance from his loved one.

During various festivals many people from outside came into the Ashram. On these occasions I walked next to him and I could picture what it was like to walk around with Jesus, surrounded by adoring eyes and people prostrating themselves, kissing Bramananda's feet, throwing flowers and garlands and money. The guru walked as if in a dream, unconcerned, talking to me as if the people around him did not exist.

I felt guilty that I, who did not believe in Bramananda's divinity, should have such easy access to him, whereas these fervent believers had to be content with a mere glance or a scrap of the earth he trod.

I asked Bramananda, 'Why do you allow these people to worship you as if you were a god, when you tell me that you are not a god?'

'I am not a god to you, but I may be to them,' he said. 'Listen, I feel that you seldom agree with my religion or my teaching. So why ask me questions? I do not care for words. Philosophy to me is mere vomiting. I talk about the *Gita* for this is what people expect of me. If you want to talk about *yoga* and the *Gita*, you have Georg to talk to. There are many philosophers apart from Georg. You can meet countless others if you like. I will not stay here much longer. What I have to teach you is not verbal. Let us not discuss any more. Come and see me in the meditation room tomorrow morning at five.'

*   *   *

The next morning my *yoga* instruction finally began. We were alone in the meditation room. Bramananda dismissed the usual Indian pre-meditation routine. He did, however, take the tiger rugs on which we were to sit.

'It is necessary for insulation,' he said. 'Before we start you will have to swear ceremonially that you will never disclose the methods and techniques that I will be teaching you over these coming months. You realise,' he continued, 'that the oath is only for the protection of the people you may talk to. The techniques are highly evolved and allowing you to talk about them is more dangerous than letting an unqualified doctor or butcher practise brain surgery.'

I had heard this argument before and had assumed that behind it there was often the simple desire of the *gurus* to keep control over *yoga*. Yet Bramananda's concern seemed genuine.

I said I would take no oaths, but I would give him my word that I would not disclose any techniques that he might judge unsuitable for discussion. With this he was satisfied.

The exercises which he would teach me in the next four weeks were not really *yoga* but preparation for *yoga*. 'After these four weeks,' he said, 'or when I judge you ready, I will awake in you the dormant *Kundalini* power.' Only then would he teach me the spinal movements, special breathing exercises and the *Kundalini asanas*.

To teach me any of these *yoga* techniques now would damage my health. Through exercise and *asanas* shown to me by Chitta Baba I had learned to sit still in a fixed posture, and had achieved some degree of concentration. For the next month, I was to learn how to regard myself as an observer.

Bramananda drew himself close to me and crossed his legs. '*Yoga*, as you know, is purification,' he said. 'In our hearts there is murder, greed, fear and avarice. These thoughts are enclosed in a small container and we never open it, for its foul smell would horrify us. So it is tucked away, repressed, yet the container is steadily leaking, constantly poisoning our mind and body. Like cleaning a dirty ink-well, we have to clean the heart by pouring in clean water, but as you pour clean water into a dirty ink-well, what happens? The dirt which was hidden and stored and invisible now turns the clean water blue. The ink-well overflows. You feel it would have been better never to have begun the cleaning. Yet this is not so; you have to keep pouring in the clean water and watch the dirty water come out—eventually the water will turn clear.

'Before you begin to do that, you must learn to dissociate your self from your mind. Otherwise, the sight of all the dirt we carry in our hearts would be too shocking.

'So this is what you will learn. Are you ready?'

'Yes, I am,' I said. I got up, stretched my legs, and sat down again on the tiger rug. Bramananda closed the wooden shades shutting out the light. His soft voice spoke, through the darkness.

'Close your eyes.'

I did so.

'Let your thoughts drift, do not check them. Watch them drift.'

I nodded and tried to do that. Yet thoughts filled my mind, making it impossible for me to relax. Bramananda seemed aware of my difficulties and sat waiting patiently in silence. As my mind finally calmed, Bramananda spoke again.

'What is it you are watching now?' the voice was still soft.

I answered, 'An ocean.'

'Excellent,' Bramananda said. 'The ocean is a trigger which will affect your passage into higher consciousness. Every symbol can act as a trigger, but men are usually aware of few of them if any. Later I will give you a trigger word, but now we can finally begin. So see the ocean again. Affirm mentally that your mind is the ocean, let your mind become an ocean.'

A few minutes passed. I said, 'My mind is the ocean.'

The soft voice spoke; 'Your mind is the ocean, but you are not the ocean. Think: I am not the mind, I am not the body, I am not the ocean. I am the witness, I watch my mind become an ocean, I watch my mind turn red and blue. Repeat. I am not the mind . . .'

I let my mind run through these courses. We practised together,

214

visualising colours and shapes, and then Bramananda said that was enough.

The next week Bramananda said he would try to teach me to share the thought vibrations transmitted by himself. He explained.

'Look at it this way. After tuning a stringed instrument to a particular pitch, strike the corresponding note on the piano and what happens? This, and only this note on the piano will cause the stringed instrument to vibrate. As you know, the air is full of radio waves which can be picked up by tuning into a particular radio frequency and heard as sounds. The atmosphere is also full of thought vibrations, emitted by all the living and the dead. The thought vibrations of Buddha, Christ, Mohammed, Krishna, and all the prophets are in the atmosphere and so are those of others. We have to be particularly careful to contact the positive and avoid the negative thought vibrations.

'I do not mean to say that the thought vibrations of Buddha have some kind of magical existence, I mean simply that his ideas are written in books, which are read by living people. By reading these books and communicating with Buddhists you can cultivate the background to this Buddhist consciousness. Buddha's thoughts, his sentiment, his rhythm can become alive in you. Generally,' he said, 'there are seven types of consciousness that we can resurrect. This is enough, for the most important frequencies can be received through those seven channels. The thoughts of Krishna and Jesus are emitted on the fifth and seventh pitch or frequency respectively.'

The switches used to tune us into any of those channels are engaged by visualising them as lotuses. So I would have to learn to visualise the lotus.

The visualisation of the lotus took many weeks of practice. Eventually, Bramananda had taught me to visualise these lotuses in different parts of the spine and head.

He called these centres *chakras*: there are seven and they correspond to the seven channels of the transmission of consciousness.

'You say that the object of meditation is to empty the mind of thought, yet I work hard thinking, training my mind to visualise these symbols. What is the object of that?' I asked.

Bramananda answered: 'It is like dusting the room. There is dust everywhere and if we tried to remove it by lifting individual dust particles we could never succeed. So we sweep it all into a dustpan and can then throw it away in one single container. It is the same with thoughts: they are scattered, hundreds of thoughts are flashing and racing around your brain, all at the same time. You focus all your thoughts on a single symbol—it takes much concentration to visualise it clearly. You have no energy to see anything else. All your thoughts gather around that symbol—say a lotus. In that moment when you succeed in focusing your thoughts you can blank out the symbol, leaving your mind empty and receptive to non-thinking perception.' I had much trouble with lotuses—only the ocean always came easily.

*　　*　　*

The days became weeks and a month passed.

I had mastered the discipline of sitting still in many *asana* postures. I had learned to empty my mind and concentrate on one particular symbol, and the process of learning the higher techniques of *Prana-yama, Kundalini-Yoga*, had begun. I used no *mantras* and skipped the introductory rituals. In many ways I was an obstinate and diffi-cult pupil, time and time again refusing to use a particular symbol or to go through a particular movement. Given any other teacher, I would long ago have been asked to leave for I often held up everybody present. Yet Bramananda put up with it. He was determined to teach me and spent an ever-increasing number of hours using all his powers to convey a particular image or a symbol to me.

It was at the beginning of the third month that he attempted the first reaction that might be understood as supernatural. We had been working for two hours. The sun had already risen, but the meditation room was still cool and pleasant.

'Do you still feel fresh?' Bramananda asked.

'Yes, I do.'

'You said once that you attended a tantric initiation where a Yogi projected light out of himself, yet you did not see it. Would you like me to materialise a ball of fire for you?'

It was amusing to hear the serious Bramananda talk of such things. I was intrigued. 'Yes,' I said. 'It would be interesting.'

Bramananda positioned himself and closed his eyes in meditation.

'Start the *Hamsa* technique,' he said.

I did so and kept it up for ten minutes.

'Feel the radiant warmth in your spine and execute the seven *Mahamudras*,' Bramananda's voice commanded.

Having done that, we both passed into *Parabasta*. After twenty minutes of silence Bramananda started to breathe extremely loudly and heavily.

'When you open your eyes you will see the divine bluish white light radiating all over my body.'

I did so.

'Now open your eyes. What do you see?'

It seemed to break Bramananda's heart but I saw nothing unusual. In the dark room his body appeared as a shadow, and I said so.

'But do you not see the bluish white light?'

'No.'

Bramananda increased his concentration and asked me to do a series of *Jyoti Mudras*. His breathing became louder still. I still could not see any light.

We finished the session by easing off and slowly recovering. This was the only time Bramananda ever tried to demonstrate the supernatural to me. I never really came to appreciate the actual act of meditating. After two months I learned how to meditate without effort or strain. It was neither particularly pleasant nor unpleasant. Still I meditated three times a day. It was the feeling afterwards that made the effort worthwhile.

With my body extremely perceptive, and purified through regular deep sleep and the absence of tea and coffee, meditation brought my senses to a razor-sharp pitch.

The day after Bramananda spent four hours trying to make me see a light I walked out, my senses eager. I remember that day well. It was almost noon as we finished. I felt a lull come over me; the bird-song quietened and nature seemed to collect itself, relax and repose. I could feel the drowsiness of the reptiles: they slowed down, their blood hardly circulating. It seemed as if wires were passed out on my body and plugged into the birds, the earth, the insects. I realised the converse experience to that which I had been going through— the heavy, sterile emptiness of a body separated from the earth, nature and life. Here the body and the mind were being charged with life, desire, joy, as if the birds, flowers and the bees were offering their energy, their *joie de vivre* to anybody willing to take it.

I would stretch out my hands and feel the warmth of the blood circulating in them. Meditation was meant to make one realise that one is not the body—yet it really made me know that one *is* the body. Soul, it seemed, was the body. Listening, hearing, touching became so powerful, so vivid. Colours rushed through my head, making me dizzy.

I tried to put into words this sensual experience, yet it was not easy. It was as if the sounds had colours and colours had texture. The red was prickly and sharp and uneven, the violet, smooth and languid. Flowers, trees, big and small, merged into each other. It was hard to differentiate between my body and the rest of nature. I tried to understand what is meant by saying, 'I am not the body'. Concentrate mentally and one really becomes the body. Perhaps it meant that one gives up the idea of seeing oneself as a separate body—for after meditation I really felt as if I were materially a part of the sounds and shapes around me.

I wondered whether I would recommend meditation to my friends. Yes, but with caution. What Bramananda told me was true, so many techniques and symbols were unsuitable to European minds that it was no wonder people become affected in all kinds of ways.

Bramananda, as a teacher, was among few patient enough and willing to adopt the exercises to suit one's individual physique. Besides, he was a friend of Georg, who asked him to modify his techniques as much as he could to suit my physiology. Bramananda had told me that he had already taught eight Europeans and was not satisfied by all the results. Some could see the lights and hear the *Aum* and experience what might be called the occult. They were very proud of their achievement, yet Bramananda said the unexpected happened—they became melancholic, slow and dreamy while claiming to be happy.

Having failed to produce the light, Bramananda tried to make me hear the *Aum* sound. We both tried hard. I could imagine the sound but I knew it was only a product of my fancy. None of the *Swami's* heavy breathing and concentration helped.

After this, Bramananda advised me to take up austerities. I was asked to discipline my body, to sit motionless for four hours a day, with two-hour intervals and to do it for two weeks. I was willing to do almost anything unless it contradicted something I felt strongly about. I agreed to austerities. The sitting-still part was hard, the joints would burn with pain and for short periods I would feel unable to walk. After a week the muscles relaxed, the pain was endurable.

Fasting was never a problem. Controlling appetite was the easiest. For two more weeks I went through other austerities—standing in the heat of the sun, maintaining difficult postures. I did all that willingly day after day, gradually getting weaker.

The fourth month in the *Ashram* was hard going. I had lost fifteen pounds in weight and my sleep was becoming irregular. Bramananda tried to teach me new techniques, but they all involved some relation to Kali, Siva and other deities, which I associated with evil. The *Swami* himself told me not to do anything that would be emotionally disturbing. There were also *asanas* which appeared undignified and unaesthetic. Of course this was often just part of the cultural conditioning by the background that I came from—but Georg said one need not deny it or destroy it and I agreed.

Slowly my progress came to a stop. Unless something in me changed, there would be very little Bramananda could teach me.

As I had subjected myself to much hunger and strain my mind was becoming incapable of concentrating on excessive meditation. My body longed for action. I wondered whether I had found myself, achieved whatever it was I was looking for. The answer was 'No'.

Towards the end of my fourth month I was suffering insomnia. Often I would stay awake the whole night, lying flat on my back on the bare wooden bed with the little candle flickering above me through the mosquito nets. I would watch the shadows of the mosquitos executing patterns on the ceiling.

The first week in January Bramananda told me to stop the austerities and give up my attempts, but I pressed on. Georg came and advised me to leave the *Ashram*.

The third week in January I stopped fasting, but by that time I found that I could not eat, and often threw up the food that I had consumed with so much effort.

I would not leave the *Ashram*—I felt the journey was incomplete, yet there was nowhere else to go. The *Ashram* seemed the final stage of my journey. What else was there to do? Go on to Burma, Nepal, climb the Himalayas? The answers were not coming. Whatever it was I wanted I was not achieving it, so I stayed.

42

The End of the Journey

It was my fifth month in the *Ashram* when I was suddenly taken ill.
I had been sitting in the garden talking to Chitta Baba when I began
to feel hot and dizzy. I remarked how intolerably hot it was to my
surprised companion. Unable to stand the unbearable heat that was
bathing my body I got up and walked towards the well, wishing to
splash myself with buckets of cold water. A few steps before the well,
I felt the earth start spinning. I felt a horrible nausea and started
swaying. My strength failed and I fell to the ground. I raised myself
on my knees but could not get up.

Inside my stomach a storm was raging—my body felt limp. I
wanted to throw up and free myself from my body which was twitch-
ing in convulsions. I felt a cold sweat break out on my forehead as
my hands started to go limp. My temperature changed rapidly from
burning hot to freezing cold so that my teeth were chattering.

I saw people's worried faces crowding around me and Georg gave
me a hand to lift me up. I grabbed it frantically somehow hoping that
he could stop the spinning. I squeezed his hand desperately.

I felt myself being carried outside the *Ashram* and laid on the
ground by the gate. Then came the sound of the ambulance and the
bespectacled face of a doctor in white.

I saw his worried look and heard him say, 'Malaria', and then he
was bending over me, a syringe in his hand, his face growing larger
and larger. I felt the drug spreading through my body, releasing me
slowly from the convulsions. As I sank into sleep, a voice kept saying something—but I was not concerned any more: the main thing
was that the convulsions were ceasing. 'Malaria ... so I've finally
been given my bill,' I thought, as I sank into a dream.

A day later I slowly came to. I recognised the smells and sounds
of a hospital but I could not open my eyes: the lids felt as if they
were glued together.

I tried to open them for a while but then gave up. It was wonderful just to lie there and not feel sick—just listening to the clock tick

away. After an hour or so I managed to open my eyes for a while but closed them again. I kept hearing a noise but could not tell what it was so I made myself deaf to it.

I heard a doctor come over, speaking softly. 'Let him lie,' he said to the nurse, 'he should not be woken up.'

I heard the footsteps going away and the door being closed. I was alone.

As I lay immobile I became aware of something stirring in me, about to emerge, I became aware of the sound—it had been there all the time loud and clear, yet until that moment I was completely deaf to it—the unceasing sound of the ocean, the roll of the surf: my trigger. The hospital must have been just by the ocean for the noise was so loud it seemed as if I were on the boat again. How could I have been so deaf to it? I had lived with this sound ever since I left Karachi almost a year ago. It was there on the boat, in my house in Puri, in the *Ashram*, yet here in the hospital I suddenly became intensely aware of it. I listened to it in a way I never could before. My mind, sharpened by months of concentration, focused on it; I caught the sound, dived into its essence and let it sink into my spine.

Never before had I been able to concentrate so well. I felt my body and consciousness dissolving, my mind becoming the ocean as my body evaporated, rising up into the sky, condensing into rain drops and falling down as rain merging into the ocean.

All became still as the awareness grew. Perception slowly crystallised; the answers finally came but in unexpected forms, taking shapes which I could never comprehend before, for I was always driven on, unable to say to the fleeting moment: 'Stop! This is it!'

I felt time dissolve—time almost tangible, time like a cellophane curtain separating events. Pictures flashed simultaneously in my head—Puri, Mauritius, Bangkok, Karachi, Zagreb, Csarda and further back into my childhood—further still dissolving into the ocean. The pictures flashed by yet amid perfect stillness. Even the ocean outside had become perfectly still. Nothing seemed to be changing yet there was a movement in the stillness, a stillness in the movement.

Again I felt the strain in Kandahar's muscles as we galloped across the steppe, his hooves hitting the frozen ground. I shivered in the cold as the raindrops hit *Project's* deck. I saw the twisted angry face of the young Thai baker swinging at me with a knife, and in the next moment heard Michelle's soft voice, singing late at night as the candle flickered in the big ochre house, then it all dissolved—I felt myself disappearing into the ocean.

Drifting far away and sinking deep. Around me were algae, coral, seaweed—I lay still on the sandy bottom, eyes wide open watching. Somewhere above me an enraged shark thrusting his teeth into a warm Dorado fish, tearing away its flesh, as it convulsively shook in its death dance, eyes staring frozen in a silent scream, gills turning blue.

A huge octopus sneaked carefully toward an unwary victim, watched by strange rosy-pink fish, indifferent as they peacefully grazed on the purple algae.

And up there through the glittering surface I watched myself on *Project*, silently unaware of being seen by myself. And then I saw myself by the Chagie River as the dogs chased the crocodile and the water turned red.

Slowly thought returns, but there are no questions, no quests— just a relaxed awareness and the ticking of the clock.

I suddenly become aware of my surroundings. I am in a big blue room, and not alone. Several floors above me there is a woman screaming in pain. Not far from me I see the earnest face of a young Indian girl, her hands writhing in silent agony as tears roll down her cheeks.

An old man in the corner is praying quietly.

I close my eyes and see the blue streak of the ocean again. There somewhere in the distance is the clear line of the horizon. Somewhere beyond that line lies Africa and further still Europe, tired old Europe.

Thousands of miles away in Zagreb it is early morning: the shops are opening, streets are filling with the clatter of the tramcars, a fat old woman is running towards the bus, her empty shopping bag flapping. A little girl comes out of the baker's shop: the bread in her bag is still warm and smelling delicious.

* * *

It has been two weeks now since I was admitted to hospital. I've moved a floor up to a bed by the window, in a bright yellow room. I am fully conscious and from where I lie I can see the previously invisible ocean. The magic has gone out of it now that I can see it: it no longer speaks to me in hidden languages but the beauty is still there. I watch the sunset's crimson colour reflected in the bay.

Georg and Father Maryan come often. Florian comes too and keeps bringing me baskets of fruit. I feel guilty about consuming all Maryan's Polish biscuits, but my appetite is enormous.

The Indian hospital staff are wonderful. I do not know how typical the Puri hospital cooking is, but I've been put on a special diet and eat like a king. There seems no limit to my appetite as I plough my way through high-calorie food.

The doctor comes often for a chat and says he hopes to release me within a week if I continue improving. I ask him whether malaria is chronic, what of the after-effects, what will become of me? 'Time alone will tell,' he says.

On Sunday comes an overseas 'phone call from my parents, there is much fuss as the staff are trying to connect it upstairs, but I am already strong enough to walk downstairs and take it. It's my father, they've heard all about it. I am not to worry, they've got me a bed in Rebro Hospital in Zagreb. I will be looked after by Dr Petricenic, a friend and a famous expert, and I must leave the Indian hospital at once. I laugh: the Indians are perfectly capable of curing me, I explain, and I am all right.

*　　*　　*

It is Thursday, March 28th. I am being released from the hospital today.

There is nothing more for me to do in Puri: the monsoon season is coming and I am leaving. The last day in hospital I wake up as usual a few minutes before the sun lifts its violet head out of the cloud-covered Indian Ocean. I feel excitement bubbling in my stomach. Since my *Ashram* days I have advanced enough to be able to control and sustain it. Observing excitement enter my body, I keep it out of my mind, my gestures and face remain calm and controlled. I take a shower and am given my clothes, a pair of jeans and a T-shirt. They feel uncomfortable.

I take my leave from the nurses. Georg is away; I left a note. Father Maryan comes to say good-bye.

Finally, I go to see the doctor. 'So you are leaving us. I hope I have been a good doctor,' he says.

We walk together to the door. It is a cloudy day. The rickshaw is already there and the servant has placed my bag in the back. I noticed the tall figure of *Swami* Bramananda standing by the porch. I put my hands together and saluted him silently in the Indian way.

He nods his head and smiles. I climb into the rickshaw, the driver pushes it down the gentle slope, runs beside it and swings into the seat.

'God be with you,' exclaims the tall *Swami,* and then he is gone.

'To the station,' I say to the driver. Around me people, shops, buying, selling, women, children, dogs, busy bustling life. I am a part of it again. My whole body just longs to immerse itself in it again.

I catch the train to Calcutta just in time. The rickshaw driver slings my books through the only free window, that of a first-class carriage. I fling myself in a moment afterwards. The compartment is empty, I sit down and relax. Behind me Puri disappears in a cloud of rain.

The monsoon season has begun.